Our Company Increases Apace

History, Language, and Social Identity
in Early Colonial Andover, Massachusetts

SIL International and
the International Museum of Cultures
Publications in Ethnography 40

Publications in Ethnography (formerly International Museum of Cultures Series) is a series published jointly by SIL International and the International Museum of Cultures. The series focuses on cultural studies of minority peoples of various parts of the world. While most volumes are authored by members of SIL International who have done ethnologic research in a minority language, suitable works by others will also occasionally form part of the series.

Series Editor

David Wakefield

Volume Editor

Doris Blood

Production Staff

Bonnie Brown, Managing Editor
Margaret González, Compositor
Hazel Shorey, Graphic Artist
Kirby O'Brien, Cover Design

Cover Photo: North Andover Old Town Center, 1988, Elinor Abbot

Our Company Increases Apace
History, Language, and Social Identity in Early Colonial Andover, Massachusetts

Elinor Abbot

SIL International
Dallas, Texas

© 2007 by SIL International
Library of Congress Catalog No: 2006926655
ISBN10: 1-55671-169-7
ISBN13: 978-155671-1695
ISSN: 0-0895-9897

Printed in the United States of America

All rights reserved. No part of this publication may be reproduced, stored in a retrieval system, or transmitted in any form or by any means—electronic, mechanical, photocopy, recording, or otherwise—without the express permission of the SIL International. However, short passages generally understood to be within the limits of fair use, may be quoted without permission.

Copies of this and other publications of the SIL International may be obtained from

International Academic Bookstore
SIL International
7500 W. Camp Wisdom Road
Dallas, TX 75236-5699

Voice: 972-708-7404
Fax: 972-708-7363
Email: academic_books@sil.org
Internet: http://www.ethnologue.com

Dedicated to the memory of Kenneth Lee Pike
1912–2000

and to all the Pikes of SIL
with gratitude for their scholarship
and their company

Contents

List of Figures and Tables	xi
Foreword	xiii
Preface	xix
List of Maps	xxv

1 "Well-Stored" Andover
       History and Language, History in Language.   1
   Philip Greven's Andover   4
   Sources   6
   Related Studies. 10

2 "From the Native's Point of View"
       Emic Social Categories in the New England
       Colonial Record. 17
   Blood and Country 24
   Company and Plantation 33
   The Bay Company and the Bay Colony 37

3 "Our Company Increases Apace"
       The Planting of Andover. 49
   Bay Colony Expansion 50
   Planting a Church-Town 56
   Planning and Recruitment for Andover:
       The Gathering of the Company 57
   The Planting of Andover 65

Who the Settlers Were: Summary Table 70

4 "Cochichawick Called Andover"
From Plantation to Town 75
Frontier Andover 77
The Plantation 79
Features of the Town Center 81
Andover in the Regional Setting 87
Growth and Fission: North and South Ends Emerge 89
Settlement and Dispersal 91
What the Tax Lists Show: Summary Table 95

5 "A Motion of Marriage"
Marriage and Alliance in Early Andover 99
Marriage in Andover 101
Marriage and Social Location 103
Old and New Social Identities in Andover Marriage Patterns . 109
Marriage in the Second Generation: Covenanters and
 non-Covenanters 112
Cousin Marriage and British Regional Backgrounds 116

6 "An Axe at Andover"
The Course of the Parish Split 123
Overview of Events: 1676–1710 127
Lines of Division in Andover: 1676–1679 129
Arenas of Conflict: 1680–1692 137
Blood, Country, and Witchcraft: 1690–1692 149
The Town Divides: 1692–1710 152

7 "As Bees When the Hive Is Too Full"
The Aftermath of the Parish Split 161
Marriage and Social Crisis: Greven Revisited 162
Samuel Phillips and the New South Parish 168
"The Peace of the Town" 173

Appendix A
Town Seals and Anniversary Banners 177

Appendix B
Documents: Seating the Meetinghouse 181
   B.1 The Beverly text: Seating the Meetinghouse 181
   B.2 The Tewksbury text: Seating the Meetinghouse 182

Appendix C
The Reverend Thomas Barnard's
      Letter to Governor Dudley (1710). 183

Appendix D
Andover Tax Records, 1679–1716 185

Glossary 205

Bibliography 209
    Sources 209
    References 213

Name Index 231

Subject Index 235

List of Figures

Figure 1 The Faulkner List. 20
Figure 2 Transcription of the Faulkner List 21

List of Tables

Table 1 Backgrounds of 37 founding families of Andover . . 72
Table 2 Taxpaying in Andover: North and South Ends. . . . 96
Table 3-a Town exogamy and endogamy, all families 113
Table 3-b Town exogamy and endogamy 113
Table 3-c Covenanters and non-Covenanters compared . . . 114
Table 3-d Marriage of the southwestern Covenanters 116
Table 4 Close-Kin marriage (CKM), generations II And III, and regional origin 118

Foreword

This absorbing book is the first study of Andover's early history in over thirty-five years. Historian Philip Greven's famous monograph, *Four Generations: Population, Land, and Family in Colonial Andover,* first published in 1970, explored long-term demographic trends in the town that unfolded gradually and for the most part beneath the surface of everyday life; Greven portrayed Andover as a generally peaceful and untroubled community. Elinor Abbot tells a very different story, uncovering a complex pattern of factional tension and conflict within the town. Andover's division into two parishes in 1710, according to Greven the result of population growth and land pressure, becomes in Abbot's retelling the culmination of a long history of division and feuding rooted in the ways that colonists organized themselves for purposes of migration and settlement.

Abbot combines her training as an anthropologist with her keen instincts as a local historian to reconstruct the ways in which the residents of early Andover categorized themselves and their connections to each other. In doing so, she develops an argument with far-reaching implications for our understanding of New England history in general. This is an engaging local history, but also much more than that, a provocative and compelling reappraisal of early American history.

New England colonists used, of course, a range of categories to define and distinguish themselves. Most of those who crossed the Atlantic as part of the Great Migration were bound together by their determination to found a holy commonwealth. Colonists also identified in terms of their nationality and more specifically the region of England from which they had migrated. On a more intimate level, most seventeenth-century New Englanders had crossed the Atlantic as members of a family. The familial household was the fundamental social unit within colonial New England. The family was responsible not only for most economic production and practical sustenance but also for the fostering of social and moral order: its hierarchical structure mirrored that of society as a whole and prepared children for their adult roles in the Puritan community. As New England families intermarried, they formed increasingly dense kinship networks that often played a crucial role in the social, economic, and political affiliations that individuals developed throughout their lives.

Abbot calls our attention to an additional category of identity and association that previous scholars of early New England have largely ignored: the company. The word appears frequently in early New England sources and the colonists themselves clearly recognized its significance as a social unit. The term company signified for contemporaries a hierarchically ordered group of people that mobilized for a specific purpose. Much of the migration that enabled settlement of New England, both transatlantic and within the northern colonies, occurred in the form of social clusters that colonists referred to as companies.

These companies were reconstituted versions of the established structural landscape in England, mobile social fragments broken off from the parent society. Each company comprised a group of families gathered around a key figure to whom members of the company deferred, sometimes a minister and sometimes a "gentleman" whose status gave him authority as a leader and patron. These self-identified social organizations gathered and dispersed, maneuvered, aligned, and competed within the evolving landscape of colonial society. The company was a moving, acting, purposeful version of social stratification through which seventeenth-century migrants to New England conveyed the hierarchical structure of their society across the Atlantic and then reconstructed it in the new world.

Historians have often drawn attention to the "middling" status of most New Englanders, pointing out that those who settled in the northern colonies included relatively few people who were either extremely wealthy or utterly impoverished. They have also stressed, quite rightly, the extent to which New England towns and congregations as well as colonial assemblies relied upon democratic processes that were quite radical by seventeenth-century standards. But we should not fall into the trap of portraying New Englanders as more egalitarian than they actually were. There remained significant disparities of social status that the colonists considered crucial to social stability. In 1636, the minister at Watertown,

George Phillips, wrote to John Winthrop, Jr., urging him to "set down" with migrants from that town in a new community, Wethersfield, in Connecticut. The Wethersfield company, Phillips wrote, desperately needed a gentleman who could provide effective leadership:

> The necessity of it is the weakness of a company without a head, [which] cannot well sway and guide itself, but is subject to many errors, distractions, confusions, and what not, which in our undertakings in this part of the world cannot but prove dangerous to the cause of religion [and] dismal to the common state, both in general and particular. (MHS 1943 vol. 3:241)

In the context of their colonial venture, Phillips opined, it was vital that the settlers reconstruct an explicit hierarchical structure with a credible "head" to safeguard order within each company.

If asked to describe what the word *company* brings to mind, most of us today would include a formal business venture in the answer, also one of the principal meanings attached to the word in early modern England. That Puritans on both sides of the Atlantic made frequent use of a word with commercial connotations should not be surprising, given their systematic appropriation of terms and concepts rooted in a market economy. Ministers had taken the powerful scriptural theme of covenant, and joined it with that of the contract, familiar to the artisans, merchants, and other commercially oriented people who formed the social basis for the Puritan movement, and used it as the guiding principle of their faith. The willingness of those planning resettlement in New England at the end of the 1620s to adapt economic ideas and mechanisms for their own ends became abundantly clear when they organized themselves for the purpose of migration as a formal trading company, the Massachusetts Bay Company (Zaret 1985).

The most explicitly structured version of company to which colonists were exposed in their everyday lives was the local militia, with its clearly defined hierarchy and formalized code of interaction. Each New England town had its own "trained band," or "company of trained men." (For use of the word company to describe local militia groups, see Shurtleff vol. 1:85, 90, 99, 109, 127, 138, 160, 165, 250, 279, 290–291, 315, 327–328.) Yet the militia was not the only local institution to be described as a company. Puritans also used the word in relation to congregations. Richard Mather defined a covenanted church as "a company of Christians, called by the power and mercy of God to fellowship with Christ, and by his providence to live together, and by his grace to cleave together in the unity of faith and brotherly love" (1643:3).

However, equally crucial to the colonizing enterprise were the informal companies of migrating families that crossed the Atlantic and settled in New England. Indeed, the Massachusetts Bay Company is perhaps best understood as a confederation of regional, parochial, and manorial companies. Various groups hailing from Puritan strongholds in England became temporarily subsumed within the Massachusetts Bay Company, but once in the new world these stratified clusters of families reasserted themselves as crucial units of association. As the colonists settled in a rapidly expanding constellation of townships, they did so as members of companies. It was not merely that colonists tended to settle in groups according to their regional and parochial origins in England. Most of these groups had a clear hierarchical structure that vested authority in a recognized leader. The affiliations that held these groups together were rooted in loyalty and deference as well as regional origin and common purpose.

Town companies did not necessarily consist of just one migratory cluster. As the colonists dispersed along the coast and into the interior, new towns were often founded by confederations of company fragments out-migrating from communities that had already been established. One group would usually take the initiative and recruit contingents from other companies. Each contingent had its own internal hierarchy on which it depended for functional coherence. If the leader of the dominant group was deferred to by the other constituent groups and their leaders, a clear hierarchy would emerge in the new town. But sometimes there was no consensus as to who should assume town leadership, in which case crises of authority and factional conflict could divide and bedevil local communities.

The early history of Andover exemplifies the importance of the company as a basic building block of colonization at the local level. It also shows the potential for conflict between constituent groups, or sub-companies, if there was no generally recognized overall leader who could unite townsfolk. Andover settlers came from three different regions of Britain. Most had migrated from either the southeast or the southwest of England; a smaller number came from northern England or Scotland. These three groups formed one confederate company in order to settle at Andover, but once there they rapidly reasserted themselves as distinct entities. Divisions within seventeenth-century Andover resulted not simply from the different regional backgrounds of its settlers but also from the specific histories of migratory companies. One group and its leadership initially enjoyed a clear ascendancy, but a series of unexpected departures fragmented authority within the new town. This led to increasingly entrenched factionalism and the eventual bifurcation of Andover into two distinct precincts and parishes in 1710.

Meanwhile, in 1692, the town produced more accused witches than any other community involved in the infamous witch-hunt of that year, including even Salem Village itself (Godbeer 1992; see his appendix B, p. 242). Historians have paid surprisingly little attention to the witch scare in Andover and its background. Paul Boyer and Stephen Nissenbaum, who argue in their famous study that factional conflict within Salem Village underlay accusations of witchcraft, mention only in a footnote that Andover produced "a disproportionately large number" of accused witches that year (1974:191, fn 12). Greven makes only brief mention of the 1692 crisis and portrays the town during the years preceding the witch hunt as largely harmonious and stable. Yet Abbot's study suggests that ethnic and regional tensions among the inhabitants of Andover, along with local loyalties that originated in company membership, may provide an important new explanatory model as we continue to seek a fuller understanding of the 1692 witch hunt.

Elinor Abbot's study shows that if we are to grasp fully the dynamics of settlement in early New England, we need to appreciate the company as an important category of identification in the society and culture of early New England. Settlers clearly recognized and valued the company as a fundamental category of belonging and as a basis for action. Abbot's book thus provides us not only with a refreshing new perspective on the early history of Andover but also with a significant and exciting new window into the minds and lives of early New Englanders.

Richard Godbeer
University of Miami

Preface

There are many ways to look back at the people of the past and their social worlds, but two distinct perspectives stand out. We can use the assumptions and categories of our own particular world to account for and judge the workings of a past society. This need not but often does result in a sort of historical ethnocentrism. How could people have actually cut off a man's ears just for blasphemy, we might ask. Even if we cannot agree, we can try insofar as possible to understand the viewpoint of people living in another time and place. Blasphemy is an offense that affects a man for eternity, they might answer, and so a mild punishment that daily reminds him can become his blessing. Both perspectives have their uses. In this book I have taken up the second approach, in common with most anthropologists. It involves the search for the emic or insider's perspective, the people's point of view in its own context. However, anthropologists usually try to grasp emic perspectives on culture and language in the process of walking and talking with the people of a living society, looking, listening, asking, and checking hunches. In this case I wanted to understand something of the history, language, and social identities of people in a small New England town of the seventeenth century. What can be done when all that is left about the people's point of view is in archives and artifacts, and there are often precious few of them?

Even when records are plentiful, however, as in the case of Andover, the question still arises: From the point of view of which people? In early Andover, for example, do we want to understand the perspective of men, or women, or children? Indians, colonists, or go-betweens? Which Indians? And which colonists? Families that suffered many troubles, or ones that flourished? Ministers or militia? Gentry or yeomen? The rich, the poor, or the middling? Masters, servants, or slaves? Those who signed the church covenant, or those who did not? People serious about the life of the church, or those indifferent, even hostile to it? Accused witches or their accusers? Secret Quaker sympathizers or those who wanted them warned out? People of English origin or people of Scottish origin? Scots who had come willingly or unwillingly to the Bay Colony? English people whose roots were in the north, the south, the west, or the east of England? All of these social identities and more emerge from the records of seventeenth-century Massachusetts towns like Andover and its neighbors. Thus the real complexity of the colony and its early towns becomes apparent.

Consider the members of just one of Andover's households that we know something about: Simon Bradstreet, tough military and civic leader of Andover and later governor of the colony; his wife, famed colonial poet Anne Bradstreet; and a servant of theirs, William Young. We catch a glimpse of their relations through records of a court case (see chapter 2). Young was whipped for an infraction and then further summoned to court for "abusive speech." He had said he "wished them hanged who had made the law giving masters the right to whip their servants." Young is recorded as having then called the whole lot of colony leaders "a company of rude debased fellows," after which he disappears from the records. Anne and Simon Bradstreet, however, will be heard from many more times. Whose story is the "real" history? None of them, and all of them. The challenge, to me, lies in trying to grasp the whole of such composite relationships evenhandedly, entering into the real complexity of other times from as many people's perspectives in turn as possible. In the same way, we would try to learn and understand a language from many different speakers of its varieties.

I have introduced Young's words above because of his use of the word company, "a company of rude debased fellows." For the colonists this was a term of strong social identity with a range of meanings; even Young's use of it in anger reflects its power to bound a certain kind of social group. There are so many uses of the word *company* in the records that I realized it was a key social term and chose to use an example of it in my title. I will explore the meaning of company for seventeenth-century English speakers, along with the meanings of several other pieces of the language of identity which the records provide.

This book is a revised version of a Brandeis University doctoral dissertation in what is best described as historical social anthropology, or worse, historical linguistic social anthropology. That work finally struggled out into the light in 1990. But for years before that, even before graduate school, I had been trying to piece together from family papers the story of a little group of young people who left Andover early in the eighteenth century. They moved some forty miles north to the wilds of southern New Hampshire to settle the town of Wilton, where I grew up. At graduate school my introduction to anthropological and linguistic perspectives at last provided me with a way to make a kind of sense out of what was in all those boxes of old books and letters in the attic. I hope to be able to carry on this odd line of antiquarian social anthropology by adding to the present volume a second one, tracing what happened once that little group got to Wilton.

During the transformation of the dissertation into a book I have incurred many debts of gratitude, but none of the people I am about to thank is in any way responsible for the book's shortcomings. Indeed, I especially urge those who have questions and additions regarding any matter here to call my attention to it. Those who work with historical and genealogical records are only too keenly aware of pitfalls in the pursuit of accuracy and of the reliance we must have on the soundness of each other's researches. As for matters of interpretation, well, that is where the fun lies, and I would be delighted to discuss them with interested readers.

I deeply appreciate the directors, staffs, and members, past and present, of both the North Andover and Andover Historical Societies, for always providing a hospitable and professional environment for us whose research interests bring us time and again to their doorsteps. Their work is the foundation that makes such projects as this one possible. My hope is that this book will be useful to them, to other researchers, and especially to the townspeople of both Andovers of all ages and backgrounds. Many people from those towns will find their seventeenth-century ancestors mentioned in this work, and I trust they will find that I treated them with care. Many other current residents may not have old roots in the towns, but I hope they will be intrigued by this book to find out more about those who once walked across the same places they walk today

I want to thank again my teachers, especially those who supervised the original dissertation at Brandeis: anthropologists Benson Saler and Judith Zeitlin, and historian Christine Heyrman. What I learned from them still stands me in good stead.

One day at Brandeis I had the good fortune to meet Richard Godbeer, then fresh from England and a new graduate student in the history department. John Demos, sizing up his interests, had advised him to go across campus to our department and take an anthropology course with Benson Saler, who then introduced us. Thus began a friendship that has lasted through many a year and many a lively discussion, as Richard expanded his scope to previously unexplored realms of early American history. He understood what I was trying to get at, offered many clarifying suggestions, and kept pressing me kindly but firmly to get the thing done. I am happy that he has been willing to write the Foreword.

I think I should also include a note of appreciation here to Philip Greven, author of *Four Generations: Land, Population, and Family in Colonial Andover,* which I first read in 1974. With a bit of tongue in cheek, I can say that without Greven this book would not have been written, at least not in its present form. I found a different story in the Andover archives than the young Greven did back then, and I spend some time here critiquing aspects of his portrayal of Andover, but this in no way diminishes his groundbreaking work with the methods of historical demography and the valuable insights into early Andover's family life that he provided.

Nor would there be any book without the influence and encouragement of many colleagues in the Summer Institute of Linguistics (now SIL International). The late Kenneth L. Pike opened up in his inimitable way to me and many others the concepts of emics and etics in his linguistics courses at SIL. We had hours of discussion about whether and how they could be applied as well to anthropological and historical materials, and this was what led me to look more closely at language in old records and thus take up the dissertation topic. My coworkers in the SIL Anthropology Department have of course taken a special interest in the revision, giving as much as they endured as I wrestled it through, tying up the printer, spreading papers everywhere, and eating up all their snacks in the late hours.

I thank the members of the SIL International Academic Editing and Publishing Services. Mary Ruth Wise, Senior Editor, is the one who consistently encouraged me (nagged would not be too strong a word) to take my dissertation and turn it into a book. I thank her and her staff for seeing it through, especially Bonnie Brown and Doris Blood, they of the gimlet eyes. Doris has stood (or sat) shoulder to shoulder with me to fix the countless things that had to be done. Thanks to Hazel Shorey, a fellow New Englander who took special care with the maps and other graphics; to Sharon Edwards who coordinated the process and gave encouragement at key moments; and to Margaret González who saw the whole manuscript through the mysteries of Ventura.

Friends and neighbors have cheered me on at every step and they are glad to see the outcome at last. Our tag line has been that victory has a thousand fathers and mothers, but we can't name them all because Prefaces have to be short. So, you know who you are! But with such friends

Preface

even defeat would never have been an orphan. They stick by through thick and thin.

To my wide extended family, thank you for the many ways you have encouraged me. Enjoy the book. You're a part of it. A special word of thanks goes to our distant relative in England, Katharine Pile, whose grandmother told her always to keep in touch with the American cousins, and so she has. I believe I learned more at Munstead, her home in Surrey, listening to her remarkable reminiscences, than ever I did from reading many books. And there at Munstead came the insight into how the old manorial companies must have worked.

Finally, I want to give thanks for my father and mother, the ones I really do wish were here to see this book and enjoy the victory. Charles and Jennie Abbot gave to us their love of the people and places of New England and of all kinds of learning and exploration. There are no more words.

Elinor Abbot
Dallas, Texas

List of Maps

Map 1:   New England Towns, about 1700. Not all are shown. Adapted from *A Map of New England,* prepared by the Hagstrom Company to show the journey of Madam Knight [from Boston to New York in 1704]. In Knight, Madam Sara: *The journal of Madam Knight.* New York: Peter Smith, 1935. Public domain.

Map 2   The New England Colonies in 1640. Adapted to show locations of some early settlements, from map at <http://www.u-s-history.com/pages/h572.html> Accessed 11/18/04.

Map 3:   Counties of England, showing number of emigrants from each county of 2646 emigrants traced. Adapted from Banks 1968 [1937]. Shaded areas show Wiltshire and Hampshire, the counties of origin of Andover's Southwesterners, and Hertfordshire, origin of the Hertford group. Public domain.

Map 4:   Regions of England. Adapted from: <http://en.wikipedia.org/wiki/Regions_of_England> Accessed 11/18/2004.

Map 5:   Hale's Map of Essex County, Massachusetts, and surrounding region (1827). The David Rumsey Map Collection.

Map 6:   Andover Old Town (now North Andover), enlargement of center from Dorman's map, *Plan of Andover* (1830). Used with permission of the Andover Historical Society.

Map 7:   Andover Old Town, center schematic, showing topographical features, waterways, early roads, and locations of meetinghouse, mill, minister's house, and ordinaries (taverns). Adapted by the author from the Forbes Rockwell map series, Andover Historical Society.

Map 8:   Andover Old Town, phase 1, 1646–1659, showing locations and owners of original center house lots. Adapted from Rockwell map series, Andover Historical Society. Used with permission.

Map 9: Andover Old Town, phase 2, 1660–1699, showing changes in house lot owners. Adapted from Rockwell map series, Andover Historical Society. Used with permission.

Map 10: Andover Old Town center (North) and emerging South center in 1692. Adapted with permission from A Plan of Andover in 1692, map prepared in 1992 by the Historical Societies of Andover and North Andover, James Batchelder, artist. Black roofs show houses of families involved in the witchcraft crisis of 1692, whether accused, accusers, or afflicted.

Map 11: Andover Old Town center (North), enlargement from Map 10.

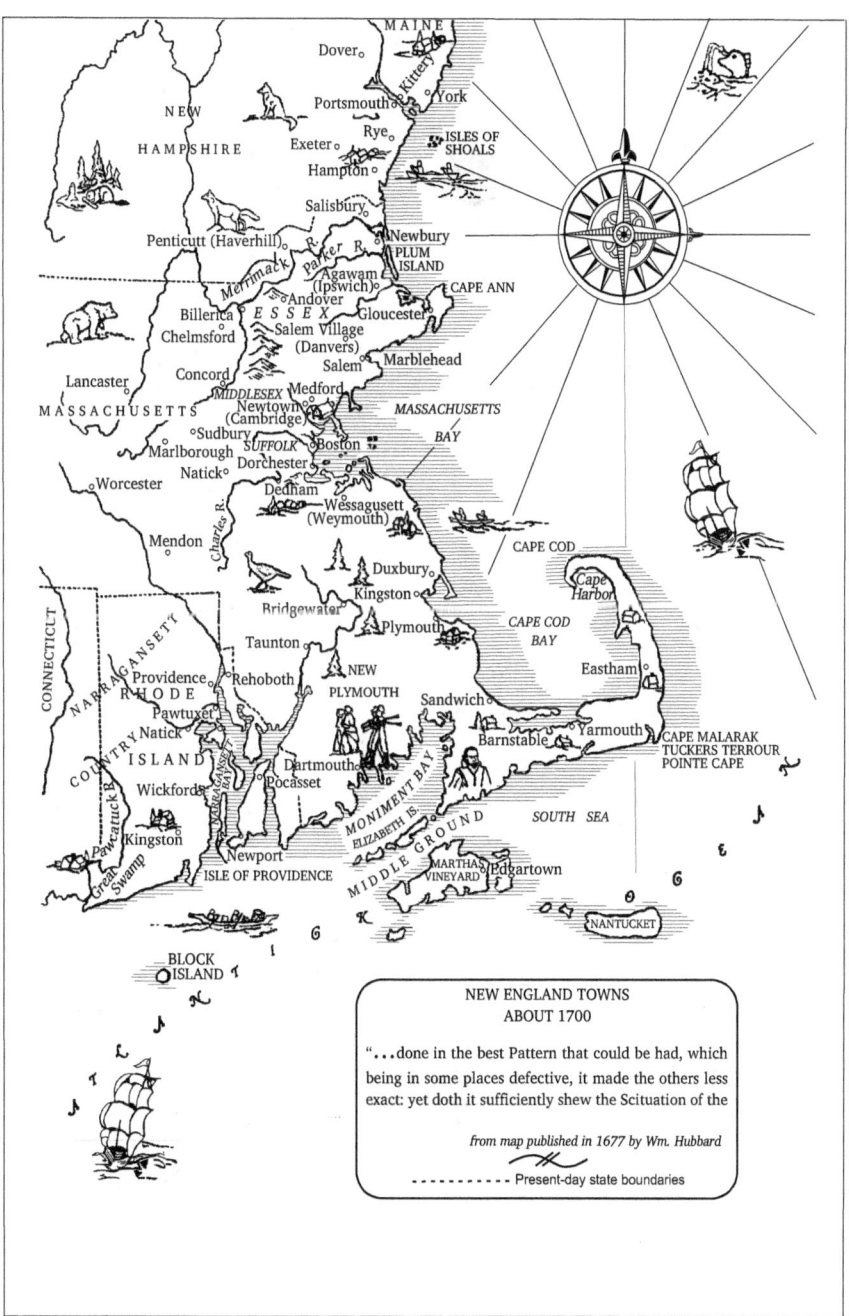

Map 1: New England Towns, about 1700

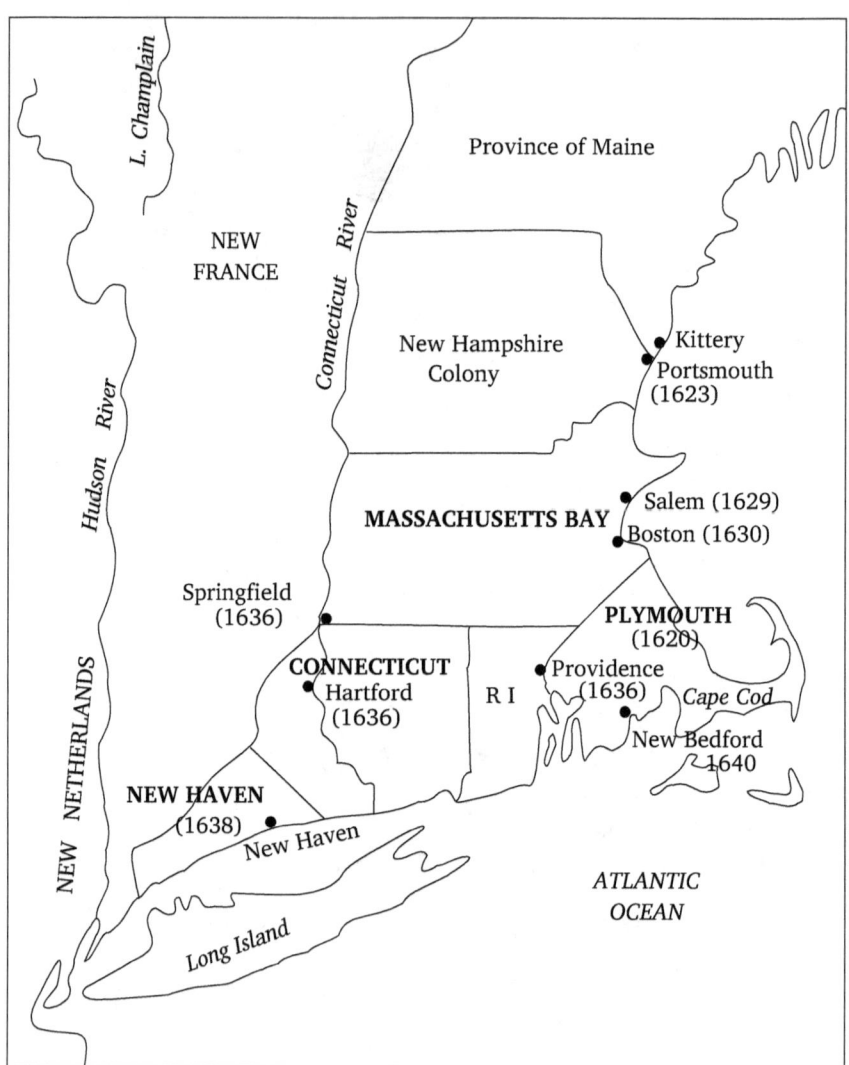

Map 2: The New England Colonies in 1640

Map 3

Map 3: Counties of England

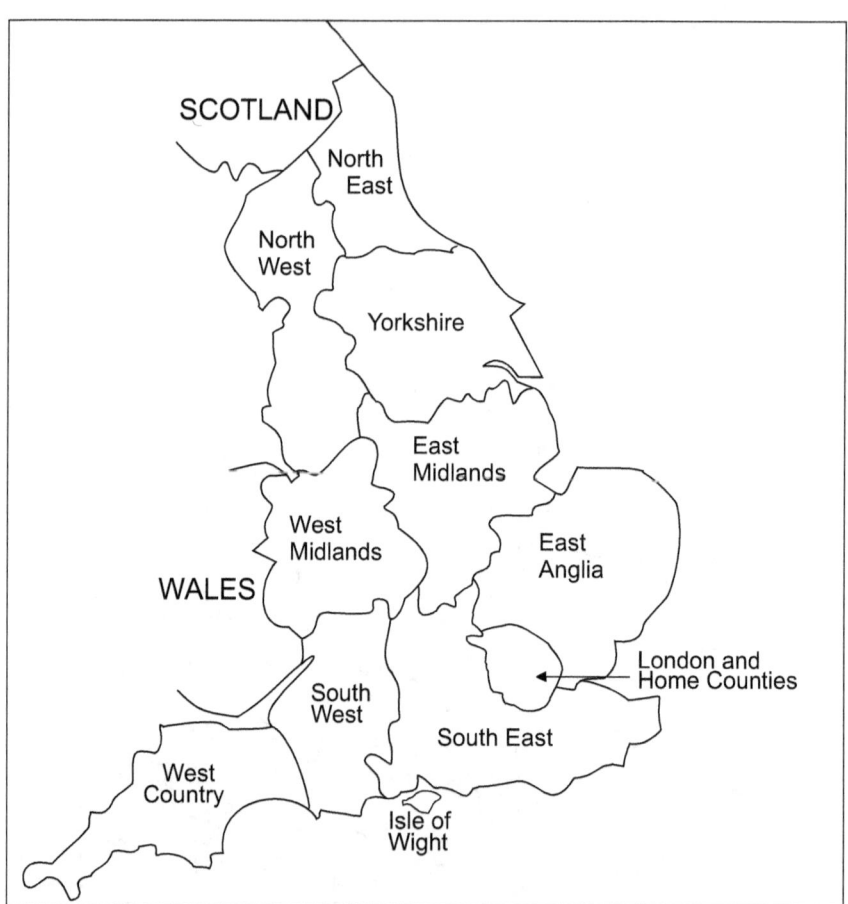

Map 4: Regions of England

(Author's note: Colonists from Wiltshire and Hampshire counties are referred to as Southwesterners in this book, although Hampshire county falls in the Southeast region on this map.)

Map 5

Map 5: Hale's map of Essex County, Massachusetts, and surrounding region (1827)

Map 6: Andover Old Town (now North Andover), enlargement of center from Dorman's map, *Plan of Andover* (1830)

Map 7   xxxiii

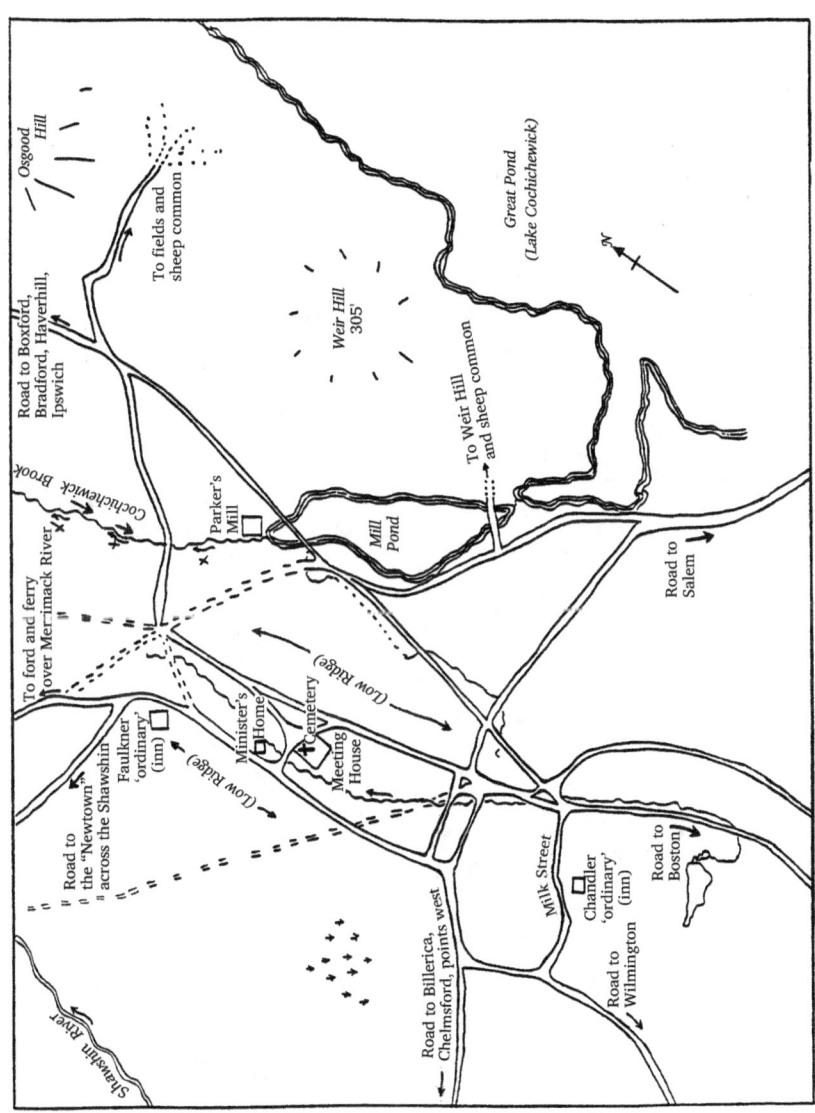

Map 7: Andover Old Town, center schematic

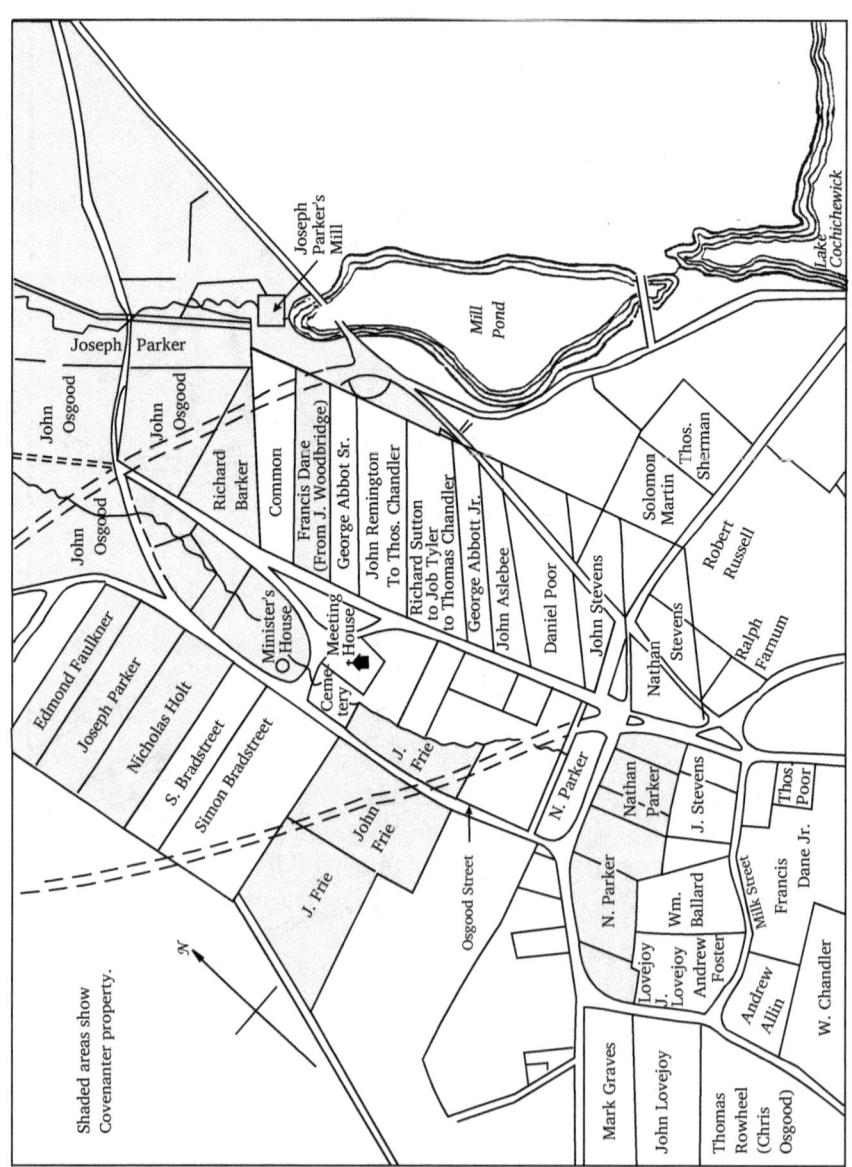

Map 8: Andover Old Town, phase 1, 1646–1659

Map 9

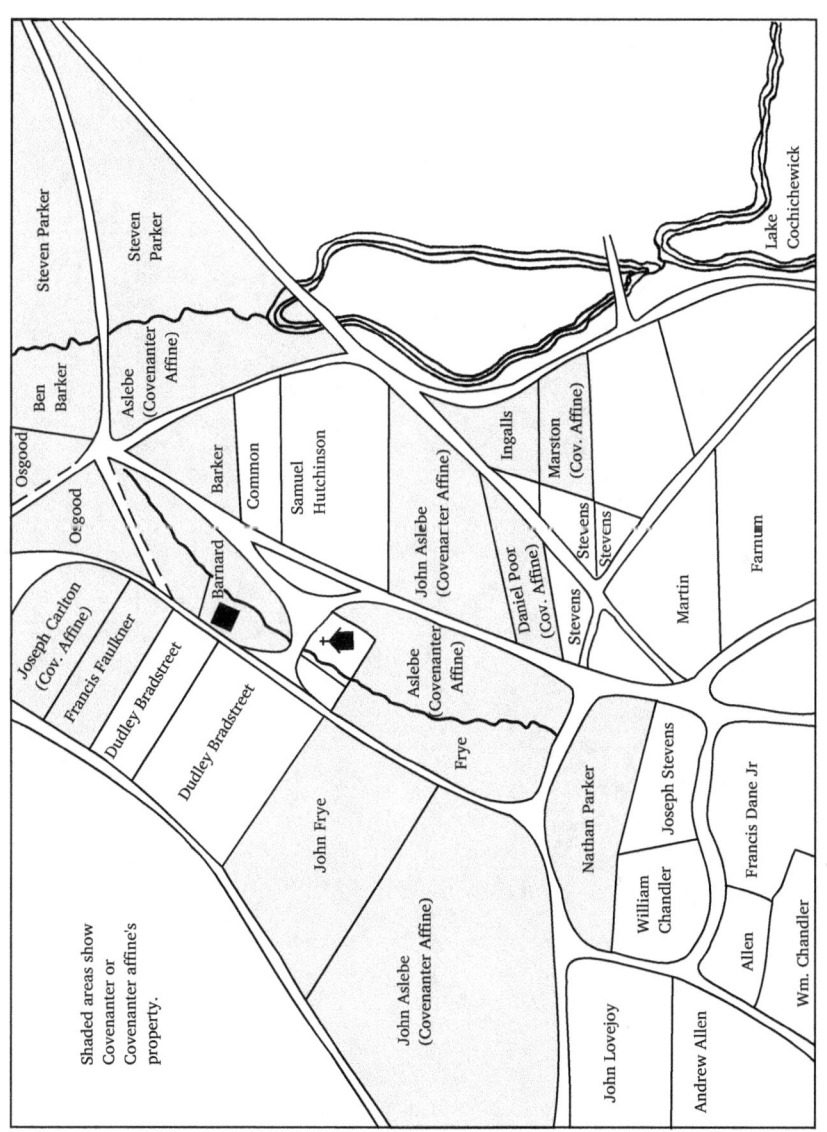

Map 9: Andover Old Town, phase 2, 1660–1699

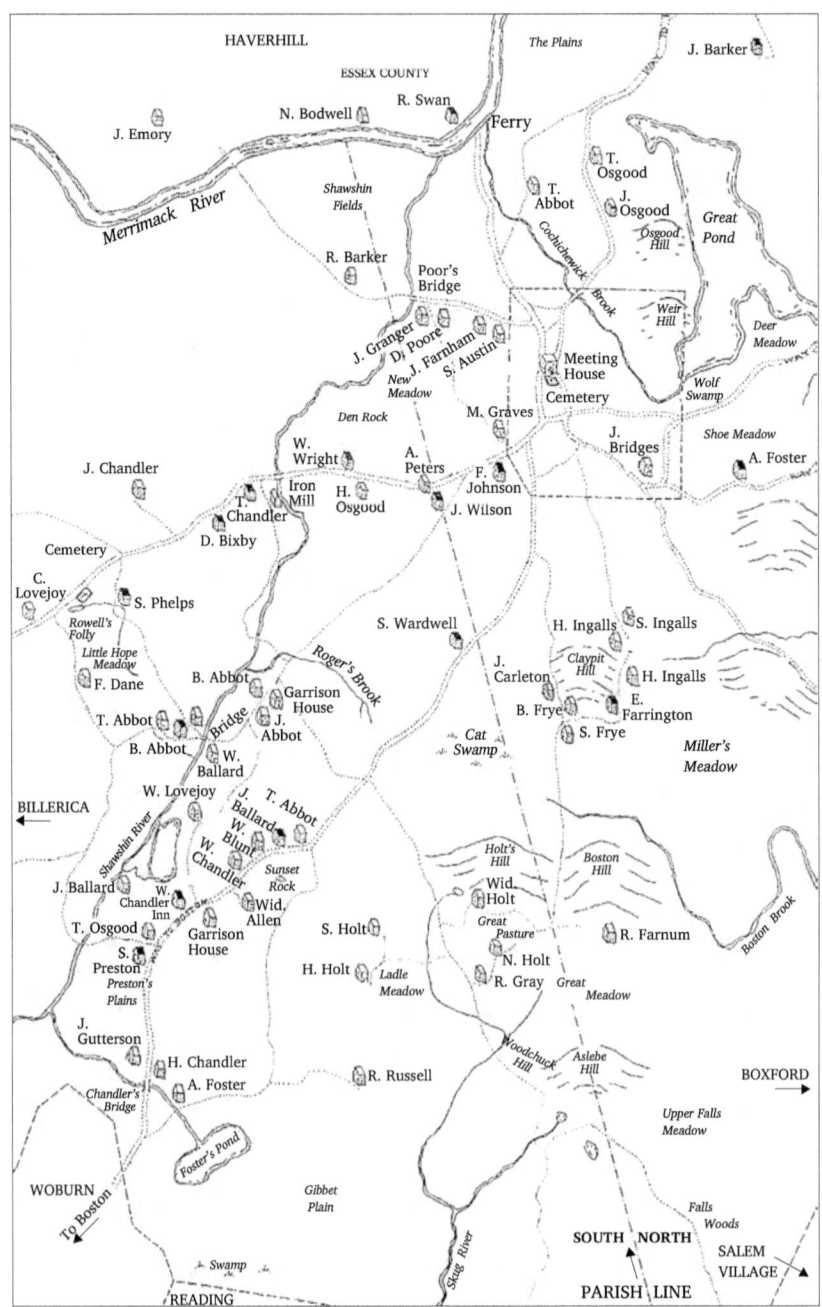

Map 10: Andover Old Town center (North), and emerging South center in 1692

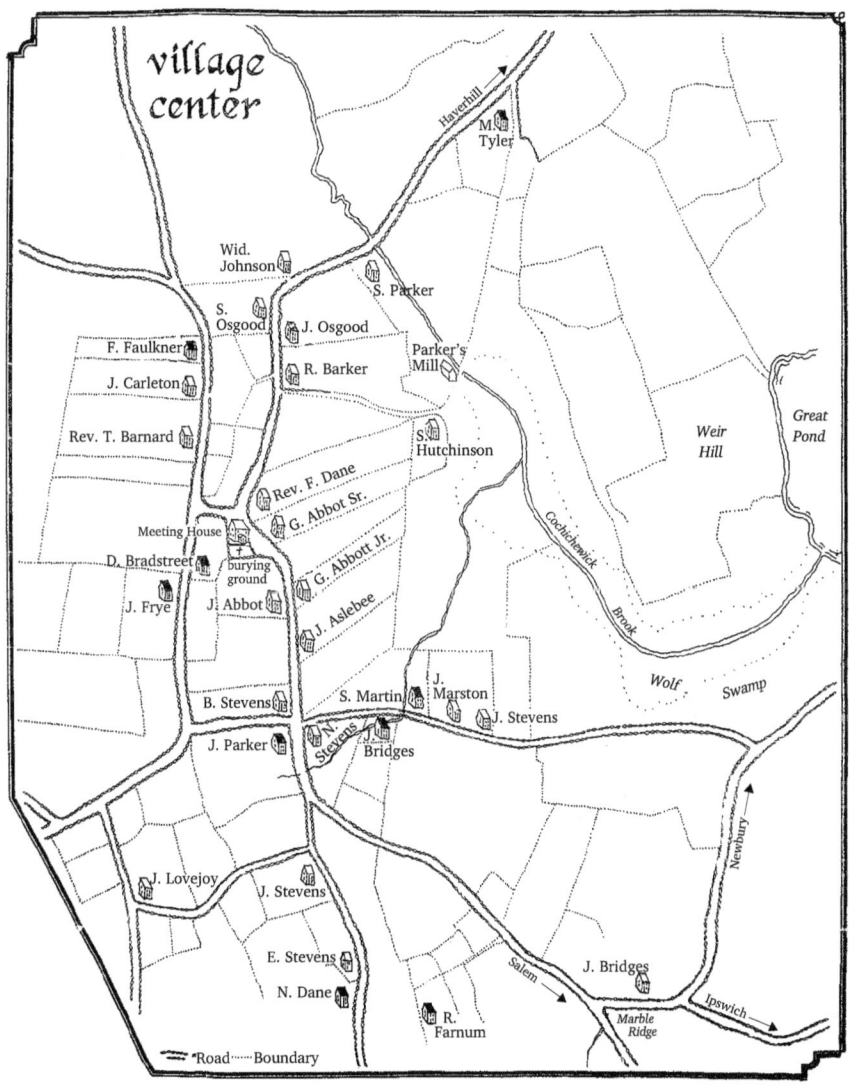

Map 11: Andover Old Town center (North), enlargement from Map 10

1
"Well-Stored" Andover
History and Language, History in Language

In the year 1663 the English gentleman, traveler, and diarist John Josselyn took a tour of the new Puritan settlements in the Massachusetts Bay Colony. It was Josselyn's second voyage to "New-England" (as he always wrote it), and he was on his way to visit his brother in the province of Maine. No friend of the Puritans, he was nonetheless curious to have a look at how their enterprise was faring. Among his many comments on this side trip he noted, "Hard upon the River Sashin where the Merrimack [River] receives this and the other branch into its body, is seated Andover, well-stored with land and Cattle."[1]

The early history of "well-stored" Andover is the subject of this book, with a particular focus on the social world of the first settlers and the language they used to talk about it. Andover was one of the first inland towns to be established in colonial Massachusetts. The Bay Colony settlements, or *plantations* as the colonists called them, began along the seacoast. Wary advance parties soon began to follow the rivers upstream to scout out the country's inland prospects. The region that became Andover had long been a favorite summer camp of local Indians, with river frontage, many ponds and streams, and a large lake. They called it *Cochichawick,* 'great water'. The English settlers as well soon realized what a choice site it was. A group of colonists hoping to plant a new church-town there and another across the river at "Penticutt" (Haverhill) began to gather in the coastal town of Ipswich to make their preparations. *"Our company increases apace,* from diverse

---

[1] See Lindholdt (1988:131). Josselyn's travel journals were first published in England in 1674. Readers not familiar with New England colonial geography can orient themselves with map 1, New England Towns about 1700, and map 2, The New England Colonies in 1640.

towns…" wrote the minister Nathaniel Ward to his old friend, patron, and relative by marriage Governor Winthrop, hoping to persuade the Governor to expedite the process of obtaining the necessary permission from the General Court. Ward expected to be the minister at Haverhill, and his son John was to be the minister at Andover.

By 1646 the representatives of Ward's company had finally negotiated the purchase of the land from a local Indian sagamore, Cutshamache, "for the sum of £6 & a Coat." Andover's nineteenth-century historian Bailey refers to "this paltrey sum" in her description of what was by her time almost a semi-mythic event (1880:26–27). Very likely Cutshamache neither understood the bargain he had made nor had any authority to "sell" the rights of other Indians to their customary use of these lands, for there came a series of Indian reprisals against the settlers during the following years. Andoverites, however, continued to commemorate the details of the purchase, incorporating into the town seal a rendition of the chief holding his new coat and his bag of money. That design was in turn taken from a large banner prepared for the town's two hundred fiftieth anniversary in 1896. For its three hundred fiftieth celebration in 1996, Andover turned to a less controversial theme featuring instead the patriotic hymn *America*, written in 1832 by a young student at the Andover Theological Seminary. Nevertheless, to this day Cutshamache still stands pointing west in his place in the town seal. North Andover, the old town, also chose an Indian theme for its seal, albeit a more generic image of an Indian in his canoe. (See appendix A for illustrations of the town seals and symbols.)[2]

Andover was apparently a thriving settlement by the time John Josselyn passed through some twenty years after the founding. But over the course of the next fifty years the town underwent an acrimonious fissioning process marked by several social and spiritual flashpoints. These included various quarrels among townsmen, attacks by Indians, and the terrors of the witchcraft crisis, which shook the whole of New England in 1692. Although that crisis is most famously linked with Salem, over forty of Andover's people were also caught up in it, and three were

---

[2]Regarding the word "Indian": although historians and others went through a period of using such terms as "native American," some now seem disposed to return to the use of "Indian" and I will do so in this book (see for example Lepore 1998). For details of the purchase of Andover from Cutshamache, see Bailey 1880:26–27. The two hundred fiftieth anniversary banner is displayed on the Andover town website at http://andoverma.gov/about/250th.php and in the Proceedings of 1896 (1896). Surprisingly, the banner with Cutshamache served as backdrop for a photo in 2000 celebrating the twinning agreement between Andover, Massachusetts, and Andover, England, and a statue of the old sagamore has been even erected in the town park in Andover, England. Online: <http://andoverma.gov/twinning/uk.php>.

executed. By 1709 the town had finally divided into two parishes, keeping a common civil government but allowing each parish to have its own minister and meetinghouse. Even then ill feeling continued. The original settlement was now to be known as the North Parish, but the minister there wrote to the Governor at Boston that his people were dissatisfied about the name, the boundaries, and other matters. Although they were the first settlement, "now they are made the lesser part," Barnard said, and he feared the situation would become "an occasion of Perpetual Discontent" (see Barnard's letter in appendix C). However, Andover continued as one town with separate parishes for nearly a hundred and fifty more years until, in 1855, the parishes took steps to become the two separate townships they are today. Still there was occasion for "Discontent," as Barnard had predicted. The old town had to settle for being officially called North Andover, while the South Parish, now more populous and the site of both the academy known as Phillips Andover (1778) and the Andover Theological Seminary (1808), kept the name Andover for itself. Some North Andover residents today will joke that "at least they got the IRS too," referring to the fact that the northeast office of the Internal Revenue Service is located in Andover.

A bare-bones summary of the town's historical milestones on a North Andover website gives no hint of the struggles outlined above: "Incorporated as Andover 1646. Split into the North Parish (now North Andover) and South Parish (now Andover) 1709. North Andover incorporated 1855" (<www.rootsweb.com/~macnando>). However, the records concerning early Andover and its place in the Massachusetts Bay Colony are plentiful enough to follow the history of that struggle in some detail. My focus here will be only on the first seventy years of the story, from the gathering of the settlers and the incorporation of the town to the parish split in 1709. What was that division about, and how did it happen? In the chapters that follow, I look at this history from the perspective of linguistic and social anthropology. That is, I am interested in the language of the records, in the settlers' own ways of talking about each other and their social world, and their struggles, conflicts, and alliances. As people from the British Isles, they used the language of their day to mark social identities, adapting or developing terms such as *company, country, blood, plantation, firstcomer,* and *latecomer* to talk about themselves and each other in the early years. Such seemingly ordinary language and its regional variation point to the associations and shifts in social identity that they recognized as they gathered and traveled from their different regions of old England, joined companies, landed in "diverse towns," formed new companies, and built new plantations like Andover.

Philip Greven's Andover

The study of early New England is by now such a well-plowed field that it might seem nothing new could be turned up. The era of colonial New England town studies has also passed, and historians may well ask what another study of an early Massachusetts town will add to the already crowded shelf of that genre. And indeed, why study Andover again? Andover's early history has already been explored by historian Philip Greven. His monograph (1970), *Four Generations: Population, Land, and Family in Colonial Andover*, based on his dissertation (1964), has become a classic in historical demography. But Andover emerges from Greven's account as a harmonious, almost a stodgy little place. He describes a community settled by a relatively homogeneous population of English colonists, whose people were not only physically but also socially healthy. Changes leading to the town's division into two parishes proceeded, in his telling, at a slow pace, generation by generation, changing primarily in response to population increase and land pressure. Although I had earlier read and reviewed Greven's book (Abbot 1974), I was surprised when I explored these same records myself some years later and found in them accounts of continuing trouble and conflict. For the first seventy years, along with the stress and crises of frontier life, the townspeople struggled to work through the particular social tensions of their new settlement. These new-world tensions were often rooted in the particular ethnic and regional tensions they had brought along from Britain. I will describe the history of Andover from this perspective, wherever possible parsing the colonists' own language for insight into their understandings of their situation. The picture of early Andover that emerges here will be quite different from the one described by Greven.

The disparity between Greven's portrayal of Andover and mine stemmed, I think, from our differing research orientations and thus from the differing units of analysis we developed out of the records. As Greven explained in his introductions (both 1964 and 1970), he was using the methods of the then-new historical demography. This approach deliberately downplayed narrative history, text analysis, and actors' perspectives in favor of uncovering long-term statistical trends. In contrast, I looked at Andover's history some years later from the perspective of anthropology and linguistics (Abbot 1985; 1990). From anthropologist Victor Turner I took the formulation of the enduring *social drama* as a way of following events over time in a community (Turner 1974). From linguist Kenneth Pike I took the concept of *etic* and *emic*, or "outsider" and "insider" cognitive categories, first introduced by him from the linguistic terms *phonetic* and *phonemic* and later expanded more widely by him and others into anthropology and related fields. Etic terms are the more general technical terms for language or social phenomena that an outside observer might use, such as glottal stop or exogamy. Emic social categories are those that are used by the speakers of a language themselves and thus are relevant to the natives or insiders of the particular social group. Clues to emic social categories can be found in the terms people use to name and categorize themselves and others. As I read the town and colony records, I looked for such emic terms in the language the colonists used and adapted to talk about themselves and each other in the social world of the seventeenth century. A glossary of such terms can be found following the appendices.[3]

Greven's *Four Generations* is rightly recognized as a classic example of the historical demographic method. His study is still an important resource and may be found on the reading list of almost any university course in early New England history. However, in the absence of other professional histories, *Four Generations* also came to stand as an accurate *social* as well as demographic history of Andover. I do not question Greven's demographic work here, especially as it is not in dispute and Greven himself soon left these early interests behind for historical social psychology (Greven 1977). But I do question the picture of Andover's history that secondarily emerged from his study, a picture that was widely accepted until quite recently. Greven wrote, "The surface of life in such towns [as Andover] seems to be unbroken in its continuity, but beneath the surface, changes gradually altered both the landscape and the lives of the inhabitants." Later he continues, "…the small rural agricultural towns like Andover probably proved to be excellent places to realize the goals of order, hierarchy, and the closely-knit community" (1970:17, 270–271). One could conclude from *Four Generations* that there were few troubles beneath the economic differences to disturb the town's unbroken surface continuity. Greven did note that Andover divided into two ends, and ultimately into two parishes, and that this process sometimes set the townspeople against one another, but the unraveling of this process was not central to his study. He relegated Andover's witchcraft crisis, which was a reverberating tragedy for the townspeople, to a single paragraph and a footnote (1970:87; 107, fn. 6).

Those curious about the early history of Andover will be left with a major misconception if they rely solely on Greven's account. And such curiosity continues about the town's early history, among both laypeople and

---

[3]See Pike 1967 for the original formulation of the terms *emic* and *etic*. See Headland, Pike, and Harris 1990, Wise, Headland, and Brend 2003, and Lett 1990 for history and examples of their use in anthropology, linguistics and other fields. See Sidky 2004 for a recent discussion of the history of these concepts in anthropology, especially in cognitive anthropology, and in Pike's debate with the anthropologist Marvin Harris over the meaning and use of these terms.

scholars. Many citizens of North Andover and Andover are strong supporters of their local historical societies and often undertake research projects sponsored by the societies. Descendants of the early settlers write to the two societies from around the world for information about their ancestors, and many maintain and exchange information through family websites. Others come to visit, trace ancestral connections in the archive collections, and walk through the greens and graveyards of the old towns. I have written this book for them as well as for scholars.

There has also been a growing interest in Andover because of its involvement along with Salem in the infamous New England witchcraft episode of 1692, perennially fascinating to lay people and scholars alike and subject year after year to new interpretations. Greven's study, as the foremost scholarly account of early Andover, was bound to figure in the debates about that event. Earlier social theorists of the witchcraft episode such as Boyer and Nissenbaum (1974) were puzzled by Andover. In their day the question was: why had the troubles erupted in a harmonious place like Andover as well as in conflict-ridden Salem? However, recent research by the town historical societies themselves make it clear that Andover's history, like Salem's, was far from harmonious, although for different reasons.[4] The present study provides some new directions for comparison. However, although I will include Andover's witchcraft crisis in the sequence of this study and suggest comparisons with Salem, it is not my focus. I intend to set the episode into a larger account of Andover's first seventy years. This will include the settlers' regional and ethnic backgrounds, the way they laid out their town, their kinship and marriage ties, their troubles without and within, their struggle to work through all that divided them, and how, following the traumatic years of the 1690s, they began to reconstruct a new social order in the opening years of the eighteenth century.

Sources

Sources for early New England history, and for this study, may be grouped into two broad categories: the literary and the nonliterary.[5] Literary sources I have used here include journals, letters, travelers' accounts,

---

[4]Boyer and Nissenbaum (1974) accepted Greven's view of Andover. Hansen (1983), Cowing (1995), and Robinson (1992) focus only on witchcraft but recognize that Andover was more turbulent than previously had been thought. Murrin (2003) provides a chronological review and critique of a number of the witchcraft studies.

[5]The archives used for this research are stored under excellent working conditions and with friendly and helpful staffs at the North Andover Historical Society, the Andover

books, broadsides, tracts, and sermons. Nonliterary sources include court records, wills, deeds and inventories, town and church meeting records, tax records, military rolls, family genealogies, and public sources of vital statistics. The Massachusetts Bay Colony is well documented, and the records pertaining to Andover are among the most extensive of the early Massachusetts towns. Over the years these records have served as the basis for town histories and family genealogies by a succession of local historians, antiquarians, and genealogists (Abbot 1829; Abbot and Abbot 1847; Moaar 1859; Bailey 1880; Fuess 1959; Mofford 1985; Abbott n.d.; Abbot 1992). These records also served Greven as a source not only for his dissertation and the book based on it but for other work as well (Greven 1964, 1972).

Literary sources relating directly to Andover are scarcer. Anne Bradstreet, wife of Andover's first civic and military leader, Simon Bradstreet, wrote poetry that is enigmatic in terms of any light it might shed on the social world of the town. Examples of Anne Bradstreet's poetry and an interpretation of her years in Andover can be found in Campbell 1891. Nathaniel Ward, the organizer of the move to Andover even though in the end he himself did not go, was the author of several important works bearing on the early colony. It was his *Liberties of New Englishmen* which was adopted in 1641 as a sort of colony code of laws by the Massachusetts General Court (it is reproduced in full on the Winthrop Society website at www.winthropsociety.org). As for other Bay Colony documents that bear both directly and indirectly on the experience of Andover and its families, two major journals from the early days of New England survive and I have drawn on them. These journals are *Of Plimoth Plantation,* Governor William Bradford's account of neighboring Plymouth Colony and the Pilgrims, and Governor John Winthrop's *Journal,* his account of the Massachusetts Bay Colony and the Puritans (Bradford 1912; Winthrop 1908). Many volumes of other Winthrop family papers have been preserved and they include related items by nonfamily members as well (MHS-Winthrop 1931). There are also the brief but important autobiographical accounts by John Dane, older brother of Andover's second minister (Dane 1894), and by Captain Daniel Denison, chief officer of the Essex County militia that had jurisdiction over Andover (Slade 1892). For the later seventeenth century there are the journals of Judge Samuel Sewall, who refers several times to Andover and who visited there at least once. In addition

---

Historical Society, the Andover Memorial Library, the Essex Institute in Salem, the Essex County Courthouse, also in Salem, and the Massachusetts State Archives, which are now kept at the University of Massachusetts, Harbor Campus, Boston. See the listing of primary and secondary sources from these institutions in the Bibliography. I thank the members of the various staffs for the hours of help and encouragement they provided at different points in the writing of my dissertation and this book.

to these, there are works such as John Josselyn's account of his voyages to New England, cited in the opening paragraph of this chapter (Lindholdt 1988). I have also drawn upon the general accounts (available online) such as Francis Higginson's *New England's Plantation* (1629) and Edward Johnson's *Wonder-Working Providence of Sion's Saviour in New England* (1654). Johnson's comments on Andover in *Wonder-Working Providence* are dated 1648. Josselyn must have read them, because the wording of his comment on Andover follows that of Johnson's quite closely. As Johnson did for many of the colony's new towns, he even wrote an "Ode to Andover" (book 3, chapter VII), a portion of which follows. In retrospect his warning about the "slipp'ry paths and dark wayes" that lay ahead for any who would trouble the town, seems prescient:

> Thou Sister young [Andover], Christ is to thee a Wall
> Of flaming fire, to hurt thee none may come,
> In slipp'ry paths and dark wayes shall they fall...

In the 1960s and 1970s there was a major shift in colonial studies in the choice and use of sources, away from literary sources and poetic emotions such as Johnson's and towards the use of materials that lent themselves to quantitative analysis. This approach stressed the use of nonliterary archives, especially tax records, land records, vital statistics, wills, deeds, and court records (although the latter, in that they are full of stories, would seem to occupy some intermediate place between the literary and nonliterary). The work of scholars such as the English historical demographer Wrigley (1966) influenced young historians of the day such as Greven to develop quantitative, especially demographic, techniques to open up these sources. Historian Gary Nash in *Class and Society in Early America* (1970) summed up the shift with a nod to the muse of history as "cliometrics." But Nash, describing the history of this historiography, also spoke of the growing realization among his contemporaries that, however much quantitative techniques had opened up the nonliterary sources and produced new insights, they were not going to be the final answer for historians after all (Nash 1970:192–193). He stressed the need to take a fresh look at the literary sources in light of what had been learned from the demographers, and to develop new ways of integrating qualitative and quantitative material. The approach I take here to the sources on Andover aims at that sort of integration.

Some of Andover's earliest records have disappeared. Probably they were burned when Indians torched the town clerk's house in 1679, because the town's tax and land records from 1679 onwards are plentiful.

Birth, death, and marriage records for the town, kept safely at the county seat, are quite complete from 1650 on, however. Many records of the larger colony also relate directly or indirectly to Andover and its people. These records contain many instances of native categories, that is, emic terms for social relationships. "Native" in this case refers not to native Americans but to the British colonists and to the varieties of English spoken by them in the seventeenth century. Using those emic categories I trace links and groupings among specific people and sets of people, following their activities over time. I also note the original formats as well as the contents of nonliterary documents such as tax and court records, which often provide a significant part of their meanings.

As historian Stephen Foster remarked, "For all their penchant for voting, New Englanders seemed unable to pass over so much as a list of names without arranging them in an order of precedence"(1971:158). Indeed, the layout of many records indirectly reveals in such ways the emics of socioeconomic rank. Town clerks in the Bay Colony did not begin to keep their tax lists in alphabetical order until the late seventeenth century, before that recognizing those of status by listing them first. Harvard College did not start listing its students in alphabetical order instead of by some criteria of social rank until, surprisingly, the year 1769. Andover's town clerks adopted alphabetical order in the 1690s. Before that, the tax lists they drew up were headed first by the names of those entitled to be called *Mister*, as for example in "Mr" Simon Bradstreet, whose name is first, followed by one or two of the other ranking citizens who were usually, but not always, the ones also paying the higher taxes. Then came the rest of the townsmen in a list that may have been random, or may have reflected an order that cannot now be determined from surviving information. Perhaps the order of names reflected the route walked by the *"tything-man"* (as the tax collector was called in the initial period when church tythes and town taxes were one and the same) as he went around from house to house making his collections.[6] Appendix D shows Andover tax lists at intervals from 1679 to 1716 but reordered from their original order to show all taxpayers listed from highest to lowest tax paid and thus how families' fortunes changed over time. Such changes will be discussed more fully in chapter 4.

These sources provide many examples of the language people used and were developing to talk about social identities in their colony and town.

---

[6]Robert Hunt (Brandeis University, Professor Emeritus) offered this practical and probable explanation for the order of names. A recent reconstruction by Gratia Mahoney and others at the Andover Historical Society of the layout of houses in the earliest settlement may make it possible to test Hunt's proposal. See Kent (1981) for a study of the role of the English village constable of the seventeenth century, a topic not commonly treated but which was helpful in understanding civic roles in early New England towns as well.

Some emic regional and ethnic labels traveled with colonists from their old society and stayed with them through the transit, such as *west-country men* (from the western counties of England, especially Dorset and its chief city Dorchester); *Southton men* (from the region in Hampshire around the port of Southampton); *Mr Parker's company;* and the *Scotties.* These terms share space in the records with terms that emerged to categorize people in the transit to the new society such as *assistants, adventurers, planters, covenanters,* and *firstcomers.* Some terms persisted, some disappeared and some, like *householder* and *freeholder* (sometimes spelled freed holder and free holder), were redefined to serve the situation. Kinship terms such as *cousin-german* (for first cousin) and *brother* (for the father of one's child's spouse) were transferred from the old to the new world, but the symbolic content of these relations changed or legal aspects of them were contested. The chapters that follow develop a broader understanding not only of social change in Andover's early days but also of the colonists' use of such language for the various social identities by which they knew and named themselves and each other as they began to reconstruct a social order.

Anthropologists often focus on language in this way in their fieldwork, searching for key terms that will illuminate native speakers' social categories and perspectives. For example, Abu-Lughad has described how Egyptian Bedouin distinguish between the *sa'adi* and the *mra'bit,* 'free tribes' and 'client tribes' in the context of a what is a major social identity for them, that is, their *gi'ma,* which he roughly glosses as 'social standing' (Abu-Lughad 1986:99–103). Compared to such exotica, it may at first seem to native speakers of English that in the language of social identity I examine here, terms like *company, country, blood,* or *adventurer* are simply obvious and familiar. However, this English is also in its way a foreign language: it is familiar English, yes, but from another society and culture which we would find decidedly unfamiliar. As Hartley's famous dictum has it, "The past is a foreign country; they do things differently there" (1953:1). So indeed they did things differently, and meant different things by what they said, in seventeenth-century Massachusetts.

Related Studies

Historian Gloria Main (2001) remarked that Massachusetts is the most studied place in colonial North America, so I had better keep my review of related studies brief. Fortunately for me, during the heyday of town studies the social historians Perzel (1967) and Goodman (1974) studied two other early Massachusetts towns, Ipswich and Newbury. Their research bears directly on Andover, because many of Andover's first settlers started out life in the colony in one or the other of these towns. They had come over in companies, groups from the same region in Britain inspired or recruited to travel and work together within the larger Bay Company. They had sailed on the same ships and tended initially to stick together once they got to the colony. O'Malley (1975) studied the town of Rowley, Andover's contentious neighbor, where some Andover families had lived previously and where Samuel Phillips, the South Parish's first minister, had lived as a boy. Gildrie (1971) studied the first forty years of Salem. These town social histories together with Greven's study of Andover provide almost a regional look in that they treat five of the eight towns of Essex County (see map 5). Still other colonial town studies done in the 1970s give comparative as well as British background material on other settlers and settlements closely related in time and space to Andover. The social historians especially probed the conflicts and sore points in the town records. Their results provide a fascinating contrast with the town histories done in the nineteenth century by local historians in preparation for the observances of the Centennial of Independence. Those writers, full of the American centennial spirit, sometimes skirted such conflicts, or paid little attention to the old world origins of a town's founding settlers other than to say they had "left England."

Competing interpretations of the importance of British regional background in New England colonial town development have been a part of early American studies at least since Sumner Powell's path-breaking study of Sudbury, Massachusetts, *Puritan Village* (1963). Powell compared in detail the pre- and postmigration information about the colonists from the various regions in England who settled Sudbury. However, he wanted to show that English customs had retained little influence in the new world, claiming that the colonists had essentially left their former habits behind. Others would later disagree with Powell, but his *Puritan Village* launched a continuing study of the influence of British regional background on particular colonial settlements (Powell 1963; Breen 1973, 1978, 1980; Allen 1981; Greene and Pole 1984; Bailyn 1984, 1986; Fischer 1989; Bailyn and Morgan 1991; Thompson 2001).

Claims for the importance of British background factors in the early development of colonial societies were not new in New England historiography, but they were surprisingly absent before the 1970s. Perry Miller, that "towering figure" (in the words of the *Columbia Encyclopedia*) who long dominated New England Puritan studies, stressed the importance of premigration *intellectual* associations. He traced the old school ties that connected New England's first ministers, many of whom had studied together at Cambridge University (Miller 1961 [1939]: ch.15 passim). Historians in the 1970s began to shift focus to *social* associations, and to what Breen called "persistent localisms," the carryovers by the colonists of the social patterns of their premigration home areas (Breen 1973, 1978, 1984). This theme was also taken up by archaeologists of early New England, especially James Deetz and his students, who began to emphasize the British regional characteristics of material culture finds at Plymouth and elsewhere (Deetz 1996). Greven began his dissertation (1964) with a useful chapter on the British regional origins of the Andover settlers, but for his book he dropped most of this material and did not follow up on its implications. Goodman, on the other hand, in his analysis of conflict at Newbury where several Andover families lived initially, pointed out the great importance of different British backgrounds in understanding colonists' alignments and factions there (Goodman 1974:39–44). Similarly, in Andover as in Newbury, differing British backgrounds and people's attitudes towards each other seems to have mattered during the early years more than any previous accounts have made clear. The settlers' use of language shows that they were well aware of the ties of kinship, friendship, and patronage they knew each other to have, as well as background factors of ethnic and regional loyalties and antagonisms or in their terms, *blood* and *country*.

Two especially influential works on the theme of British regional background bracketed the 1980s. David Grayson Allen's study, *In English Ways,* a touchstone for the new direction, opened the decade in 1981. David Hackett Fischer's *Albion's Seed: Four British Folkways in America* (1989) closed it. Allen compared five New England towns, including Newbury and Ipswich, relevant to Andover as noted earlier because of their subsequent relation to Andover's history. Groups from different parts of England had settled each of the five towns. Allen explored how the differing cultural backgrounds of the colonists had affected the way towns developed, especially in agricultural and legal custom. He concluded that the variation among New England towns was closely related to this English background factor. Powell's work had opened up the way for New England historians to pay closer attention to English background. Allen developed the theme, but in quite the opposite direction. Specifically challenging the sweeping generalizations of his predecessors, Allen claimed that, far from leaving all behind, the colonists reconstructed much that was familiar to them from their regional English worlds. Summing up the significance of his findings for the "new" colonial history that would emerge in the1980s, he writes:

> The conclusion that the New England communities continued the laws and customs of old England would hardly seem arresting had not American historians agreed to the contrary for the past eighty years. Frederick Jackson Turner and others, reacting to the so-called Teutonic school, contended that the mere act of leaving the feudal and early modern institutions of England and settling in the hostile and primitive environment of North America brought forth a new man, the American man. Even a work such as *Puritan Village* reflects this whiggish bias. [Powell spoke of] "a startling transformation." The townsmen, said Powell, had had to change or abandon almost every formal institution that they had taken for granted. (Allen 1981:4)

David Fischer in *Albion's Seed* continued to stress British regional carryovers, but he expanded the range from New England to the American colonies in general, identifying four colonial subcultures or "folkways." New England's regional subculture he traced to the Puritan strongholds of East Anglia. But Fischer's generalization obscures the crucial point that colonists came from Puritan strongholds in other regions of England as well, and were sometimes at odds with the East Anglians. Still other early New Englanders, even in early Massachusetts, did not come from English Puritan strongholds at all and did not identify themselves with them. Andover's early social groupings show all these variations.

Other folkways that Fischer identified were the "Middle Atlantic" colonies, settled from the English midland counties with a strong Quaker influence, and the "Cavalier coast" stretching from Virginia on to the south settled by colonists supportive of the monarchy if not of Anglican church traditions. Finally, for his fourth folkway Fischer describes a category of settler he calls the "Borderers" or "backcountry people," found all around the colonies. They had their origins in the north England counties, in Scotland, Wales, the Marches of the Welsh border, and in Scots-Irish Ulster. Fox (1978) referred to these peoples as the "Celtic fringe." Even in 1674, Josselyn considered them as a distinct social category, calling them the "Old Brittains" to distinguish them from the English colonists (Lindholdt, ed. 1988:90). These people lived, as Bailyn and Morgan (1991) put it, on the cultural margins of the First British Empire. Their experience and their impact on colonial history was now being given a more prominent place in early colonial social history, as well as in the history of the American Revolution. Several of the settlers who were key figures in Andover's history had roots in such regions. Following Josselyn and Fischer, I will refer to them variously as *Old Britons* or as *Borderers*.

Given, then, that there is already this long line of research on old world origins of the colonists, my point cannot simply be that the particular

British regional backgrounds of individuals or families influenced the nature of particular colonial settlements such as Andover. We already know that. Nor is it enough simply to identify the British regional factors at work in the founding and subsequent social drama of a particular colonial town. I propose that in addition to the role of individuals, families, towns, and British regional backgrounds in shaping colonial social structure, we look at the role of another, larger kind of category to which most colonists belonged or had belonged. They called this the *company,* and they often identified and named themselves and others in its terms. Company affiliation was connected with regions of Britain, and with groupings with which people initially identified themselves and each other as they traveled to and through the colonial social world. As I will describe below, the colonial companies at all levels of organization, both formal and informal, played key roles, both competitive and cooperative, in the migration histories of people to the colonies and once there in the complex processes of their settlements.

What was a company? Colonization in early New England was carried out by segments of local British social structures of various sorts, breaking off and recombining to make up the units of emigration and colonization. These segments were drawn from the three key social domains, the manor, the parish, and the military. These were the long-standing focal social orders of feudal life still dominant in seventeenth-century Britain (see the discussion of these in Duby 1980 and even in Homans' earlier classic on the thirteenth century English village (1970 [1941]). Interlocking vertical social hierarchy characterized each of these orders. Although colonial society can certainly be analyzed in terms of class structure, upper, middle and lower, that would not be an emic analysis. I have not yet found texts from this period where colonists identified themselves, *emically,* as members of some sort of horizontal class. Rather they seem to have thought of themselves, at least initially, as still belonging to groups organized in a sort of vertical structure of interacting roles and statuses, in which they and the others had their places and knew what they were, but together they formed a unit.

Such vertical structures were well described by the British social historian Perkin (1972, chapter 2 passim). What has not been so strongly emphasized is the extent to which they were mobilized into founding units to carry out British colonization. People initially came to the British North American colonies in large and small sets or segments of such structures, with already established ties among individuals, families, and extended families of patronage, work, kinship, and friendship. These relationships worked themselves out in various ways during the first phase of the colony while the British social world they derived from remained an influential part of people's living memory. Most people had traveled together as subgroups in these kinds of units to the colonial arena and continued to appear together in the early records. Their collective social identities and actions included smaller subsets such as "Mr Rogers' company," a minister and his entire parish that simply up and left Rowley in Yorkshire to found a town in Massachusetts (and give it the same name). Others were "Mr Parker's company" settling Newbury, and "Mr Ward's company" made up of people coalescing out of their former companies to form around a new leader for the purpose of settling Andover. The one company which was supposed to encompass and command the loyalty of all was the Massachusetts Bay Company, the legally chartered, stock-issuing company that founded and administered the Bay Colony. Once in the new world, individuals and families often continued, however, to live and act within the framework of the activities, rivalries, and recombinations of their subcompanies, small and large.

In summary, what the colonists moved in and called a *company* was an English emic term for a type of social grouping with, as we shall see, a range of meanings but a core sense. In etic terms, it is a language-specific term for a type of hierarchical structure/action unit (to use the terminology of Giddens 1984) that would be common to many societies. Giddens made a useful and important distinction between the *action* of social structures and the function of them. The company as a structure/action unit operated above the level of individual, family, town, or region in British colonization dynamics. The *military* company or local militia was the most obvious and formal type. A structure in equilibrium, such as a *manor* or a *parish*, could become one type of company, a mobilized form of that structure, ready to act when leaders like Winthrop and Parker recruited and organized willing companions for a venture.

Company loyalties and rivalries and continuing tensions within and among segments of the old companies lay close to the surface of events in colonial Andover as elsewhere in the Bay Colony. Etically, a sociologist might say that a hierarchically stratified vertical social cluster mobilized into an action group; emically, *a company gathered*, in the language of the English-speaking colonists. Companies were, and are, vertical slices of some portion of the social hierarchy, a social (and analytic) category different from family, household, kindred, community, town, or class, which have been the usual units of analysis for colonial studies. The importance of the company has occasionally been noted if seldom treated as a unit for analysis in colonial studies. Cawston and Keane (1968 [1896]) gave a sweeping history of companies starting in 1296 AD. Staloff (1998) devoted his prologue to the "struggle for the company" in Massachusetts, but did not seem to see it as either a broadly operating unit of action or as a category term for various social identities. Yet it was the continuing purposes and operations of hierarchical, vertically organized companies, formal and informal, large and small, that shaped colonists' loyalties and identities in Britain. Companies drove the processes of migration, initial settlement, cooperation and competition once in the new world. So clear are the facts of this from the records that it is astonishing to realize the degree to which a subsequent ideology of American classlessness once obscured them. That ideology demanded from its historians for a long time a picture of new, pure, farmer-artisan egalitarianism and individualism, existing from the beginning.

2
"From the Native's Point of View"
Emic Social Categories in the New England Colonial Record

The final goal...is to grasp the native's point of view, his relation to life, to realize his vision of the world. (Bronislaw Malinowski 1984 [1922])

If we are going to cling—as in my opinion we must—to the injunction to see things from the native's point of view, where are we [as historical anthropologists] when we can no longer claim some unique sort of psychological closeness, a sort of transcultural identification with our subjects? (Clifford Geertz 1974)

The quotations above from two anthropologists writing fifty years apart, Malinowski and Geertz, point to the background for the aim of this chapter: to clarify the concept of emic social categories and to highlight several such categories that emerge from records relating to Bay Colony and Andover history. Malinowski was one of the first proponents in anthropology of grasping "the native's point of view," the goal that Kenneth Pike, arriving at the problem by a field linguist's route, would later call getting the emic perspective. What was a rather radical proposal in Malinowski's day had become a well-accepted goal for many linguists and anthropologists by the time Geertz wrote fifty years later, even if it is now questioned by some who doubt the possibility and even the desirability of such a goal.[1] But in any case, as

---

[1] For example, see the work of the late Marvin Harris, who developed his own meaning of Pike's emic/etic concepts to argue *against* trusting the native view (Harris 1968, especially chapter 20, "Emics, etics, and the new ethnography"). Although the later Pike/Harris debate (see Headland et al.1990) is fascinating, it is clear that Harris never spent much time trying to analyze and speak unwritten languages as did Pike, nor did Pike work as much on the emics of culture and society as he did on language.

Geertz pointed out, seeing things from the native's point of view, important as it may be, raises particular problems for historical anthropology. In live fieldwork situations such as Pike's in Mexico, or Malinowski's in the Trobriand Islands, a researcher who wants to explore native categories can walk and talk at length with people, live amongst them, learn and explore language, and supplement conversation with observation. But what about the point of view expressed in the language of natives of past societies? How can one recover with any assurance the views of people whose language and culture can be explored only in archives, such as the people of a seventeenth-century village in colonial Massachusetts? I hope to show that despite the limitations of learning from "informants in the archives," as Brown (1980) calls them, it is both possible and worthwhile to construct emic perspectives from the historical documents that relate to early Andover and the larger colony.

In the opening chapter, I proposed that company affiliation was a major category by which the colonists identified themselves and one another, not only as they gathered and traveled but as they dispersed and settled. Discussion of the company and other reference terms of social identity will frame and focus the narratives and analyses in the following chapters. Such terms, though common enough in daily language, reveal some of the categories colonists used to refer to (and, I assume, think about) their own and each other's identities and actions, past and present. Some identities that they brought along from Britain spanned the transition from the old society to the new. Some were terms for new identities that gradually arose, submerging the old ones as colonial society developed. I will give the term company extra attention in this chapter, exploring it as the key organizing social unit of the British colonial migrations to America and of the societies the British established there.

In addition to the company, the terms *blood, country,* and *plantation* and the relationships they entailed are especially relevant for this study. Ethnic language such as *scottie* and kinship language such as *brother* and *cousin-german* are examples of other emic categories around which symbolic and social, even legal, controversy developed. As the colony grew, the settlers of each town also developed vocabularies of social identity specific to the situation in their particular places. In Andover's case, for example, the records yield emic social category terms such as *covenanter, freed holder,* and *house holder* as well as the paired terms *firstcomer* and *latecomer, North Ender* and *South Ender,* all of which marked components of settlers' social identities by linking them with crucial phases of the settlement process.

The oldest surviving list of names for Andover is a key text for understanding the town's initial social order. The original is called the Faulkner List and considered a priceless town document. Kept in an Andover bank vault, it cannot be viewed, but it was photographed for inclusion in the town's *Proceedings of 1896*. A facsimile of the Faulkner List from the *Proceedings* is reprinted here as figure 1, with a transcription of the names and additional notes facing in figure 2.

The Faulkner List is named for Edmund Faulkner, Andover's first town clerk, in whose handwriting it is. Other town records supply the important information that this same order of names was used each time there was a new drawing for lots in the divisions of the town's common land (Andover Town Records, hereafter ATR: 24, November 1662). The list is doubly valuable because it names an important social identity, the *freeholder* (or *freed houlder* as it is spelled in the original) and indicates the specific set of men in that category. The social hierarchy within the set is shown by the list order. Furthermore, the list also shows a change of category terms written in by a later clerk (in different handwriting but date unknown) who emended *"freed houlders"* to *"house houlders."*

It should be noted that the Faulkner List that Greven and I used, shown here in figure 1, is quite different from the list reproduced recently in Mofford (2004:4). Her illustration is labeled "List of the first twenty-three Freeholders. Individuals are listed in the order they came to Andover." But there are some forty names on the list, in a very different order from the one Greven and I used, and it is dated January 1672. The caption seems to read "the names of those which ? houses ? betwixt their neighbours, according to our order." As I so recently noticed it, I have not yet inquired about its provenience from the Historical Society staff. In any case, I will continue to use the Faulkner List as shown on the next page.

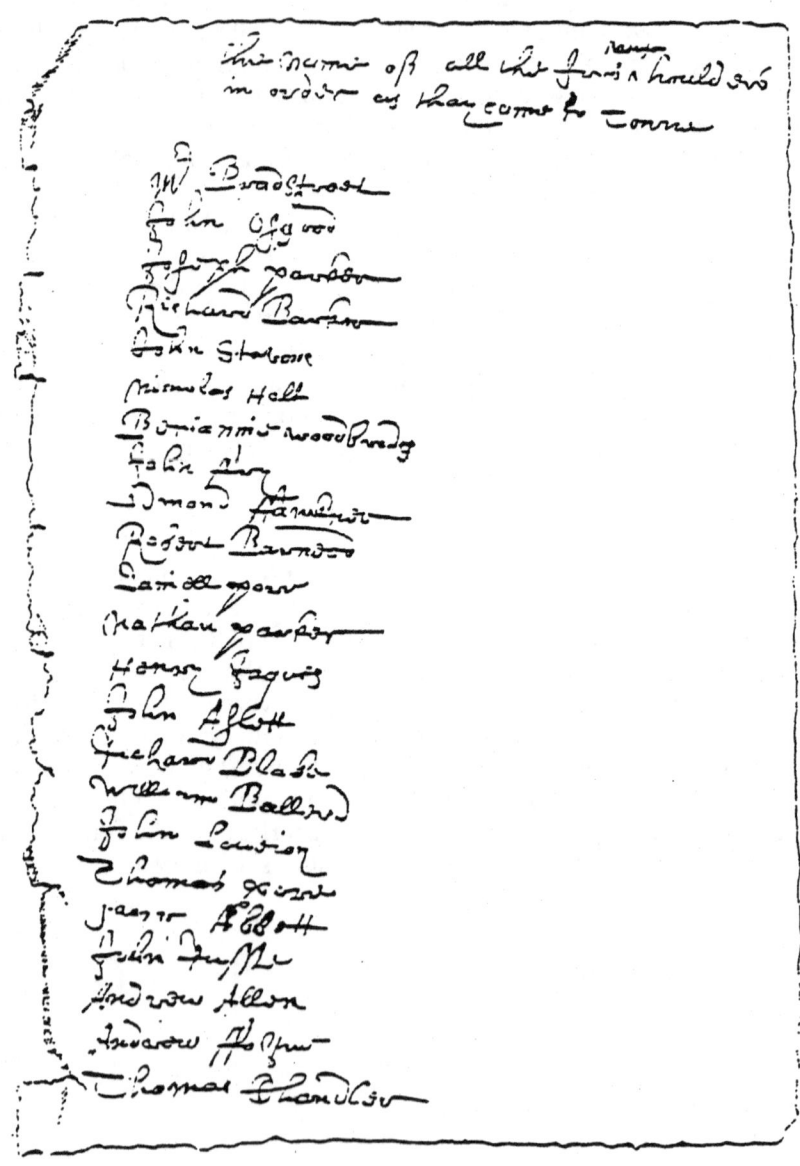

Figure 1. The Faulkner List of the first twenty-three Freeholders in Andover in the order that they came to town. Photocopy courtesy of the Andover Historical Society (reduced size).

"From the Native's Point of View" 21

house
The name of all the freed /\ houlders*
in order as they came to town

Mr Bradstreet
John Osgood**
Joseph Parker
Richard Barker
John Stevens
Nicholas Holt
Benjamin Woodbridge
John Fry
Edmond Faulkner
Robert Barnard
Daniel Poor
Nathan Parker
Henry Jaques
John Aslett [or Aslebe]
Richard Blake [Black]
William Ballard
John Lovejoy
Thomas Poore
George Abbott
John Russe
Andrew Allen
Andrew Foster
Thomas Chandler

---

* The word "house" inserted above "freed" is in a different handwriting.
**I have italicized the names of the men who were the original Andover Covenanters.

Figure 2. Transcription of the Faulkner List

The minister John Woodbridge would have been the first signer of the Covenant, but he was not a freeholder like the others, as his house and lot were provided for him by the town. Thus his name does not appear on this list.

From the beginning, the division that would eventually become the two parishes of Andover was present in that group of twenty-three. The lines of loyalty (and of division) can in turn be connected to these families' prior associations with different migration companies, and before that, with their different British regional background associations. The first fifteen men and families on the Faulkner List remained in the old town, later the North End, except for one man, Nicholas Holt (about whom more will be said later). The eight families on the second half of the list would form the core, first of the South End, and later the South Parish, when they all moved to the other side of the river. Greven was able to work out the list of initial acreages allotted to each Firstcomer, and his list shows that as a group the future South Enders, although they were Firstcomers, all began life in Andover with less land than the North Enders (Greven 1970:46; also shown in the final column of my table 1 at the end of chapter 3). Of the twenty-three men on the Faulkner List, three did not stay long in town, selling out their shares to others and moving away. Twenty remained and established their families in Andover. Some have descendents still living there today, even on portions of the same land. These twenty became known as the *Firstcomers* when a term was soon needed to identify and differentiate them from those who came after the founding year of 1645 and who were called, logically, the *Latecomers.*

These explanations are needed here because the research population for this study is made up of the twenty Firstcomer families and ten of the best-documented Latecomer families. I will explore their relationships and their changing language of social identity across seventy years, spanning the first three generations of their lives in Andover.

Before turning to the specific story of Andover, however, let me summarize how a Massachusetts Bay colonist might have been identified by a succession of emic terms of social identity in the English language of his day. Some of these have already been introduced; here they are put in the context of changing social identities of a particular colonist. Drawing on material in Abbott (n.d.:Osgood), Bailey (1880) and Osgood (1894), I will use the career of John Osgood, who became a leading citizen of Andover and his family after him. The town was named for Osgood's old home town of Andover in Hampshire, a southwestern county of England. The hill in Andover near where his family settled is still called Osgood Hill, which may be reached from Osgood Street. When John Osgood lived in old Andover, England, he would have had such old world identities as *yeoman,* for his social rank, and perhaps he was known as a *Southton* or *So'ton man,* as those who lived in the region around the port of Southampton were and still are called (Sewall 1976; Hansford 1998, personal communication). Then as tensions in England rose against those who wanted to "purify" the Church of England, Osgood would have been labeled with the pejorative *Puritan,* since he was not sympathetic with the *Cavaliers.* Osgood joined the exodus to New England, sailing for Massachusetts as a member of *Mr Parker's company* of other Southwesterners from the Hampshire region. That company identity persisted from embarkation through the landing in the Bay Colony and during his initial years in the Parker Company's plantation at Newbury. Then, however, Osgood and others left Parker's troubled settlement and joined *Mr Ward's company,* forming from segments of several companies and "increasing apace" as more settlers gathered to plant the proposed new plantations at Andover and Haverhill. Osgood moved with his family to Andover, and his name is second on Faulkner's list of *freed houlders,* after the gentleman "Mr" Simon Bradstreet (whose name is always preceded on lists by "Mr"). Over time, Osgood appears in the Andover records variously as a *freed houlder* and a *house houlder,* a *covenanter, firstcomer, representative,* and a *North Ender.* He died before there was a North Parish. His former identities as a yeoman, a puritan, and a Southton man faded away into irrelevance in the new society. Of Osgood's old world identities, however, one seemed more enduring: his social identity with others from his home region in the southwestern counties of England. The evidence is indirect, found in his family's continuing solidarity with other families from that region in forming their marriage alliances (see chapter 5) and in acting together in decisions about town affairs. But solidarity of this sort among the several families of southwestern England origin seems to have persisted in Andover for at least the next three generations.

As families like the Osgoods uprooted themselves, traveled, created new towns, and built a regional society, how did these old and new social identities disappear and emerge in the following generations? Can this process be tracked through the changing language in the archives? These have been among the guiding questions for this research. In the rest of this chapter I use the records of the Bay Colony and Andover to introduce and develop the meaning of several emic categories, using them to provide a narrative sense of the larger gathering, voyaging, and settling process of the Bay Company in Massachusetts. The next sections explore use of language, first the set of terms *blood* and *country,* and then the set *company* and *plantation.*

I have given the term *company* more attention than the others, to underscore what I believe is its importance as a seminal unit in British colonial expansion. *Company* and *plantation* are linked terms, however. A plantation was one of the possible purposes and outcomes of a company's formation and action. In the colonists' words, one of the actions a *company* could take in the colony was to "set down" and "plant" a new settlement, a *plantation* which soon would be called a town. The discussion of the various uses of the term *company,* including the Massachusetts Bay Company itself, leads into the next chapter, where I explore the structure and workings of the particular company recruited to plant Andover.

Blood and Country

Would-be colonists, before gathering into and identifying with a company, identified themselves and others by categories of identity and belonging according to what they called their own and one another's *blood* and *country*. They used these terms in ways suggesting their importance as identities in early colonial society in general, as well as in particular cases of conflict such as town splits, quarrels, and witchcraft. Although these terms are still very familiar in English usage today, it is important not to miss the aspect and force of meaning they had for seventeenth-century English speakers. Edward Johnson, in *Wonder-Working Providence,* vividly pictures a composite shipside farewell scene as a company of colonists gathers to board ship and leave England for what he called the "Western World."

> Brethren, Sisters, Uncles, Nephews, Nieces, together with all Kindred of blood that binds the bowels of affection in a true Lovers knot, can now take their last farewell, each of other, although natural affection will still claim her right, and manifest her self to be in the body by looking out at the Windows in a mournful manner. Among this company, thus disposed, doth many Reverend and godly Pastors of Christ present themselves, some in a Seamans Habit, and their scattered sheep coming as a poor Convoy loftily take their leave of them as followeth: "What doleful days are these, when the best choice our Orthodox Ministers can make is to take up a perpetual banishment from their native soil, together with their Wives and Children." (Johnson, in Jameson 1910:53, spelling modernized)

"All Kindred of blood" binding the "bowels of affection in a true Lovers knot" sounds almost painfully intense. Just what it meant to Johnson and his contemporaries in terms of mutual kin obligations is not exactly clear here, but what is clear is the image of the strength of the shared blood of kindred and the profound attachment to one's "native soil." That native soil was not all of England, but "one's country," which for seventeenth-century Britons meant not a political entity but a local place, a region. Blood and country correspond to what I will call ethnic and regional identities. Blood and country, as terms for the ethnic and regional loyalties and antagonisms of the home society, played a continuing role in the life of the new colony as they did in the life of the mother country.

While *blood* and *country* identities may have overlapped, they do not seem to have been interchangeable terms. According to some seventeenth-century observers, the inhabitants of a certain country or region might acquire at least some of their characteristics through the local soil, water, and customary foods (see for instance the views of John Aubrey, cited in Allen 1981:82–83). However, the influence from one's blood was inherited, fixed, and perhaps even eternal. As the Puritan minister Cotton Mather famously opined, "The Line of Election for the most part runs through the Loins of Godly Parents" (cited in Morgan 1944:102). The term blood as sign and symbol is found in contexts ranging from the family to the nation and race. Even more then than now the idiom of blood was invoked to account for similarities, distinctions, and obligations, between nations, peoples, and families.[2] Charles Morton, a Boston minister, wrote a testimonial in 1689 for a young cousin of his in England that "he is of my blood, for his grandfather and my father were brothers, and therefore I can do no less..." Although the minister had never even met this cousin, he still felt obligated by blood and promised to use his influence in his behalf (MHSC 5, vol. i: 436, in Cressy 1987:276).

The metaphor of shared blood could be extended to various levels. When the colonial militias defeated the Pequot Indians at the battle of Narragansett in 1637, Winthrop wrote in his journal, "Life was offered to all who had not shed English blood" (Winthrop 1908 vol. i: 227). Since Winthrop would have been well aware that there were Scots in the militias, his use of "English blood" perhaps becomes in this context a pan-British Isles contrasting category to "Indian blood." As such, even the blood of Scots and other non-English who had fought alongside the English might have been included under "English" blood. As for the Indians, they seem to have referred to all the colonists as "English," although they may have made distinctions among them that have not yet been explored. Aside from their role in the militias, the non-English, especially the Scots, usually seem to have occupied a strange, intermediate place in the colony, ethnically and socially, as Fischer also asserted. They were called *Borderers* or *Old Britons* by contemporaries such as Josselyn.[3] Scots were probably the most numerous of the non-English people in the colony. But whereas some Scots had come over willingly as coreligionists with the Puritan reformers, others came as bondservants. Later, after the English civil war (1642–1651) had brought Cromwell into

---

[2]See Schneider's "cultural account" of contemporary American kinship (Schneider 1968) and the stress he places on the idiom of blood. See also Leyton 1975, du Boulay 1984, and Sabean 1984 for studies of "blood" concepts in Ireland, Greece, and early modern Germany.

[3]The term "Old Brittains," as Josselyn, the seventeenth-century traveler, called them, probably subsumed bloods or ethnicities on the British Isles not considered English. It was used by Josselyn as an Englishman (or Norman?) to distinguish between English and the older ethnic layers of Irish and Scots (Lindholdt 1988:90). Robin Fox (1978) calls this the "Celtic fringe"; Hanson (1985) uses "the non-English New Englanders"; Jones (1991) continues the theme of Scots-Irish in the early period as culturally marginal. See also McDonald (1986) for an insider's analysis of the tension between old Celtic and English identities in contemporary Britain. Chadwick Hansen (personal communication 1987) thought there were ethnic issues in the witchcraft crisis at Andover that were not present at Salem.

war against the Scots, some came as Scottish prisoners of war, sent to the colonies to be sold on the docks (Banks 1928).

Although there is no direct language about English-Scot relations in Andover records, such relations were reflected in the town layout and later emerged as likely factors in town friction. The Scottish families lived initially in the same neighborhood and in a section of town later shown on school district maps in the Andover Historical Society as *Scotland*. In Andover's history, Scottish blood and country may have mattered in particular, for many of those first involved in the witchcraft crisis in Andover, both accused and accusers, were of Scottish background or from the northern border counties of England (see chapter 6).

The language in court records about cases from towns near Andover sheds light on the general position of Scots in the colony and its towns, on the attitudes of others towards them and on their view of themselves. One of the most provocative fragments of insight into the idiom of blood in relation to Scottishness comes from a case about a quarrel that came before the Ipswich Court in 1671. Here John Gould deposes regarding the temper of the controversial Mr. Gilbert, minister of Topsfield (two towns away from Andover). Both men, then, though Scots, were not among those who had come as laborers or bondservants but were among those who had allied themselves with the Puritan migration and held ministerial posts in the Bay Colony. Gould deposed:

> Soon after Mr Gilbert come from the Court...he did say...that they that sat to judge would say it was the Scotties blood and the Scotties fumes that fumied up into his head...but if ever the godly...do come to heaven they shall bless god that ever they did see a Scot man. At a further time this deponent saith that Mr Gilbert did use the words of being gaged [highly agitated] at that time after he came from the court when he spake of Scottish blood & Scottish Fumes. (ECQCR iv:370)

The Scots emerge from the colonial records with a mixed report. In this example from Topsfield a Scot is the minister, albeit struggling with his "Scotties blood and fumes." But about the same time, Judge Sewall in 1670 reports with curt brevity: "A Scotchman and a Frenchman kill their Master, knocking him in the head as he was taking Tobacko. They are taken by Hew and Cry, and condemned: Hanged" (Sewall 1973:10). The judge continued to note ethnic distinctions in his diary. "Mr Brown the Scot preached at the Boston church," he records as late as January 1687 (p. 131).

Militia records also provide insight into the ethnic relations of the colony and how Scots (as well as other ethnic groups) were categorized. In 1652 the General Court ordered that "all scotchmen Negers and Indians inhabiting with or servants to the English...shall be listed and are hereby enjoyned to attend trainings." In 1656 the court repealed that part of the law requiring that domestic Indians and blacks take part in military training, but the Scots were to stay in the militia (Millar 1967:52ff.). Unfortunately, nothing survives of the rationale for this decision by the Court. It may have been due to Scots' reputation as fighters (see Webb 2004, *Born Fighting*, for a popular account of early Scots and Scots-Irish in America). Whatever their status in the context of Britain, perhaps the Scots had come to seem less foreign in the new world than they had in the old. They could now be seen in comparison to such new contrastive ethnic categories as "Negers and Indians." Scots themselves, however, apparently felt their alien status and the need for mutual aid. Lockridge (1970:81) notes that the few Scots who settled in Dedham in the 1660s were "by implication second-class citizens." The Scots community in Boston established the Scots Charitable Association in 1657, signing a compact that was renewed for years after by their descendants. It provided that "the poor strangers and families and children of our Nation [Scotland]...may be more orderly and better relieved—being flesh of our flesh & bone of our bone" (Hardwick 1962:5–6).[4]

Town layout, growth, and neighborhood names reflected ethnic as well as regional ties in the colonial towns, including Andover. The Scots had their own neighborhoods, often together with other non-English people and Borderers such as the north Britons and Welsh. Old neighborhood names in the early towns still survive, such as "Scot Hill" in Ipswich, "Scotland Road" in Newbury, "Scots Corner" in Kittery, as well as the "Scotland" school district in Andover, testifying to the locations of the enclaves. In Andover, the initial territorial arrangements in fact recreated a miniature version of the map of Britain. Recent houselot reconstruction done by members of the Andover Historical Society in 1992 and 1995 (available at the Society office) show that people of English origins, albeit differing ones, lived in the east, central, and southern sections of the center of the village at first, while the Scots, other Borderers, and old Britons lived in the Celtic fringe around the north and west edges. (See map 8. See

---

[4]This association was the first ethnic self-help group to be established in the Bay Colony. Surviving records reveal something of the Scots' view of their situation in the colony in the words of the compact the founders signed. There is as well a valuable list of the names of the founding members (among whom were several of the Scots of Andover, as will be made explicit later). Not all Scots in early Massachusetts had come as servants or prisoners; some were apparently free and even prospering by the 1650s and in a position to start a fund to provide aid "for ourselves being Scottish men and for any of the Scottish Nation whom we may see cause to help." Twenty years later the original compact was renewed by forty "Scotsmen and sons of Scotsmen now Inhabitants of Boston and the colony thairof [sic], being of one accord to give..." (Hardwick 1962:5–6).

also HH Andover 1946 and Rockwell n.d., which these later projects built upon.) In the second and third generations, some of these families would eventually be assimilated into English-origin families by marrying in. Other "fringe" families would remain further marginalized in the outlying parts of town.

Colonial historians have assessed differently the matter of ethnicity and regional loyalties and antagonisms in early Massachusetts. Boyer and Nissenbaum did not explore these issues in their Salem study, although they mentioned an account of the negative reaction to Welsh ironworkers in Rowley (1974:124–125). However, Stephen Innes, a colonialist with an interest in early ethnic relations, noted many such incidents from the court records for early Springfield, Massachusetts. Innes found that, although the number of Scots in Springfield was not great, "their impact on the community was considerable." In Springfield, he discovered, most Scots were probably of that group of prisoners from the English Civil War, defeated by Cromwell and sent to be sold into indenture on the docks of Charlestown in 1652. William Pyncheon, Springfield's founder, had bought a number of them. Because the Scots were in the Bay Colony for the most part involuntarily, "their personal commitment to Puritan norms was minimal" as Innes wonderfully understates it. They flouted the laws, played cards, got drunk, caroused, and fought. All of them appeared before the Springfield magistrate, most more than once. But they were allowed to remain in the community, Innes finds, because they were such good artisans, especially at the indispensable art of blacksmithing (Innes 1983:9–10, 143ff.).

Seemingly small issues could spark ethnic antagonism in Springfield. Innes recounts a court case of 1659 in which John Henryson complained against Thomas Miller for "detaining a cart which he sayth he had right to" and "using reproachful speeches." Miller then hit him and called him a "Scottish Dogg." Later Henryson and his wife were summoned to court for having card parties in their home. Henryson's defense is worth noting. He did not know there was a law against card-playing at home, he said, and besides, it was recreation for his wife "to drive away her melancholy. I was willing to do anything when my wife was ill to make her Merrie," he said (Innes 1983:144). Here also is a glimpse of the anguish of a woman doubly isolated, not only sick and stuck in a remote frontier town, but a "Scottish dogg"as well.

John Demos noted factors of regionality and ethnicity in his work on New England, but inconsistently. In his review of witchcraft cases in New England other than those in the 1692 outbreak, he did not consider the evidence to be very strong for an ethnic factor in the accusations, despite citing several cases to the contrary. He goes on to say, "But otherwise most of the witches seem to have been of solidly English stock..." (Demos 1982:71). Here he may have been applying his own view of relevant social categories to these people rather than trying to uncover their view. I find little evidence of any emic category like "solid English stock" in the thinking of people in either seventeenth century England or New England, although as noted above, facing a common Indian enemy may have helped raise a new sense of the common blood of greater Britain. Later in the same volume, however, in his chapter on witchcraft in Hampton, New Hampshire, Demos did note that "differences in English origins," (that is, in region or country, rather than "stock"), weighed heavily in that town's factional history leading up to the witchcraft accusations. One of the two quarrelling Hampton ministers, who was of southwestern England origin, accused the other, an East Anglian, of "abuse of the power of the church." Notably, he further accused the church members of "cleaving to him" not because of the rightness of his position but because of "[their] being his countrymen and acquaintances in old England" (Demos 1982:318). English regional loyalties had carried over (in the accuser's view) to affairs in the colony and it became an issue in the trial. This Hampton case is relevant here, for the settlers of Hampton and Andover had much in common. In both towns, those on one side of a factional dispute had come from this same region in old England. In both cases, they had at first been part of Mr Parker's infamous company, the deeply divided community that had earlier split up at Newbury.[5]

As for *country* or regional identity, as people distinguished it from ethnic or *blood* identity, there are clues in the records, and together with comments from the historians, they show how regional and ethnic associations continued from Britain into the reconstruction of the colonial society. The colonists referred to the place they came from as their country, but they did not necessarily mean England or Britain. Often they meant the shire or county, or even a particular region within a shire or county (see Dudley's letter below, referring to Winthrop). Thus among the identities that settlers had upon arrival in the new colony was their identity as belonging to a "country" or region within Britain. Many colonists traveled as a set of passengers, connected to a regional leader who had recruited a company of his extended family, friends, workers, and other local connections to organize and outfit the voyage. Fellow voyagers were often family members, servants, and neighbors from the same country in this sense.

The colonization of New England and the implicatures in the colonists' writings about their own and others' origins cannot be understood

---

[5]See Goodman (1974) for an account of early Newbury, the town where many Andoverites had been living before coming to Andover, and Perzel (1967) for the town of Ipswich, from which Newbury had been settled.

without a good sense of the counties and regions of Britain being discussed here, the sides that people of different regions took in the momentous events of the seventeenth century, and the networks of relations among specific persons from those regions. Then it becomes possible to understand something deeper of what lies beneath the words of the early letters and journals as the colonists commented about events and one another. (See map 3, Counties and map 4, Regions.)

The backgrounds and relations of John Winthrop and Thomas Dudley are a key example of such forces within the Bay Company. They were the leaders of the two main regional entities that sailed with the first fleet of the Bay Company. Map 3 shows the numbers of migrants from each English county. Governor Winthrop came at the head of the contingent from Suffolk and Essex Counties in East Anglia, where Puritanism was strongest. Dudley, the next governor, was a native of Northampton. That is part of the area of England known today (if not in Dudley's day) as the East Midlands. However, Dudley had most recently been living in neighboring Lincolnshire, where Puritanism was also strong.[6] Dudley had long been a part of the patronage network of the Earl of Lincoln, and under Lincoln he had developed a patronage network of his own. This included Simon Bradstreet, also a Lincolnshire native, who was Dudley's ward and later his replacement in the earl's household. Eventually, Bradstreet married Dudley's daughter Anne (the poetess), and so became his son-in-law as well. Dudley's background and status in the colony are of special interest to this study because his two sons-in-law, Simon Bradstreet and John Woodbridge, later led the company that settled Andover. Although Dudley's and Winthrop's contingents were both from the east of England, they were from different *countries* in the sense of counties or regions explained above, Dudley from the East Midlands, Winthrop from East Anglia. They and their people operated somewhat separately and even contentiously during Massachusetts' opening years in the 1630s. However, as Dudley and Winthrop and their people related to new companies of settlers arriving to join the colony from the West Country and from the southwest region of Hampshire and Wiltshire, they seem to have consolidated in an identity, if unnamed, as being from the east of England.

A remarkable letter survives, written from Massachusetts by Dudley back to the Countess of Lincoln, the wife of his company's chief patron and financial backer. He tells her of the background and early activities of the Bay Company, the voyage, the landing at Salem, the colonists' disappointment at what they found there, and their subsequent dispersal south to Boston harbor. The language of Dudley's letter, a long segment of

---

[6]For more on specific members of the Lincolnshire network, see Cook 1956; for an overview of the Puritan gentry families, see Cliffe 1984.

which appears below, opens up an emic or insider's view of the Bay Company in three important ways. First, he describes how the Bay Company leaders while back in their local "countries" had acted to recruit and mobilize people into subcompanies, organized for action and incorporated into larger, socially stratified units that were *above* the level of household, nuclear, and extended family groupings. Second, as the head of a company himself, a man accustomed to being in charge, Dudley uses the language of his authority to describe the new situation, as in "we sent" ships over, men to explore, and so on. Third, he uses the term country both in the sense of the new unexplored land they were going to, and as a local regional identification when he speaks of Winthrop, "well known in his own country." Dudley writes to the Countess:

> [In the] year 1629 we sent diverse ships over with about 300 people and some cows, goats, and horses, many of which arrived safely [this was the forerunner fleet of John Endecott and the New England Company]. These by their too large commendations of the country and the commodities thereof invited us so strongly to go on that Mr Winthrop of Suffolk (who was well known in his own country and well approved here for his piety, liberality, wisdom, and gravity) coming to us, we came to such resolution that in April 1630 we set sail with four good ships....[We] arrived in June and July where we found the colony [Salem] in sad and unexpected condition, above eighty of them being dead the winter before, and many of those alive weak and sick; all the corn and bread amongst them hardly sufficient to feed upon a fortnight, insomuch that the remainder of the 180 servants we had before sent over, coming to us for victuals to sustain them...whereupon necessity enforced us to our extreme loss to give them all liberty, who had cost us about 16 or 20 pounds a person furnishing and sending over.
>
> But bearing these things as we might, we began to consult of the place of our sitting down, for Salem, where we landed, pleased us not. And to that purpose, some were sent to the Bay to search up the rivers for a convenient place....(Vaughan 1972:60–61, spelling modernized)

When Dudley remarked that Winthrop was "well-known in his own country," he meant Suffolk, not England. It is another instance of how, in Underdown's phrase (1973:20) for the seventeenth-century English "country meant county." Many colonists emigrated not only with family members, but also in the company of their "countrymen," that is, people from a local region of the same county, and these allegiances to custom and countrymen were often strong. Goodman (1974) in the opening chapter of his study of Newbury stresses this point, remarking that, even by the time he was writing, colonial historians had only begun to develop the implications of British country (county) loyalty. That is, not only migration, but also exploration and establishment of new territories in the colony were most often done in groups based on these old regional relationships.[7]

Colonists often noted their own and others' regional backgrounds, even if they seldom felt they needed to specify the attitudes they had towards people in those categories. Of special interest is Winthrop's reference to "the *west-country people*" when he notes in his journal of June 1630 that Bay Company men were not the only ones exploring the harbor. "We lay at Mr Maverick's and returned home on Saturday. As we came home we came by Nataskott, and sent for Capt. Squib ashore (he had brought the west-country people, viz., Mr Ludlow, Mr Rossiter, Mr Maverick, etc., to the bay, who were set down at Mattapan)..." (Winthrop 1908 vol. i:50). The "west-country people" were of the Dorchester Company, which had landed about two weeks before the Bay Company and were in the process of "setting down" and making their initial encampment. West-country people had been earliest on the scene already at Plimoth Plantation. They were in Massachusetts already at Salem. Winthrop's note highlights regionality since his Bay Company was made up largely of people from the east of England, East Anglia, Essex, and Lincolnshire. Eventually, this Dorchester Company mentioned by Winthrop would be absorbed into the larger Bay Colony, but not without some conflict between the westerners and the easterners who made up the two original companies.[8]

As Dudley told the Countess (see his letter above), Winthrop and his entire company had originally expected to join the settlement at Salem and form one large community there, but they found conditions so discouraging that they soon moved down the coast to what is now Boston Harbor to look around. To summarize the course of events as noted by Winthrop during the next months of 1630, the advance party for the Bay Company could not find a place with suitable water to sustain a single large town around Boston Harbor. So in a major change of plans, Winthrop reluctantly gave permission for the company to regroup into its smaller

---

[7]In Judge Sewall's time the colonists still remained attuned to each other's country, especially to those who were from one's own home region. Sewall, who came from Hampshire near Southampton, noted in his journal for 1675 the visit to his house of another "Southton man," as they called themselves, who had gone to school not far from where Sewall himself had studied as a boy. Sewall also reports in 1685 of meeting other "Hampshire men" on the ferry to Salem (Sewall 1973:10, 61).

[8]For an account of Winthrop's struggle with the west-country men of Hingham, see his *Journal (MHS 1931* vol. ii:229–245) and Waters' analysis in his study of Hingham (1968). According to Waters the initial country loyalties of the men of Hingham faded with the rise of the new realities of the colonial economic order.

companies, explore the terrain, and "set down at desirable places" along the Charles and Mystic rivers. The smaller companies had been recruited into the larger Bay Company, most of them gathered around regional gentry as company heads. Winthrop had wanted each new plantation to be headed by a *person of quality,* that is, a member of the gentry (see Brown 1954, and see Hotten 1962 [1880] for continuing use of this term). But were there enough gentlemen?

A further problem with the multiplication of settlements was that according to the Puritans' plan, each settlement would need a minister, but only two ministers had come initially with the Winthrop Fleet. Making the best of it until new ministers could arrive, the leaders set one of the two at Charlestown and the other, George Phillips, at Watertown (the grandson of this George Phillips appears later in the story of Andover). Until there were more ministers, the new plantations had to be situated so that the people could get to one or the other of the two meetinghouses. These plantations would be headed by the gentlemen and modeled on the feudal-manorial structure that was foundational to the life that Winthrop and the gentry knew. This unexpected change of circumstance and the recourse to the manorial model gave the beginning of the Bay Colony and especially the Boston harbor settlements their particular initial imprint.

The next wave of arrivals would bring with it a different form of the company. This was the church- or parish-based company, formed by a minister at the head of a group of his parishioners. Ezekiel Rogers and a group of families from his former parish of Rowley in Yorkshire were such a parish-based company and they planted a town (also called Rowley) on the Merrimack some six years before Andover was founded. Such parish-based companies hailing not only from the same county or "country" but from the same church began to make their way to New England in the 1630s and 1640s, and so the parish model joined and in some ways rivaled the manorial model for planting new Massachusetts towns (Winthrop 1908: entries for 1629 and 1630, passim).

Company and Plantation

What kind of a unit was the *company*? It was at heart a voluntary association, *com pan,* sharing bread. Giddens' formulation (1979) of a structure/action group as compared to a structure/function group fits a phenomenon like the company, which was not a social institution, yet was clearly a key unit in the founding of New England colonies and towns (indeed, of British colonization in North America).[9] To form a company, then as now, was to mobilize a more or less willing group and move it toward and through some common, shared enterprise or purposeful action. After that action, it might take further action, or disband, redefine its enterprise, ally with other companies, segment off into subcompanies to take up different purposes, fall to internal quarreling, or settle down and transform itself into a permanent unit. The colonizing companies that came to New England did all these things, as well as sometimes settling down to start a plantation where the establishing of institutional *functioning* would supercede the imperatives of *action.* Or, in current military company language, it demobilized.

Companies mobilized and acted in four main social arenas: economic, civil, military, and ecclesiastical. These arenas were often closely interconnected activities in the colonial companies. Companies could be formally organized, like the East India Company or the Massachusetts Bay Company, with a charter, stockholders, governor, and secondary leaders or assistants. Military companies with their ranks and officers could be more or less permanent and formal as with a standing army or a local militia. A company could also be a temporary, informal, companionable group gathered for a less well-defined purpose. And, except for some military contexts where men were conscripted, companies were voluntary organizations; the main participants (if not all their dependents and servants) *chose* to join or leave them. In the ecclesiastical domain, the New England ministers used the term company to mean the social basis of a church: "...a company of People combined together by holy Covenant with God and with one another," "a company of saints by calling" (from the Cambridge Platform of 1648, in Vaughan 1972:100; Miller 1939:435). Companies could be made up of networks of kin and non-kin, friends, associates, workers, masters, and servants. A company might be referred to and identified by place of origin, of destination, of purpose, or by the name of its head person. But in all cases companies were groups organized essentially voluntarily, for a purpose, under direction, with a hierarchical structure and with an internal rank or stratified order corresponding to the larger system from which it was recruited.

Whatever else characterized a company, therefore, it was headed, hierarchical, had a purpose, and generally, membership was by choice. The history of the Plymouth, Dorchester, and Bay Companies as they

---

[9] Giddens' way of thinking of groups in terms of structure/action rather than, or along with, structure/function has influenced the way I came to look at groups and group processes in colonial social reconstruction. I am grateful to Dr. Sherwood Lingenfelter, now of Fuller Seminary, for pointing out to me its usefulness when I was working on my dissertation. See also Giddens 1984:293–297. Also see Abbot (1916) for a precurser in this line of thinking, relating structure, function, and causation.

mobilized for colonization shows also that the relationships among the people within such clusters could be old and complex. The Earl of Lincoln, for example, never did set foot in New England but was the interested patron of an advance party of three hundred or more people, over half of them servants (see Dudley's letter above). Matthew Cradock, the first appointed governor of the Bay Company, never got there either, although he had sponsored a company to Massachusetts and their settlement at Medford was considered to belong to him, (Winthrop 1908, vol. i:66, 67, 119). When men of Parker's Company petitioned for permission to settle at Newbury, colony records show that the General Court at Boston "reserves the right to take order that the said plantation shall receive a sufficient company of people to make a competent town" (RMBC 1853, vol.i:146). This text sums up the sequence that a group of Bay Colony settlers expected to follow, from *company* to *plantation* to *town.*

In 1636 George Phillips, minister at Watertown, wrote to John Winthrop's son urging him to "set down with the plantation here." Phillips' language shows how the Watertown company, the unit of structure and action sent by Winthrop to settle there, had moved into its plantation phase. Phillips told young Winthrop that Watertown had been in disorder without a proper gentleman to head it ever since the sudden departure of Sir Richard Saltonstall, who had decided to return to England. The minister went on, " A company without a head cannot well sway and guide itself but is subject to many errors, distractions, confusions and what not...dangerous to the cause of religion, dismal to the Common state...and a disturbance to the Church estate..." (MHS 1943, vol. iii:241–242; see also Thompson (2001).

Other texts taken in chronological sequence from Governor Winthrop's Journal show companies in action—also in competition—in several different contexts during the early years of the colony, starting with the arrival of the first ships of the Winthrop fleet at Salem. (See map 1 for places mentioned in the following excerpts.)

> June 14, 1630. In the afternoon we went with most of our company on shore [at Salem] and our captain gave us five pieces [a five-gun salute]. (Winthrop 1908, vol. i:50)

> July 6, 1631. A small ship of sixty tons arrived at Natascott [Dorchester]....She brought ten passengers from London....They came with a patent to Sagahadock [southern Maine], but not liking the place, they came hither. These were the company called the Husbandmen and their ship the Plough....Most of them proved familists [a sect the Puritans deemed heretical] and vanished away. (p. 65)

> Sept 6, 1631. About this time last year the company here set forth a pinnace to the parts about Cape Cod to trade for corn, and it brought here above eighty bushels. This year again the Salem pinnace...was by contrary winds put into Plymouth, where the governor [of Plymouth] etc. fell out with them, not only forbidding them to trade, but also telling them they would oppose them by force, even to the spending of their lives, etc., whereupon they returned, and acquainting the governor of Massachusetts with it, he wrote to the governor this letter here inserted. (p. 67)
>
> August 1632. The Braintree company, (which had begun to sit down at Mount Wollaston) by order of court, removed to Newtown [Cambridge]. These were Mr Hooker's company. [Hooker, a minister, was not yet in New England; this was the advance party of one of the first of the minister-led companies.] (p. 90)[10]

The role of the military form of the company would only increase over time in Massachusetts with the increase in importance of the town militias (see Shy 1963). Although membership was not always voluntary but required, in other respects the military company epitomized the type: "companionable" yet hierarchical, it was an action-oriented structure with a clearly defined rank order and a clear purpose. Each town was required to have its own militia company, referred to in records as a *trained band* or *trainband*. In Andover the men of the Frye family soon became leaders in the town militia and their names appear as officers for several generations. An undated Frye family document clearly lays out the ranks of the militia company: "Mr Fry was one of the first settlers in this Town and his offspring men of Great Note; there was Corporals, Sergeants, Clarks, Ensigns, Lieuts, Twelve Captains, Majors, Colonels, and Major Generals..." (in Bailey 1880:88; spelling modernized).

The struggle among local, regional, and central centers for control of military resources was present from the beginning. At first the Governor urged that leaders of local militia companies be appointed from the central authority in Boston. But not all in the towns were in agreement. Soon after the landing, Winthrop noted in his Journal for May 8, 1630: "A proposition was made by the people that every company of trained men might choose their own captain and officers; but the governor giving them reasons to the contrary, they were satisfied without it" (Winthrop 1908 vol. i:79). Later, however, Winthrop had to change his position, for the local

---

[10] Born in Leicestershire, fellow of Emmanuel College, the chief Puritan stronghold at Cambridge University, and lecturer in Braintree, Essex, after he emigrated with his followers, Hooker never quite grafted into the Massachusetts Bay Company. After a few years in the Bay Colony, in May 1636 he took his company from Cambridge to "sit down" at Hartford, in Connecticut Colony, a poignant departure described later by Winthrop (Winthrop 1908 vol. i:90). See map 2.

companies did get the right to choose their own leadership after a crucial standoff between Winthrop and the militia of Hingham (see Winthrop vol. ii:229ff. and Waters' (1968) discussion of the event). As Indian and French hostilities increased, the importance of both the town militia companies and county and regional military organization increased as well. The intense company life of the town militias during their combined maneuvers with those of other towns soon elevated the military order into probably the most important integrating force for men at the town and county level and in the colony.

Bay colonists, then, moved and acted in the context of these various sorts of companies with their various purposes and levels of organization and permanence, gathered around some leader as head, whether governor, minister, or military officer. The ties they had as members of a company usually included immediate or extended family members and friends or fellow countrymen from the old world, but the ties were broader than that. Whatever the nature of people's ties and activities in their other roles at other levels, here they acted at the level of the company.

Note that colonists also used the term company in a negative way. They might speak of Indian parties as "devil's companies" or as "a company of rogues and blackguards" (see Slotkin 1973, Norton 2002, and Karlsen 2003 for notes on instances of such usages). And the servant of Simon Bradstreet, brought to court in 1656 for protesting being whipped, dared to call his master and the magistrates "a company of rude debased fellows" and said he wished them all hanged (in Bailey 1880:415; see also Towner 1962, and my Preface).

The Bay Company and the Bay Colony

People who joined the companies gathering for migration from Britain to North America had a variety of reasons for wanting to migrate. Many of those joining the Massachusetts venture were drawn to the prospect of escaping England to found a religious community run according to their beliefs. Others were adventuring, with mainly economic motives. Sympathizers with the religious motive came from several pockets of Puritan dissension in Britain. Many, as Fischer (1989) said in his discussion of the New England folkway, were from East Anglia, especially Suffolk, Norfolk, and Essex. But they came also from Lincoln and Hertfordshire, from Northampton and Leicester in the midlands, and from Gloucester and Dorset in the west. Many also came from around London. Later a wave of immigrants arrived from the south counties of Wiltshire and Hampshire. There were Scots from Scotland and Ulster Scots from northern Ireland. Although the East Anglian contingent may have been the dominant one, as Fischer makes the case, there were many smaller companies and clusters of families from other British regions who settled Massachusetts and the larger New England colony (see map 3).

The Massachusetts Bay Company received its royal charter and began to prepare itself for the Atlantic crossing in what would ultimately be a fleet of eleven ships that became known as the Winthrop Fleet. In the spring of 1630 the Winthrop Fleet finally set sail for Massachusetts, as both Winthrop's and Dudley's accounts describe. A wave of migration followed that would bring some twenty thousand people to the colony during the next ten years. Many of the passengers were somewhere on the spectrum of that religious persuasion that had come to be known derogatorily as "puritans" for their desire to "purify" the Church of England, and they were leaving an atmosphere of increasing hostility and persecution in England. They consciously drew upon biblical metaphors, calling the venture in their sermons an "exodus," and speaking of entering the "new Canaan." John Winthrop preached aboard ship the sermon that gave the colonists the famous "city on a hill" metaphor, which marked their collective identity as a chosen, special people, albeit burdened with special responsibilities because of it (Winthrop 1630). Years later, when London burned in the year 1666, many were quick to see a connection between that wicked city they had left behind, the date of the fire, and the mysterious number 666 of the beast in the Apocalypse.

However, whatever their views on these matters, the voyagers were also part of a formal, chartered trading company traveling under the title of "The Governor and the Company of the Massachusetts Bay in New England." The charter members took the royal patent with them by Winthrop's design in an unprecedented move.[11] With the patent or charter in hand, they claimed the right to settle and trade in a region designated as extending from three miles south of the Charles River to three miles north of the Merrimack River (map 1). The western boundary was unlimited. To the north in what are now Maine and New Hampshire were the huge grants previously made to a royalist, Sir Ferdinando Gorges, who opposed the Puritans. The men of the Bay Colony would soon be at odds with Gorges' men. Crowding down from the north on Gorges were the French

---

[11] It was not usually permitted for such chartered companies with overseas operations to take their charters with them. They were to be left in England in the hands of the home-based board of trustees. For an earlier perspective and details of how the Massachusetts Bay Company happened to take its charter along and the ramifications of that act, see the colonial historians, for example, Palfrey 1882 and Adams 1893.

in Canada. To the south of the Bay Colony was the Plymouth Colony, which had now survived as a plantation for ten difficult years. Plymouth would be the Bay Company's closest, if not always sympathetic, neighbor (see above, Winthrop's entry for September 6, 1631).[12] Later, after the restoration of the monarchy in England, all the New England colonies would, by royal decree, reluctantly have to undergo consolidation into one Province.

The passengers on the Winthrop Fleet were not the first arrivals. In 1629, the leaders had sent a forerunner fleet known as New England Company, sometimes called the Endecott Company. Led by John Endecott, they were mostly from the West Country of Dorset and Devon. Six ships with three hundred men, eighty women, twenty-six children, one hundred forty head of cattle, and forty goats left England for Massachusetts in May. Some eight weeks later they landed at Naumkeag, which became known as Salem. Far more men than women and children traveled in the Endecott Company, and this was due to the presence of the many artisans and laborers recruited for the voyage. That there were eighty women and the children is nevertheless remarkable and sets off the purposes of the New England colonists from other colonizing ventures of the time. Their colony was meant to be a permanent home, with families establishing it, not a rough and ready trading outpost. Some idea of why the composition of this company was as it was may be gathered from the specifications in a prospectus called the "New England Tracts," probably authored by John Winthrop. This tract was circulating in England in 1628 among potential colonial "*adventurers*" (the term for financial backers of a "venture"). In one section, the author specifies "the means of effecting this work" with a fascinating estimate of the amount of money, workers, and animals that would be needed.

> Means the First. The Raising of a sufficient stock to the value of £10,000 by the adventurers of such voluntary persons as God shall be pleased for the former weighty ends to move to the forwarding of the work: wherewith might be transported 200 Carpenters, Masons, Smiths, Coopers, Turners, Brickburners, Potters, Husbandmen, Fowlers, Vignerons, Saltmakers, fishermen and other laborers; 100 Kine and Bulls, 25 horses and mares; by whose labors in 3 years space may be provided at least for a thousand persons dwellings and means of livelihood besides. (MHS 1931 vol. ii:147)

The author listed the workers needed by their trades, but such a listing can obscure what would probably have been the internal hierarchy of

---

[12] The Plymouth Company was made up mostly of Separatists (many from the west country of England. They unlike the Puritans, had decided to sever ties completely with the Church of England rather than try fruitlessly to "purify" her).

such a group of workmen. The two hundred men were probably recruited as crews already familiar with each other from particular locales and their guilds, with previous associations and experience of life and work in hierarchically organized mixed work and patronage crews. While expected to work together on the project envisioned by the chief adventurers, such a group of artisans and laborers would have also had ties to their own particular employers, sponsors, or patrons. Each crew would also have had its own set of ties to particular sponsors among the adventurers.

John Winthrop describes how he and his brother-in-law Emmanuel Downing, as organizers of the East Anglians, continued to plan for the colony.[13] They journeyed from their country estates in Suffolk to the Lincolnshire estate of the Earl of Lincoln, there to confer with the earl and Thomas Dudley about the proposed venture. Lincoln was a major financial backer of the colonial venture. Dudley was the earl's former steward. He had left the earl's employ, bringing in his former ward and future son-in-law Simon Bradstreet as his replacement. Though now an active member of the congregation led by Puritan preacher John Cotton in nearby Boston (also in Lincolnshire), Dudley still held his place as an important link in Lincoln's network of patronage. Although Winthrop, Dudley, and later Bradstreet became the chief leaders of the Bay Colony, they at this point represented the two dominant, and at times contentious, regional contingents from Suffolk and Lincoln.

Winthrop (n.d.) had already been circulating a general letter among his Suffolk and Essex circles "encouraging such whose heart God shall move" to join the "undertakers of the intended plantation" in their venture. A letter of October 20, 1629, from Winthrop to his wife shows Winthrop and his son in the process of organizing their Suffolk company, recruiting colonists through the networks of local families connected to their manor and its demesne. As proper gentry, the Winthrops were careful to look after those within their purview of responsibility. He writes to his wife, "Let John [John Junior, his eldest son] enquire out 2 or 3 Carpenters: and also know how many of our neighbors will go, that we may provide ships for them" (MHS 1931 vol.ii:161). Winthrop's planning for the new colonial plantation reflected the organizational pattern of manor life familiar to him and to others of his status. When Winthrop tried to continue the old role of head of the manor in his new position as colonial governor in Massachusetts, some in the colony may have chafed under his governorship, but not necessarily because they had become instant democrats. Perhaps

---

[13] A good general account of patronage in seventeenth-century Britain is found in "The Old Society," chap. 2 of Perkin's classic *Origins of modern English society, 1780–1880 (1972)*. Downing's life and contribution to the venture is described in one of the few biographies of him, by Simmons (1959).

it was as much because they had come from different counties, or countries, and so their loyalties were to other company heads or, as at Rowley, to the headship of their ministers.

Nathaniel Ward, the minister who would later plan to lead the move to Andover, was a native of John Winthrop's Suffolk country. Before the migration he was also actively involved in the recruitment process. At the time of writing the following letter to Winthrop, Ward was minister in a parish in the neighboring county of Essex. The letter is especially important as it shows the prior relationship between Ward and Winthrop, and how Ward served as a channel of patronage both to and from Winthrop. As described in chapter 1, once in New England Ward would call upon Winthrop again, this time to plead for himself and his company to be granted the official permission over rival companies to settle Andover. Here, still in England, he writes to Winthrop close to the time of the fleet's departure. His wording shows the use of company in its wider sense:

> January 16, 1630. Sir, I purpose to see you this next week at London if God permit. In the meantime I intreat you to reserve room and passage in your ships for 2 families, a carpenter and Bricklayer, the most faithful and diligent workmen in all our parts, one of them hath put off a good farm this week and sold all, and should be much damaged and discouraged if he finds no place amongst you. He transports himself at his own charge. There is a pair of sawyers also especially Laborious, all of them will come to you upon Monday or Tuesday. I pray let them discern your hearty desire of their Company...Nathl. Warde, Stondon, Essex. (MHS 1931 vol. ii:192)

The previous texts and discussion shed light on the nature of the social order, the gathering of companies, and the role of patronage, kinship, and hierarchy in the relationships of would-be colonists, as they were getting ready for their journey. The following selections from Winthrop's journal and other sources show something of the historical sequence of the next phase. They relate incidents from the voyage, the landing at Salem, and the subsequent process of settlement around Boston and vicinity. After following the colonists on their voyage and early days in Massachusetts, in the next chapter I will take up the stories of the group that went to Andover.

The voyagers, with all their old world social identities and networks, now entered a transitional period, even what ritual analysts call a liminal period, aboard ship. Victor Turner (1969) described liminality in the context of rites of passage as the threshold stage between old and new statuses. The colonists were in many ways like initiates, passing through a ritual of status change. They would emerge at the end of their eight weeks' passage transformed, to take up new roles on a radically new environmental stage. Of necessity they would reproduce some form of their old social status order, yet they would be transformed by the rigors of the passage, by initial adjustments to the new environment, and by responses to the unexpected.

An entry by Winthrop describing shipboard life shows the statuses of the old world structure in operation:

> April 23, 1630. About eleven of the clock our captain sent his skiff and fetched aboard us the masters of the other two ships, and Mr Pyncheon, and they dined with us in the round-house, for the lady and gentlewomen dined in the great cabin. (Winthrop 1908 vol. 1:35)

Note the mention here of "the lady" and "gentlewomen." There was only one "lady" on the Winthrop Fleet and this was the Lady Arbella Johnson. Again, Winthrop's journal provides the background of these family and friendship ties. She was the sister of the Earl of Lincoln and the highest-born member of the company. The flagship on board which this dinner took place had been renamed *Arbella* for her. She was the wife of Sir Isaac Johnson, also of Lincolnshire, who together with the earl, his brother-in-law, was a major financial backer of the Bay Company enterprise.

The Earl of Lincoln was one of the few English noblemen sympathetic to the Puritan cause. His home in Lincolnshire where Winthrop and Downing visited him was near Boston, a city that was a center of Puritanism under the preaching of John Cotton. As persecution of the Puritans rose during the 1620s and 1630s, Lincoln and several other Puritan nobles grew very interested in the New England enterprise. Lincoln's mother's brother, Lord Say, was one of them. Allied with another relative, Lord Brook, Lord Say was about to finance a voyage along the Connecticut coast with a view to possible relocation there, should the situation for Puritans in England grow threatening for even the nobles. Lincoln began to gather a *company* along with his sister and brother-in-law Johnson. It included a group of kin, friends, retainers, and servants attached to them through a series of segmentary hierarchical relationships. This company would be an advance party that was to explore and prepare a place for the rest of Lincoln's household and the earl himself in case it should be necessary for him to flee England.

As for the "gentlewomen" dining with Lady Arbella in the great cabin, they would have included the daughters of Sir Richard Saltonstall of Yorkshire. They would have also included the wives of the men of the upper gentry, who stood just below these titled men, such as William

Pyncheon of Essex.[14] At this and other on-board meals, dining in their separate cabins, the men and women who were the elites of the major regional and parish clusters were establishing the hierarchy which would make up the Bay Company leadership. But it was "the lady," recognized with deference by all as the social peak of that particular and temporary social microcosm on board the fleet, who provided a social center for the group as a whole. She as the earl's daughter and her husband (not quite as highborn) were expected to continue to hold this top position in the new colony.

However, both Lady Arbella and Sir Isaac died within months of landing in Massachusetts. Their deaths left an unexpected social void at the top of the Bay Company, a vacancy that was never again filled by a figure like the lady Arbella who could symbolize in the manner of the old society a unified social structure for the whole group. The early deaths of Sir Isaac and Lady Arbella had consequences for the subsequent restructuring of the whole Massachusetts enterprise. The loss so soon of those expected to continue as the joint heads of the Bay Company not only reoriented the inner structure of the powerful Lincolnshire contingent, but also the relations between it and the other subcompanies of the fleet. Other changes at the upper levels occurred at an early point in the colony's life, but none so significant. Sir Richard Saltonstall, the knight from Yorkshire, was soon at odds with other leaders on several points of polity and went back to England. None of the lesser nobility who came to the colony in the beginning stayed beyond the first year. As for those in the category of gentry, William Pyncheon moved on with his company to western Massachusetts and founded what is now the city of Springfield. Other gentry went home to England, some when it became apparent from Cromwell's victories that conditions at home were improving for the Puritan cause. The deaths of Lady Arbella and her husband meant that the gentry, such as Dudley, Winthrop, and Bradstreet, moved into the top strata of the Bay Colony's central social order, thus rising to a level in New England that they would never have had in the home country. Their rivalries and reconciliations not only with each other but in their emerging relations with the ministers and military leaders, created pushes and pulls on the loyalties of colonists, many of whom were allied with one or the other of the two companies at some level.

The central social order of the Bay Colony, like its parent society, can be seen as three intertwined sub-orders—civil, military, and

---

[14]Pyncheon was not happy for long in Winthrop's Boston. Innes (1983:136–141) traces his career, which is of special interest in view of the fact that he bought many Scots prisoners as bondsmen to take with him to Springfield. They formed one of the best-documented early Scots ethnic enclaves there.

ecclesiastical—interrelated but each with its own system of hierarchy and offices.[15] Much of the early life of the colony was spent in the working out of these hierarchies, filling and defining their roles, and hammering out the power arrangement of each one and how they would work together as a whole. John Winthrop provides a picture of this structure as it was at Salem, as he records the momentous day of the fleet's landfall there. Here are the assistants, the gentlemen, the women, the captain, the people in their companies, in their social identities, in their roles, in their orders: the structure in action.

> June 12, 1630. Landing at Naumkeag [Salem]. Mr Pierce came aboard us, and returned to fetch Mr. Endecott at about two of the clock and with him Mr Skelton and Capt. Levett. We that were of the assistants, and some other gentlemen, and some of the women, and our captain returned with [the men of Salem] to Naumkeag, where we supped with a good venison pasty and good beer...in the meantime most of our people went on shore upon the land of Cape Ann which lay very near us and gathered store of fine strawberries. (Winthrop 1908 vol. i :49–50)

Although, as Dudley reported, many of the Endecott Fleet had died that first winter and food was scarce in Salem, Salem put out the best it had for the new arrivals. The rule of rank is captured in a vivid moment of contrast in Winthrop's account: the captain, the assistants, some gentlemen, and some women are taken to eat venison pie and drink good beer in the town, while the others wait on shore gathering wild strawberries, albeit "fine" ones.

Other points should be noted about this text. First, Winthrop makes the distinction between the two categories of colonists in his company: "we" (the gentry, assistants, and other leaders) and "our people," the others. It was for him the essentially birth-mediated dual structure of nobles and commoners. Second, a social organization had emerged at Salem based on the three main hierarchical orders (found in some form in most societies): the social, military, and ecclesiastical. This organization was manifested by the three men, Endecott, Levett, and Skelton, who came to meet the Winthrop Fleet leaders. Endecott was the governor, the social and civil authority. It may have been a difficult moment for him for he was about to relinquish his authority to Winthrop. Captain Levett was the military man, an experienced professional soldier of uncertain spiritual status but certain essential skills, the sort whose role was to become crucial and

---

[15]This was an understood ordering of society. Later at Andover the Boxford men used specifically the three orders (as described by Duby 1980 and fn. 16) in their request for relief in their "civil, military and ecclesiastical matters" (for Boxford, see Perley 1880).

problematic in the colony as dangers mounted.[16] Skelton was the first minister at Salem. These three men appear together here to welcome Winthrop and his company as heads of the civil, military, and ecclesiastical orders in the settlement.

Despite the welcome at Salem, Winthrop was shocked and dismayed at the difficult straits in which they had found the people. He further records that he and those with him found Salem "not to our liking" and they did not linger long before moving further south to Boston harbor and the area around what is now Charlestown. Mathew Cradock's men had already established a settlement near there at Medford. But by now many of Winthrop's people were already falling ill themselves. By the end of August, only two months after landing at Salem, Lady Arbella had died and her husband, Sir Isaac, followed her a month later.

With the Johnsons gone, Winthrop and Dudley, the two dominant men of the Suffolk and Lincoln contingents, suddenly and unexpectedly became the colony leaders. Their uneasy relationship set the tone of civil government in the early Bay Colony and has long fascinated colonial historians. Although their differences might be attributed to a matter of personality and leadership style, Dudley, who according to some historians had a connection to royalty, may have considered himself higher-born than Winthrop. This may have contributed to his chafing under the latter's leadership.[17] Dudley was also, after all, part of the Earl of Lincoln's company, having been for many years the earl's steward. So in terms of the Winthrop fleet, his loyalties lay not with Winthrop, nor at first with the Bay Company per se, but with the higher-ranking Lincolnshire company led by Sir Isaac and Lady Arbella. Their deaths so soon after arrival meant that the Lincolnshire party quickly had to regroup as far as its leadership went. Dudley took charge. This set him and the Johnson loyalists at a level opposite Winthrop and his East Anglian people. Without the Johnsons, there was no man of higher rank to whom Dudley and Winthrop could both defer, and under whom they could work out their relationship with each other.

Dudley and Winthrop almost came to blows one evening in 1632 when Dudley questioned the basis of Winthrop's authority. The incident

---

[16]See Winthrop's *Journal* for an account of the Colony's problems with some of its military leaders, Captain Underhill (1908 vol. ii:272–275) and Captain Patrick (vol. ii:153–154). Duby (1980) points out that this three-estate structure was an old theme in the culture of Britain. He cites the famous dictum of Alfred the Great, "Give me men to work, men to pray, and men to fight, and I will build the kingdom."

[17]Roberts (1987:101) discusses possible royal lines among the immigrants, including the likelihood that this was the case with Dudley. Roberts does not discuss what difference this might have made in the hierarchical relations of the central social order. However, to the colonists it may well have been an issue.

marked a critical moment in the life of the colony. As Winthrop in 1630 had reminded the company in his famous shipboard sermon, "A model of Christian charity," they were on their way to found a new kind of society. If the leaders now could not set the example, what was to become of the followers? It was not (directly) a theological point at issue here, but one of rank, authority and rivalry between men in the social and political hierarchy. Winthrop tells the story in his journal, referring to himself as the governor and Dudley as the deputy.

> After dinner the deputy proceeded in his complaint...and demanded [of Winthrop] the ground and limit of his authority, whether by the patent or otherwise. The governor answered that he was willing to stand by that which he propounded, and would challenge no greater authority than he might by the patent. The deputy replied, that then he had no more authority than every assistant (except power to call courts, and precedency for honor and order). The governor answered he had more; for the patent, making him a governor, gave him whatsoever power belonged to a governor by common law or the statutes, and desired him to show wherein he had exceeded [his powers]; and speaking this somewhat apprehensively, the deputy began to be in a passion, and told the governor, that if he were so round, he would be round too ["round" meaning outspoken in a summary and uncompromising way]. The governor bade him be round, if he would. So the deputy rose up in great fury and passion, and the governor grew very hot also, so as they both fell into bitterness, but by mediation of the mediators they were soon pacified. (Winthrop 1908 vol. i:85–86)

It would have been a great addition to this story if the method and substance of the "mediation of the mediators" had been described as well. Several years after the quarrel recounted above, however, the two men found another route to mediation. Winthrop's eldest daughter was married to Dudley's eldest son. This alliance was certainly seen as a sign, if not a means, of reconciliation between the colony's two chief families. It was so noted by Winthrop a few years later in the following entry, which also records the establishment there at Concord of perhaps the first public monument in British North America.

> April 24, 1638. The governor and deputy went to Concord to view some land for farms, and, going down the river about four miles, they made choice of a place for one thousand acres for each of them. They offered each other first choice, but because the deputy's was first granted, and himself had store of land already, the governor yielded him the choice. So at the place where the deputy's land was to begin, there were two great stones, which they called the Two Brothers, in remembrance that *they were brothers by their children's marriage,* and

> did so brotherly agree...that a little creek near those stones was to part their lands. (Winthrop 1908 vol. ii:269–270, emphasis added)

In customary seventeenth-century English kin term usage, the fathers of a bride and a groom called each other "brother" after their children's marriage (see Glossary). Like the Old Testament patriarchs who set up stone altars at important junctures (and they may very well have been modeling themselves after those patriarchs), Winthrop and Dudley intended that these "two great stones" would always remind themselves, their families and followers, and future generations that by means of both the symbolism and the reality of the marriage alliance they had established peace between their houses. The theme of marriage and family alliance among the families of Andover will be taken up in greater detail in chapter 5, and again in the final chapter, where marriage becomes a visible symbol of peacemaking between factions in Andover. Here the stage is set for it with this prototype social drama in the neighboring town of Concord, symbolically naming and symbolically marking the uniting not only of two people and two families, but also of the two great rival companies within the Bay Company.

Winthrop's account here of the exploration and staking out of lands around Concord also marks the beginning of inland settlement in the expanding Bay Colony as crowded settlers began to look for ways to move out from the coastal towns. Rowley would be settled in the following year, 1639. Forays into the Andover region were already under way. In the next chapter, I continue the story of how Governor Winthrop's old friend, the minister Nathaniel Ward, gathered together a new company to set down a plantation at Andover, drawing upon ties of country, blood, and marriage in the process.

3

"Our Company Increases Apace"
The Planting of Andover

> [May 1639] To the Worshipful Governor Winthrop at Boston:...One more request, that you would not pass your promise, or give any encouragement concerning any plantation at Quichichacke or Penticutt, till myself and some others either speak or write to you about it, which shall be done as soon as our counsels and contrivals are ripened.
>
> [Later that year] Sir: We are bold to continue our suit concerning the plantation I lately mentioned to you; our company increases apace *from diverse towns, of very desirable men, whereof we desire to be very choice: this next week, if God hinder us not, we purpose to visit the places & forthwith to resort to you, & in the mean time we crave your secresy, & rest Your Worships. We have already more than 20 families of very good Christians purposed to goe with us.*
> (Nathaniel Ward's letters to John Winthrop; my emphasis)

These excerpts from letters written by the minister Nathaniel Ward to Governor Winthrop provide insight into the ripening "counsels and contrivals" of the company making plans to establish plantations at Quichichacke and Penticutt, Ward's transliteraton of the Indian names of the regions that later became Andover and Haverhill (Massachusetts Historical Society Collections 4, vol. vii in Bailey 1880:4). At this point the organization of the move was still under the headship of Ward. The minister was related by marriage to Winthrop, and his relationship with the governor went back to pre-emigration days in East Anglia, their home region in England. A leading Puritan minister, Ward had come to the Bay Colony a few years after the Winthrop Fleet to be minister in the new town of Ipswich.

In those days, Ipswich seemed likely to become the leading settlement of the Bay Colony (map 1). The Governor's son was expected to take over as head of this settlement. But then, according to the early historians of the town, the excellent natural harbor at Ipswich was discovered to be filling with sand (Felt 1834). Ocean currents had shifted and so men's plans had to shift as well. Winthrop's son decided to move elsewhere. Ward, disappointed and concerned about his own prospects, was also ready to leave Ipswich. From the letters cited above, it is clear that he was forming his own company to cope with the changed situation, drawing upon the old patronage relationship between himself and Winthrop to further his cause and that of the "more than 20 families of very good Christians" gathering around who "purposed to go" with him.

In this chapter I trace the story of Ward's company, its relation to other companies, and the initial phase of their settlement at Andover (even though by then Ward himself had returned to England). This action of a company was what the colonists called *setting down a plantation,* the first step towards official incorporation as a church-town. Enough information emerges from the records on thirty-six of the first families at Andover to follow at least some of their steps and experiences through town and colony history to the town split in 1710. A summary (table 1) of the basic information on these families may be found at the end of this chapter.

Bay Colony Expansion

With more and more shiploads of colonists arriving every year and crowding the coastal settlements, the Bay colonists were feeling land pressure and cautiously exploring possibilities for starting inland towns. Winthrop tells us that as early as 1634 some men of Newtown (later renamed Cambridge) sent scouts west and north on an exploratory foray, and that they explored the Merrimack River region that was to become Andover.

> May 15, 1634. At the general court at Boston...those of Newtown complained of straitness for want of land, especially meadow, and desired leave of the court to look out either for enlargement or removal, which was granted; whereupon they sent men to see Agawam [Ipswich] and Merrimack, and gave out they would remove...(Winthrop 1908 vol. i:124)

Winthrop went on to note that the Bay Colony's leaders were anxious to start a line of settlements along their northern border to counter the French, who were beginning to make Indian alliances and southern encroachments from their Canadian outposts. The Governor's military advisors warned especially about the coastline north of Salem, believing the colony vulnerable to attack through the excellent but unguarded harbor at Ipswich.

As for the region inland along the Merrimack River that the Cambridge scouting party went to see, it included the Cochichawick tract. On the one hand, the scouts reported, it was "well-watered and a place of goodly prospect." On the other hand, it was remote and near the Indians, who had long-established camping and fishing grounds around the lake and streams of Cochichawick. Nevertheless, the General Court took upon itself the right to set aside this land and held out strong inducements for settlers to go there.

> 1634. It is ordered that the land about Cochichiwick shall be reserved for an inland plantation, and whosoever will go to inhabit there shall have three years immunity from all taxes, levies, public charges and services whatever, military discipline only excepted. (In Abbot 1829:11; see also RCAMBC 1904 vol. i)

Even with these inducements, no group ventured a permanent settlement at Cochichawick for almost nine years.

However, local historians say that unauthorized settlers, not mentioned by Winthrop or the Court, were already living in Andover before the official company of settlers arrived. One of these squatters was Job Tyler. One Tyler family tradition has him as probably from Cranbrook, County Kent (Brigham 1912). Only one other Andoverite, Latecomer John Johnson, is thought to have had roots in Kent. Other genealogists suggest that the Tyler family, though perhaps most recently from Kent, was actually of Welsh background (Abbott n.d.: Tyler; Johnson). How Tyler got to Massachusetts or to Andover is not known, but he and his family quarreled often with the official settlers. As will be described in later chapters, his relations with them were thorny from the beginning, and he makes a number of appearances in the General Court records. Tyler himself eventually left town, but his kin and step-kin stayed on, living at the town margin in what is now Boxford, and were among those accused in the witchcraft crisis (Bailey 1880:46–48; also see HH Andover 1946, Map #24-II).

As colonists learned where the desirable tracts of land in the colony lay, they began to compete for them. Permission to plant towns had to be obtained from the Court, but the securing of the rights to new settlements was carried out at the level of company connections and patronage ties. Ward's letter at the head of this chapter shows how Ward "craved the secrecy" of his old friend the Governor with regard to his company's "counsels and contrivals" for the lands of Cochichawick. Other texts provide insight into relations between incoming companies and already settled plantations. Such was the case with the initial arrangements for Andover.

The town of Rowley adjoined the Andover tract at the east (see map 5). Established earlier, Rowley was unusual among Bay Colony towns in that it was composed mainly of a company all from the same town in Yorkshire, in the north of England, led by its minister. Early negotiations over the Andover land (Cochitawit in the text below) included an attempt to fend off perceived encroachments by Rowley and its troublesome and powerful minister.

> October 8, 1640. At this court Mr Ezekiel Rogers, pastor of the church in Rowley, moved for further enlargement for taking in a neck of land upon Merrimack near Cochitawit...The court was very doubtful what to do in it, having formerly granted a plantation at Cochitawit, and did not yield his request. Whereupon...he grew into some passion...the next day he came...and did freely and humbly blame himself for his passionate distemper, and the court knowing that he would not yield from the justice of his cause accepted his satisfaction, and freely granted what he formerly desired [i.e., the rights to the neck of land]. (Winthrop 1908 vol. ii:16)

Ezekiel Rogers is here shown in a characteristic "passionate distemper" as he attempts to expand the borders of Rowley, already the largest town in Essex County. Although Rogers later agreed to host the first meeting of the new Andover church, relations were never too cordial between the two towns. Andover later complained to the court about Rowley taking this land, and got some of it back. The disputed area later became the separate town of Boxford.[1] The Boxford district became a marginal, isolated neighborhood somewhat like sections of Salem Village, whose residents lived far from the meetinghouse at either Andover or Rowley. Boxford later figured in the witchcraft crisis as several of the families involved lived there. This was also where Job Tyler had settled, according to Andover tradition an unauthorized "squatter" (not the colonists' term) living by the river before the official settlers arrived (Bailey 1880:46–47). Among those of Boxford involved in the witchcraft crisis, as mentioned above and further discussed in chapter 6, were Job Tyler's descendants, in-laws, and step-relatives.

---

[1]See Winthrop's *Journal* (1908:117) for an account of a quarrel in 1643 between Rogers and Thomas Dudley, who told him that as a minister he should stop butting into civil affairs. See O'Malley (1975) for a history of Rowley and biography of the volatile Rogers. See also Perley (1880, 1893). Parkhurst (1952) has a map of early Boxford house sites, keyed to Perley 1893. O'Malley outlines Rogers' stormy career in Rowley. She says that there is a town tradition that Rogers was preparing Rowley as a place for Oliver Cromwell and his entourage to live in exile in the event they had to flee England. The tradition says that during his life as tutor and private chaplain in England, Rogers had had close connections with kin of Cromwell and hinted that he expected these friends of high status might be joining the Rowley group. Thus he was anxious to expand the town's territory and get hold of the valuable frontage on the Merrimack River.

Early Bay Colony Plantations

The foregoing provides a glimpse of the many issues surrounding town and church planting in the early days of the Bay Colony and of Andover's particular experience. Surprising variation existed in circumstances of origin among Bay Colony towns, but it was not until the 1960s and 1970s that social historians began to do serious comparative research. The interests of Harvard intellectual historian Perry Miller in Puritan thought had long dominated the field of New England colonial history (Miller 1961 [1939]). As interest in social history rose, Miller's focus on "the New England mind" was set aside as historians took up new lines of research in the early New England economic, political, and social worlds. Studies of particular town histories were part of this new emphasis. Eventually, the idea of "the New England town" also came to be seen as a generalization obscuring important variation in the conditions of the early settlements.[2]

The neighboring towns of Rowley and Andover, for example, had very different origins. As just described, Ezekiel Rogers and members of his parish from Rowley, Yorkshire, in the north of England, founded Rowley, Massachusetts. Alarmed by growing tension between King Charles and the Scots, Rogers and a group of twenty parish families hired a ship and migrated together in 1638. They were skilled in sheep-raising and wool production, and they planned to make their living as suppliers of mutton and woolens to the new colony. Along the way this Yorkshire company had gathered in a few non-Yorkshire families, but the minister and his parishioners formed the social center (O'Malley 1975).

In contrast, Andover was planted by clusters of families from different regions of Britain. Each cluster had many internal connections, but not necessarily ties to the other clusters. The minister Nathaniel Ward, having organized the company, was their common connection. Ward never saw Andover, as far as we know, and returned to England. The new town had two ministers in quick succession. Again, by contrast, Rowley's minister was a strong personality who had sailed with his congregation and directed events in Rowley for its first thirty years. Although there was friction between Rowley and its neighbors, that town never went through the sort of bitter split that Andover did.

No two town histories were alike in New England, but there were certain features that were common to them all. As already discussed, early records of most towns, including Andover, show that the founding group of families often began to refer to themselves as the *Firstcomers* or sometimes with a

---

[2]For earlier studies very useful in their detail, see Sly (1928) and Haskins (1960). For a recent review, see Heyrman (1984), especially the first chapter, and her treatment of Marblehead and Gloucester as quite different from towns in the rest of the region.

different focus, the *Proprietors*. One term stressed priority, the other property rights. These categories came into use as it became necessary for the first lot-holders to define a contrast with the *Latecomers*. Within the group of Firstcomers, however, there was often another social identity, the inner circle of *Covenanters*. This term marked neither priority nor property-holding but a religious distinction, murky as it turned out to be, between those who were Covenanters, and those who may have been Firstcomers but had not signed the covenant. This was the case in Andover.

Forming a Covenant Community

Thus did new social identities develop, as the colonists continually devised such language for themselves and each other, as well as continuing to use the category terms they had brought along from the old world. Especially important in the beginning was the nature and role of the *covenant community*.

The Puritan preachers and scholars and their followers were eager to act on their longing to put into practice their vision for a regenerated society. So they were driven, or inspired, to take the great leap into the "wilderness" of New England which they often in sermons equated with biblical Canaan. Perry Miller's aim as a historian (see chapter 1, Related Studies) was to document the intellectual history of this movement. The covenant community was its social vehicle. Winthrop and the Bay Company leaders had originally intended to settle in one large community, perhaps even to join Salem, but once on the scene in Massachusetts, they found that this would not be possible. Winthrop's company had to separate into its subordinate companies and then into scattered settlements along the coast. It was not long before boatloads of new arrivals crowded the sea and river ports, and the pressure was on to move out and start new settlements. The General Court soon realized that they had to set the conditions under which permission to start new settlements would be granted. A firm policy was needed, especially to define the criteria for land-holding rights, for freeman status, and for voting rights.

Much has been written about the complexities of the early social, political, and economic development of the Bay Colony and the workings of the Court, which need not be reviewed here except for some general points.

Towns in the Bay Colony began as church-towns. In order to found a town, a minister and at least ten men were needed to make a covenant, and this covenant group would be at its center. Perhaps the Puritans modeled this after the synagogue tradition, which they understood well from their studies; a synagogue also required a minimum of ten men and the rabbinical teacher. In a decision that caused great controversy between the colony and the Crown (and which the Crown eventually forced the colony to reverse in 1664 after the Restoration), the General Court ruled that no man in the colony could vote unless he held the status of *freeman.* However, no man could be granted freeman status unless he was a *covenanter,* a covenanted church member. And in order to be a covenanter, he must be a covenant member of one of the Puritan *congregational* churches. To be granted covenant-church membership he was required to be approved as to his spiritual condition. For this he must give his public testimony, a confession of faith before the congregation or the elders, and then be tested on it through questioning by the assembled ministers. The man would then be granted or denied membership in the covenant group. Women and children at this point were considered covered by their husbands' or fathers' covenants, an issue that becomes important later in the story.

Thus in line with the Puritans' attempt to insure a godly citizenry, a man's right to vote in the Bay Colony was made dependent upon church membership, which was in turn dependent upon the defense of his faith he gave before an approved minister. But—and here was the rub—the only approved ministers were those of the Puritan persuasion. The Anglicans, Baptists, Quakers, and others in the colony were not approved, and there were mixed opinions about Presbyterians.[3] However, all still had to pay taxes for the support of the Puritan ministers. This taxation was justified because in Puritan social theology the minister's labors benefited all in his parish, whether they appreciated it or not. However, restriction of the franchise plus compulsory taxation eventually got the Puritan leaders of the Bay Colony into trouble as an early version of taxation without representation. They got by with it during Cromwell's time, but after the Restoration, the Anglicans of the colony particularly protested to the Crown, and the Crown forced the colony to change its policy.

---

[3]Goodman (1974) discusses the church conflict at Newbury. Although the congregationalists made room for the presbyterian sort of Puritanism to some extent, it was not in the mainstream of Bay Colony ecclesiology, and presbyterian-congregational friction continued to grow. Parker was more presbyterian in outlook, and that fact was part of the controversy with the church at Newbury. If John Woodbridge had been influenced by his uncle Parker, perhaps he had presbyterian leanings which contributed to his short stay at Andover (see Woodbridge's son's correspondence with Richard Baxter in England on these issues in Stearns (1937).

Planting a Church-Town

The Bay Company's first intent had been to live in one big community, but this soon proved impossible (see chapter 2), and the General Court (which consisted of the Governor, the Assistants, and the Deputies) had to develop rules about how new towns could be planted. The early type of settlement is more appropriately called a church-town. The Court determined that no company could start a plantation without Court approval and without a covenant community. This body must be made up of at least one approved minister, preferably two, a *teaching minister* and a *preaching minister,* and at least ten men who were covenanted church members and thus enfranchised. Only men of the covenant could vote in their town or in the colony elections. One of the laymen was chosen deacon or ruling elder. The minister was then ordained to lead this particular new church-town; it was not considered a general ordination good for any future post he might hold. Ordained ministers of the neighboring towns conducted the ordination ceremony. At a later date, in a separate act from the covenanting of the church, the town was named and incorporated. One of the covenanters would be voted representative to the Court. Others could and did join the company in planting a town without entering the covenant and becoming church members, but their civil privileges were restricted even though they were taxed for the minister's home and living.

Each town, then, began as a church; it was not to "have" a church, but to be a church. Following the parish model with its geographical basis, there was to be one church meetinghouse to a town as a territorial unit. The meetinghouse served all town functions and was a garrison as well. But in contrast to the old world they had left behind, here in the new colony each congregation would call its own minister, who would be ordained by a group of his peers as described. Thus there would be no handing down of favors from above by a corrupt episcopate or appointments to "livings" that soon became mere sinecures. The congregation would raise its own rates to pay its minister. Furthermore, as noted earlier, all townspeople would pay for the minister's support, whether or not they were among the covenanter church members.

Missing, however, from the social planning of the Puritans was a practical solution to the problem of town growth as it affected the church and the policy that there be only one meetinghouse. In the vision and words of the ministers who drew up the Cambridge Platform of 1648, new churches would hive off as naturally "as bees when the hive is too full" (see chapter 7). But the hives of humans in most cases proved more quarrelsome internally than this symbolic counterpart in the world of nature.

Initially, the Court had required that for safety and public order people must live no more than a mile from the meetinghouse, or they would be fined. This rule gave rise to the classic settlement pattern still visible in many New England towns today, including Andover Old Town (North Andover), of homes around a rectangular town green with a church building at one end and the graveyard beside it. The one-mile requirement soon began to prove impossible for lack of house-lot room, and it was lifted. However, the difficulties that arose as people had to build homes farther from the center did not go away. The long walk or jolting ride to the meetinghouse became longer and longer for more and more families. Sections of expanding towns began to petition the Court for permission to establish themselves as separate parishes. The original town center's residents often opposed this petition vigorously. And for some reason the Court exacerbated friction in town after town during the late seventeenth and early eighteenth centuries by refusing to grant permissions for new parishes within towns until social tension had become very high. This happened in Andover. In the following section I return to the story unfolding there.

Planning and Recruitment for Andover: The Gathering of the Company

Nathaniel Ward and his company, "increasing apace," waited at Ipswich for an answer from the Court on their proposal to set down plantations on the Merrimack River at Andover and Haverhill. Ipswich was an important port of entry for the Bay Colony and a center for recruiting, grouping, and regrouping as settlers organized to move on. Newcomers arrived, provisioned themselves, and moved on from the port. The Parker company, planning to start a new plantation to the north at Newbury, passed some time there, resting and reprovisioning. The group that ultimately went to Andover was composed of sections of three such companies that passed through Ipswich in the 1630s, each of which had come from different regions, or countries, of Britain. These three regions were East Anglia (especially Essex and Suffolk counties), the southwest counties of Hampshire and Wiltshire, and Hertfordshire, just east of London (map 3). In addition, there were settlers not from England proper but from other regions or countries and blood as well, people from the "Celtic fringes" in the far north and west, from Wales and the Borders or Marches, from Scotland, and from Ireland. The Bradstreets, although Andover's most eminent family, were the only ones from Lincolnshire in Andover. Perhaps the lack of "countrymen" allies led to the brevity of their stay in Andover.

Ward's Company: The East Anglians

When the Court and its military advisors decided that the harbor at Agawam (Ipswich) must be protected, they assigned Governor Winthrop's eldest son to form a company and start a new settlement there as soon as possible. Ipswich, with its fine harbor and the Governor's son at its head, was expected to become the chief port in the colony. The settlement was named Ipswich in honor of the port in Suffolk County from which Winthrop and many of the East Anglians had sailed. Ipswich was expected to emerge as the political center. It would surpass Boston, named for the old city in Lincoln County and a reminder of the power of the Lincolnshire contingent. (See Allen 1981, chap. 5 on Ipswich, also Kimball 1823 and Hammatt 1980 [1880–1889] for detailed accounts of early Ipswich. See also Rutman 1965 for the rise of Boston)

In anticipation of the rise of Ipswich, several prominent men with their families, servants, and retinues moved there from the Boston Harbor settlements, including Thomas Dudley and his son-in-law Simon Bradstreet. Nathaniel Ward joined the exodus of Puritan preachers now sailing to Massachusetts from Suffolk to accept a call to the Ipswich church, as did John Norton, another Puritan firebrand who became his assistant. But things did not work out as planned. Young Winthrop decided not to stay in Ipswich, despite petitions from Ward and others urging him to do so (see Dunn 1962 for a history of the Winthrops). He planned to take a post on Castle Island in Boston Harbor. Ward catalogued the growing decline and decadence in Ipswich, especially among the youth, now without Winthrop's ameliorating influence. He said in a petition to the governor in 1637 (reprinted in Waters 1905:50) that he feared for Winthrop's future on the island. That post would not permit him to "maintain him & his company comfortably," he opined, but would prove "on sundry occasions mutable." Ward went on to say that the "the distance we are set in hath made us earnest for the company of able men & loathe to lose them when we have obtained them."

But young Winthrop could not be prevailed upon to stay in Ipswich, probably because the damage to the harbor was already becoming apparent and the future of the port thus uncertain. When Ward saw that Ipswich was not thriving as expected, he decided to organize a move for the sake of his family and followers, and to start two new plantations inland opposite each other on the banks of the Merrimack. He would be the minister at Cochichawick (Andover) and his son John the minister at Penticutt (Haverhill). His son-in-law, a young physician finding it difficult to make a living in Ipswich, would join them. Mr. Simon Bradstreet, in Ward's congregation at Ipswich, would be the gentleman and civic leader at Andover. A son of old Sir Richard Saltonstall would fill the same role as Haverhill's gentry leader. To this end, Ward began to recruit two companies through kinship, friendship, and his congregation at Ipswich, companies that would make the move inland and begin these new plantations. At this point he wrote his letter of appeal to Winthrop, cited at the opening of his chapter.

Now I will introduce in more detail the members of these networks that were drawn together to form the larger Ward company. When the lines at Andover later fell out, they fell out around these old groupings.

Parker's Company: The Southwesterners

To review, Massachusetts was colonized by waves of settlers from Britain's different regions or "countries." Roger Conant, John Endecott, and most of those first at Salem were West Country men from the region around Plymouth and Dorchester. Lincolnshire people and East Anglians dominated the Winthrop fleet. The arrival of Mr. Thomas Parker and his company in 1634 signaled an influx of Puritans from still another region of England, whom I call Southwesterners, from Wiltshire and Hampshire and the adjoining Newbury region of Berkshire. Southampton was their port of departure (see maps 3 and 4). Winthrop notes,

> May 1634. The week the court was, there came in six ships, with store of passengers and cattle. Mr Parker, a minister, and a company with him, being about one hundred, went to sit down at Agawam [Ipswich], and divers others of the new comers. (Winthrop 1908 vol. i:125)

Different in custom from people of Lincoln, East Anglia, or the West Country, the Southwesterners were first encouraged to move immediately up the coast to strengthen the settlement at Ipswich, as Winthrop notes. They "sat down" at Ipswich for the first year, where they would have met Ward, before setting off a few miles north to found Newbury (map 1). There they remained while they sought permission to plant towns of their own around the mouth of the Merrimack. Newbury, and later Hampton and Salisbury, all grew out of this southwesterner company (Perzel 1967, Allen 1981). Parker led the move from Ipswich to Newbury as the town's first minister and was soon embroiled in divisive controversy over church polity (Coffin 1977 [1845]; Goodman 1974). A cluster of families from Parker's group, chief among them John Osgood's family, eventually left Parker to become the core of the new company Ward recruited for Andover.

Since it was from Newbury that the dominant group of the original Andover company came, these people and their connections need a closer study. Allen included Newbury in the five towns of his study of the transferal of English local law and custom to Massachusetts. His estimates that most of the Parker company had come from towns in Wiltshire and Hampshire within thirty or forty miles of each other (1981:82–84). Despite this surface homogeneity, however, the new settlement at Newbury was contentious and conflict-ridden from the beginning. Analyzing what is known of the settlers and their backgrounds, Allen found that the home region was highly stratified economically, although it had been suffering from a severe recession in the period prior to the emigration. Allen states, "One of the clearest traditions that these people brought with them was the propensity to establish a rigid, stratified society." According to Allen, Newbury had the greatest inequalities in wealth of any of the five towns in his study (pp. 89–90).

Once Parker had established his church-town at Newbury, he persuaded other family members to come over from England. Four of Parker's nephews (his brother's sons, Joseph and Nathan Parker, and his sister's sons, John and Benjamin Woodbridge) arrived on a later ship and joined their uncle in Newbury along with other Wiltshire and Hampshire people. It was John, the elder Woodbridge brother, who became the first minister at Andover when, as it turned out, Nathaniel Ward was unable to make the move after all.

John Woodbridge had begun preparations for the ministry at Oxford, but withdrew when the university was ordered to require an oath of allegiance to the established church. At this point he left for Massachusetts to assist his uncle Parker. Nathaniel Ward, looking for more "choice families" and a young minister to assist him at Andover, drew upon his connections with the Parker company that had briefly "set down" with him in Ipswich. He recruited Woodbridge, his brother Benjamin, and their cousins, the two Parker brothers, as well as several other Southwesterner families of Newbury. Woodbridge had just further cemented his status and strengthened his connection to the Ward company by marrying a daughter of deputy governor Thomas Dudley. Since Simon Bradstreet was also married to a Dudley daughter, this meant that Woodbridge and Bradstreet were not only Andover's town leaders as minister and gentry but also were brothers-in-law and were part of one of the dominant extended families in the Bay Colony (Bailey 1880:416–420; on Newbury, see Goodman 1974).

The company that Ward was recruiting from among the Southwesterners was a network of ties by blood, marriage, and patronage. As well, they shared common experiences in England as religious dissidents and as shipmates on the voyage over. Bradstreet and Dudley, however, for all their initial influence, did not maintain it in Andover. Perhaps there were too few other Lincolnshire people in Andover. But Lincolnshire had been another *country* and another *company* to begin with: the arena of action for the Lincolnshire group in the colony really remained at Boston Harbor. In any case, it was not that group, but another Southwesterner, John Osgood of the old Parker company, who moved into a leading role in the new town. His family held that place after him for many generations (Abbott n.d.: see Bradstreet, Osgood, Parker, Woodbridge genealogies).

Norton's Followers: The Hertfordshire Families

Yet another subset of Ward's group was made up of members of families that had gathered around the minister John Norton, first in England, then in the Bay Colony. Norton had arrived in Ipswich in 1639 to be Ward's assistant. He and his followers did not refer to themselves nor were they referred to as a company in the sense we have been describing. They did not gather together intentionally in a group under his leadership. Rather, individuals spoke of themselves as having *sat under* his ministry. A noted Puritan preacher, Norton preached for a time in the market town of Bishop's Stortford, about thirty-five miles east of London in the county of Hertfordshire.[4] There he had made a strong impression on a young man named John Dane (and perhaps on John's younger brother Francis). John Dane's *Narrative* of 1682, one of the few surviving personal documents from this period, is a fascinating account of his life in Hertfordshire and his move to the Bay Colony (Dane 1894).

Dane's story provides valuable background to Andover's early history because his younger brother Francis would soon become the second minister at Andover and a key figure in the next fifty years of its history. Through Dane's account we see how loyalty to the minister Norton influenced him, his brother, the rest of his family, and several other Hertfordshire families, first in England, then in the Bay Colony. Following Norton from his preaching days in Bishop's Stortford, Hertfordshire, these families found their way to Ipswich and into Ward's company, for Norton had become Ward's assistant. There they gathered, awaiting permission for the inland move. Again, applying imagination to the description below of kinship, friendship, and

---

[4]I am not following Allen (1981:118) in calling the Hertfordshire people East Anglians, as it is not historically a part of that region. Powell (1963) referred to Hertfordshire as part of the East Midlands. The shire is now considered one of the Home Counties (the nine around London), but there was no such category in the 1700s. I will just call them here the Hertfordshire group, since they did not travel as a company.

patronage connections among the Hertfordshire people allows us to enter the social world of this close-knit group.

According to his account, John Dane, eldest son of his family, had worked as tailor and then butler in the household of Sir Francis Barrington. Barrington was a prominent Essex County Member of Parliament and a Puritan who had also been the patron of the Reverend Ezekiel Rogers of Rowley before Rogers emigrated (see fn. 1, this chapter). Around 1639, as the English civil war loomed, Dane decided to go to Massachusetts. He acted against his parents' wishes, he says, but they changed their minds and later joined him with the rest of the children. Dane went first to Rocksbury (now Roxbury) where, he noted, he had friends who were already established. They gave him a piece of land for his garden. Dane later heard that John Norton and some of his followers were now in Massachusetts and that Norton was preaching at Ipswich, assisting Nathaniel Ward. Dane decided to move to Ipswich to "sit under" Norton again. The rest of his family—mother, father, a sister, and his younger brother Francis—joined him there in Ipswich when they came from England.

Those friends at Roxbury who helped Dane out were probably the Hertfordshire families he knew from home in Bishop's Stortford. The Chandlers and a young man named George Abbot were already in Roxbury. Abbot who was eighteen, may have been William Chandler's bondservant or otherwise supported by Chandler, as he was soon to marry Chandler's daughter. These people were all from Bishop's Stortford and had come over on the same boat the year before Dane came. Very likely all three families knew each other and had sat under the persuasive preaching of Norton during his years in Bishop's Stortford.[5]

Within a few years, the kinship ties among these three families—Dane, Chandler, and Abbot—had grown more complex. William Chandler died, and John Dane's mother died. Widow Chandler then married the widower Dane, John's father. Danes and Chandlers were now step-kin. They moved to Ipswich with the younger children, joining John there (Chandler 1883). Francis Dane, meanwhile, was studying for the ministry at the new

---

[5]An older Abbot brother named John may have preceded George Abbot and the Chandlers to Massachusetts, much as John Dane (who was from the same town as Abbot and the Chandlers) preceded his siblings. Note that earlier, in 1636, a young man named John Abbot was accidentally shot dead at Concord by a Matthew Bridges. This incident may also shed light on why the eldest son in the senior male line of the George Abbot family was named John for the next ten generations, even though according to the early naming custom we would expect the name of the eldest son to be George (See Walne 1978 and Moriarty 1931 for early Hertfordshire immigrants; see RCACMB 1636 vol. 1:66, 71 for the account of the investigation of the shooting of John Abbot. See also Main 1996 for more on naming children in early New England).

school, Harvard, over in Cambridge. Once at Ipswich, members of these Roxbury families were recruited into Ward's company for the plantation at Andover. George Abbot married the eldest Chandler daughter, and this couple joined the group. The name of the oldest Chandler boy, Thomas, sixteen, also appears on the list of first settlers. Since young unmarried men were not allowed to live alone, he probably went with his sister and brother-in-law to the new town.

John Woodbridge, Andover's first minister, left the settlement after only a year and returned to England. The tide was turning in the Puritans' favor there and a number of the New England ministers decided to return. Francis Dane was called to Andover as Woodbridge's successor. Unfortunately, no evidence survives about why or how the choice of Dane was made. But this change meant that the control of that influential position of minister shifted from the Southwesterners to Dane and his connections, the Hertfordshire group. Meanwhile the town's political leadership (selectmen and representative to the Court) remained in the hands of Southwesterner families.

Soon another Chandler brother arrived, William, married to Francis Dane's brother's daughter. Chandler would ultimately become embroiled in a dispute over his right to have a tavern in his part of town (Bailey 1880:70–71). The petitions that have survived regarding this dispute show how people with roots in these two different home regions or countries, Hertfordshire or the southwest, lined up either for or against Chandler.

The cluster of Hertfordshire families had been drawn together, first in England and then to New England, by their loyalty to the charismatic preacher John Norton. The Hertfordshire company began as the smaller of the two regional groups recruited by Ward and his East Anglians. The larger group, the Southwesterners, mainly from Wiltshire and Hampshire counties, had broken off from Parker's company at Newbury. Each group was characterized by a regional basis, loyalty to a central figure or head, and an internal network of kinship, marriage, friendship, and work or employment ties. In addition to these three groups, which can be considered as groups with some inner cohesion, there were other residents of Andover with still different social identities but without such strong initial group cohesion.[6]

---

[6]Greven in his discussion of these families (1964:37–42) postulates a different sequence of arrival. He does not develop the connection with John Norton.

The Scots and Old Britons: Other Countries

The rest of the people in Ward's company came from several different backgrounds and places, and very little is known about some of them. But at least three families who were among the first settlers of Andover are referred to in records as Scottish—the Allens, Fosters, and Russes—although there is little known about them for sure (see Abbott n.d. on each of these families). We do not know whether they had any previous associations or had been living in the same town prior to their moves to Andover, or how the Ward-Woodbridge network happened to include them. They may in fact not have been of the Ward company at all. Their move to Andover may have been more closely linked with the second minister Francis Dane, who in turn was linked to them by marriage. His wife's sister had married into one of these Scots families, the Allens.

The Dane family itself may have been partly, or recently, Scottish in origin. Indirect evidence shows that the Danes were willing to side with and associate with Scots. A court case in Ipswich reveals anti-Scot sentiment and records that John Dane was a sympathetic witness for the Scots of Ipswich in the hearing.[7] On the basis of this, and more direct genealogical evidence that some of Francis Dane's children after him married with Scots families, it may be that the Danes were part Scot, or at least a social broker family through which the Scots families could become incorporated into a company like Ward's. The Danes may even have been an anglicized Scottish family. If this is so, then it may lend support to the thesis that there was an ethnic aspect to the witchcraft accusations years later in Andover, centering as they did so largely around Dane's family (see also Summers 1927 for a provocative early discussion of the association of witchcraft with Scots).

To review the discussion in chapter 2, Scots had a mixed reputation in the colony. Cotton Mather praised the Scots theologians and other coreligionists as welcome members of the new colony. On the other hand, there were those who, along with others of Celtic and Old Briton stock,

---

[7]The immediate issue was the one that probably more than any other seemed to set the colonists against one another: straying animals. Nathaniel Browne brought a complaint against Samuel Lomas for assault on the highway. Lomas had also threatened to kill Browne's pigs if ever they came on his land. Browne was a Scot, and the depositions of those who testified in his behalf center on Lomas' outspoken dislike of Scots. Daniel Davison said that on an earlier occasion when he had gone to Lomas' house to complain that his swine were trespassing in his, Davison's, corn, Lomas had called him a "Scotch rogue" and told him to get off his land or he would knock him down, "he having a ten pound Rock in his hand." Alexander Thomson, a Scot also, said he had heard Lomas call Davison "a limb of the devil saying that all Scotchmen were hypocrites and devils." Among the others testifying in Browne's behalf, that is, with the Scots, was John Dane (ECQCR 1679, vol. vii: 360–361).

came as servants or bondsmen, lived on the social and cultural margins of the colony, and had little stake in and were even hostile to the Puritan experiment. Bailyn and Morgan (1991) called them "strangers in the realm." To these were added the Scottish prisoners of war, sent over by Cromwell after his victory in the war with Scotland. They were sold on the docks at Charlestown and Boston (although none went to Andover). We do not know whether such marginal folk as Job Tyler, Thomas Carrier, Andrew Foster, and their families felt any sense of social identity as a group. Though living on the physical, social, and cultural margins of the town and colony, they nevertheless came to play key roles in its story. Without intending to blur the very real distinctions in their backgrounds, I will continue to call them the *Borderers*.

The Planting of Andover

By spring of 1640, Nathaniel Ward had gathered together his "choice men" and their households and hoped to be able soon to move the company out from Ipswich and Newbury to plant Haverhill and Andover. The Reverend Ward and Sir Richard Saltonstall were to lead Haverhill; Mr. Simon Bradstreet and the Reverend John Woodbridge were to be the civic and spiritual leaders at Andover. John Winthrop was now no longer governor; Thomas Dudley had been elected. The Andover group had powerful connections to the new governor; he was the father-in-law of Bradstreet and Woodbridge. Ward's company received its official permission to go.

> May 13, 1640. The desires of Mr Ward and Newbury men is [sic] committed to the Governor [Dudley], Deputy Governor, and Mr Winthrop senior, to grant it to them provided they return answer within three weeks from the 27th present and that they build there before the next Court. (MHSC 5 vol. i, in Bailey 1880:5)

But although the land around Cochichawick was set aside and the Court's permission, even orders, given to start building, still the group delayed. The reason appears in a letter to Winthrop of March 1641, not from Ward this time but from John Woodbridge.

Nathaniel Ward, as it turned out, had given up the idea of going to Andover himself due to his failing health. He decided instead to return to England, leaving his son John to carry on with the planting at Haverhill. Responsibility for the Andover negotiations had fallen to John Woodbridge. The new young minister and his company were faced with another boundary dispute with Rowley. Rowley's minister Rogers had already asked for an extension of Rowley's border into the neck on the Merrimack, and the court had granted it, as recorded in the text above (see also Winthrop's entry for October 8, 1640). Now, complained Woodbridge to the Court, Rogers was laying claim to even more land in the Cochichawick reserve and "proving himself so great an annoyance that will quite cut off any hopes of being a plantation there."[8] Woodbridge went on to urge Winthrop to help resolve the controversy in favor of the Andover company, hinting that the Bay Colony might lose colonists (including himself) to "Long-Island" if something was not done soon.

> March 1641...the reason why I desire your speedy advice is because some of our company have sold themselves out of house and home and so desire to be settled as soon as may be...some with some resolution affect Long-Island intending speedily to be gone thither if they settle not here, and for my own part I have strong solicitations thither, by some not of the meaner sort...(MHSC 5 vol. i, in Bailey 1880:6).

Dispute over the covenant

Ward's decision to return to England, the boundary dispute with Rowley, and other unrecorded issues apparently impeded the move for yet another three years. At last Woodbridge and the Andover company held a first gathering as a church, hosted by the apparently reconciled neighbor Ezekiel Rogers in the Rowley meetinghouse. Now a new difficulty arose. The members could not agree on the covenant. According to Winthrop's journal, this first organizational meeting of the church broke up in conflict. It took a further year before the planting of Andover could proceed. Winthrop describes the course of events.

> September 19, 1644. Two churches were appointed to be gathered, one at Haverhill and the other at Andover, both upon Merrimack River. They had given notice thereof to the magistrates and elders, who desired, in regard of their far remoteness and scarcity of housing there, the meeting might be at Rowley, which they assented

---

[8]Woodbridge said that Rogers was claiming the land to replace acreage that had gone to former Governor Henry Vane, who had established himself on a farm in Rowley. At this time the colony was still in an uproar over the "antinomian controversy" with Mrs. Ann Hutchinson and her followers, whom Vane had supported. Vane and Winthrop stood opposed to each other. The Hutchinson faction was exiled to Rhode Island, and Vane later returned to England to the aid of Cromwell, but it may be that at this point Woodbridge saw in the threat from Rowley more than an issue of land—a possible land base in the Bay Colony for a faction of which Woodbridge disapproved (see the account of controversy in O'Malley 1975).

unto, but being assembled, most of those who were to join, refused to declare how God had carried on the work of his grace in them, upon this reason, because they had declared it formerly in their admission into other churches; whereupon the assembly brake up without proceeding, etc. (Winthrop 1908 vol. ii:199)

And at last, a year later

> October 8, 1645. A church was gathered at Haverhill upon the north side of the Merrimack, and Mr John Ward chosen and ordained pastor. About the same time a church was also gathered at Cochichawick called Andover upon the south side of Merrimack, and Mr John Woodbridge ordained pastor. (p. 262)

The first church in Andover began, as it would end, in conflict. The issue, if it is not clear from the text, was as follows: If a company wanted to set down a new plantation, or church-town, it was required by Colony law to have a minister and at least ten covenanting members. Both the ordination of the minister and the signing of covenant were to be done afresh for each new congregational situation. But at the Rowley meeting it became clear that some in the Andover company did not wish to declare again "how God had carried on the work of his grace in them." They said that the public profession they had made earlier when they had covenanted with their previous church was sufficient (probably in Ipswich or Newbury, or perhaps in Bradstreet's case, Boston). Others in the company apparently thought that a new church/town required a new covenant and commitment by all founding members in relation to that body. Some of the Andover group apparently changed their minds or at least acquiesced and some did not.

No surviving record exists of who was at the Rowley meeting. Nor is it on record who objected to making public profession again. But it is possible to make a good guess because we know the names of the ten Covenanters and there are two important omissions from the list, leading settlers Simon Bradstreet and John Stevens (see figures 1 and 2, pp. 20–21). Were they the men who would not make new professions of faith? Prominent among the Andover founders, neither of them is listed among the Covenanters. Bradstreet had earlier been at Boston and Ipswich, Stevens had been with the Parker company. They had probably made their covenants there. There must have been some distinction arising between making a Christian covenant with a group of people, and confessing faith and repentance, although they were supposed to be done together. The bruises from the quarrel at Rowley apparently remained for some time, because it was still another year before the move to Andover was finally made (Bailey 1880:416–417). Tension must have continued between those at that meeting who had signed as Covenanters and those who did not.

However, as the next wave of settlers began to arrive in town, this identity as a *Covenanter* began to submerge somewhat beneath the need for new social distinctions and thus identities. Especially important became the distinction between the twenty-three *Firstcomers* (whether or not *Covenanters*) and those who came after, called the *Latecomers*. The Faulkner List of the settlers "in order as they came to town," also established the order in which land acreage was later allocated and lots chosen.

Setting down at Cochichawick

Cochichawick, *great water,* was the Indian name for the Andover area, and indeed a large lake dominates the region (maps 5 and 6). From the point of view of the colonists in the late 1630s, restless in the crowded port towns, questionable morals (evidenced in the Ipswich town records) and a growing shortage of nearby farmland made things difficult. Inland regions like Cochichawick looked like very desirable territory despite remoteness and proximity to the Indian frontier. Overland, Cochichawick would be a day's rough walk or half a day's horseback ride to Salem or Boston. But its location near a major ford of the Merrimack River meant access across and upstream to Haverhill, the settlement to be co-founded with Andover at the river's upper navigation point. Equal access also existed downstream to Newbury Port on the sea, and thence to points along the coast. Not only was Cochichawick reported to be well-watered, with fresh springs, a lake full of fish, ponds, and streams with suitable mill sites, it was rich as well in the land resources valued by the colonists including bottomland, upland, woodland, clay pits, and swamps. And a less common but prized resource was on hand there: bog iron ore. That meant that they could forge metal tools.

With such bounty, it is not surprising to find that there was competition for the region. Before Ward's company formed, other groups from the older towns had been requesting the official permission of the Court to "set down" there, as the colonists called it. Among them were the men sent to look from Cambridge, as noted in Winthrop's journal above. Rowley also wanted to add parts of this desirable tract to its township. But under Dudley as governor, it is not surprising that the group led by his two sons-in-law, Bradstreet and Woodbridge, received the permission to start.

The next step was to complete negotiations with the Indians who camped and fished in the area. The records show that the minister John Woodbridge took the lead at this point with the help of Mr. Edmund

Faulkner, formerly of the Parker company at Newbury. Like Woodbridge he was a Southwesterner and formerly of Newbury, England as well. Faulkner and Simon Bradstreet were the only Andover Firstcomers listed with "Mister" before their names in the records, a term which indicated their gentry status. (Ministers were also called "Mister." See Dawes 1949 for a early discussion of the use of titles in the colony.) Woodbridge and Faulkner drew up a document for rights to the land by which the Indian Cutshamache, "sagamore of ye Massachusetts came into ye Corte May 6, 1646, and acknowledged [that] for the sum of £6 & a Coat...he had sold to Mr John Woodbridge in behalfe of ye inhabitants of Cochichawicke now called Andover all his right interest and privilege in ye land 6 miles southward from the town, two miles eastward to Rowley bounds...and northward to Merrimack river." Included in this agreement was a clause to the effect that the Indians who frequented this site especially "Roger and his *company* [my italics] may have liberty to take alewives in Cochickawicke River, for their own eatinge; but if they either spoyle or steale any corne or other fruit to any considerable value this liberty...shall forever cease" (in Bailey 1880:27).

One wonders what the sagamore understood as to either the long or short-term implications of this document. Bay Colony records and the Andover historians say that Cutshamache received six pounds and a red coat in exchange for Cochichawick. However, a Faulkner family tradition says that twenty gallons of rum was an unofficial part of the bargain as well (Abbott n.d.: Faulkner 1–2).[9] If so, it was a highly illegal part, for it was by then strictly forbidden to give or sell liquor to the Indians. Faulkner was in fact listed as a vintner and obtained the first tavern license in Andover, so the family tradition may have some truth to it. Faulkner remained a major figure in Andover history. He was the town clerk and held that office for many years. But Faulkner's house and his family were later targets of a raiding party of Indians who may have felt particular animosity toward him as they came to realize the meaning of written contracts, and what exactly Cutshamache had signed away at Cochichawick.

[9]According to an earlier historian of settler-Indian relations, the sagamore Cutshamache was already troubling the inland Massachusetts tribes by his willingness to accept the Europeans' attribution to him of more power to act on their behalf than they, the other Massachusetts, considered him rightfully to possess (Perley 1912). Thus when the representatives of the would-be settlers approached Cutshamache, he may knowingly or unknowingly have agreed to arrangements that Roger did not know of, understand, or accept. Roger seems to have been perceived as having violated the terms of the agreement and thus forfeiting his right to his plantation. But when the Indians later raided Andover, killing several people, they made a special point of burning down the town clerk Edmund Faulkner's house and the records. They seem to have thought, not unreasonably given their experience with written contracts, that by destroying the papers they destroyed the agreement (Abbott n.d. Faulkner: 1).

Faulkner's family was also one of those most deeply and tragically affected later by the witchcraft crisis.

Although Simon and Anne Bradstreet were the leading gentry family in Andover, they were virtually alone there in being from Lincolnshire country. Bradstreet became more and more active in colony-level administration and matters at the Court, and after the death of his wife he soon moved to Boston. Their son Dudley Bradstreet remained to carry on his father's role in the town as he could. But it was Woodbridge and his Newbury companions, with their common roots in the southwestern counties of Wiltshire and Hampshire, that formed the core of dominant families in early Andover, both as Covenanters and Firstcomers. So, when Woodbridge left unexpectedly after only a year, the Southwesterners lost control of the ministry, though not of the other town offices. The Covenanters remained a strong force. The new minister, Francis Dane, was from the east, a Hertfordshire man, and gradually the cluster of families related to him coalesced into a unit of its own. This cluster included the intermarried Chandler, Dane, and Abbot families, who had sailed together, been together at "Rocksbury" (now Roxbury), then Ipswich, and then on together to Andover. Certain of the Old Britons or Borderers had also begun to ally themselves with the Hertfordshire families through marriage.

In the next chapters, I will follow the fortunes of these Andover families and regional clusters of families as they settle, marry, and endure crises of several sorts, and finally struggle their way through to the parish division. To follow this process it will be essential to understand and keep in mind the settlers' old world regional identities and groupings and how they affected these initial arrangements. To this end I have prepared table 1 at the end of this chapter, designed as a reference summary of information about the Andover families who are the cast of characters in this unfolding social drama.

Who the Settlers Were: Summary Table

Table 1 displays information about thirty-seven of the first Andoverites. The Firstcomers section lists the first minister, Woodbridge, and the twenty-three men who are called variously Covenanters, Freed holders, House holders, and Firstcomers, along with background material about them in various categories. The Latecomers section lists the second minister, Dane, and an additional set of twelve of the families called Latecomers, with their background information.

The Firstcomers section lists the people in the order they appear in the earliest known list of names, the Faulkner List. This may be compared with Greven's list of them, which he has rearranged in alphabetical order (1970:46) *"The names of all the freed houlders in order as they came to town."* The word *house* is written above in a different hand above the word *freed houlders*. The Faulkner List is a prime clue to the specifics of the early social hierarchy in Andover and the order in which they drew lots for subsequent divisions of territory (review pp. 20–22).

In the Firstcomers section, the names of the ten who were also the Covenanters are shown in italics. Four Firstcomers, including two of the Covenanters, left Andover soon after arrival, selling their lots to others. Then after one year the minister Woodbridge left. These names are shown here in table 1, but will not be appearing in future chapters.

The Latecomers section includes Dane and twelve Latecomer families. Not enough additional information is available to trace origin or genealogy for two Latecomer men. They are shown on this list for other reasons, but do not remain in the research population. Given these omissions, a research unit remains of thirty families for which there is considerable documentation, though in places it is unfortunately patchy and incomplete. These are the families I will follow through Andover's first seventy years until the parish split, looking at the words, activities, and marriage patterns of these "informants in the archives" for three generations.

Table 1 (pp. 72–73) provides a reference summary of basic information about the founding families of Andover. This summary enables the reader to take a closer look at their regional and ethnic backgrounds, at the interrelationships among them, and at the new social categories developing among them.

To summarize: at the baseline date of 1645, the group of twenty-four Firstcomers or Householders in Andover was composed of both Covenanters and non-Covenanters. Although they came from the southwest and the east of England, and the Celtic fringes, twelve of the first fifteen names on the list were from the southwest counties of Hampshire and Wiltshire. The Covenanters were older, married, and had started families, while many of the non-Covenanters were either just married or single. Some were bondservants to others, as, for example, was John Lovejoy to John Stevens. Thus some time would elapse before they would be mature enough to challenge—if they wished to—the dominance of the Southwesterner and Covenanter group, or numerous enough to outnumber them in the vote.

Latecomers seem to have come to Andover on the basis of a connection with some family among the Firstcomers. Henry Ingalls, for example, had

Lincolnshire connections to the Bradstreet/Dudley families. Ralph Farnum's daughter may already have been married to a son of Nicholas Holt when he moved to Andover with the rest of his family (Abbott n.d.: Ingalls; Farnum). The relationships among the Southwesterner families (formerly together in the Parker company at Newbury), and between them and the Hertfordshire group, dominated the early history of Andover's social organization. Bradstreet, though a town leader, was almost alone in Andover as a Lincolnshire man. As for the Old Britons, they found themselves somewhat excluded from civil life, they did not marry with the English, and thus they built up their own neighborhood and interrelations. The history of the structure and actions of these groups can be described from several perspectives, at the family, neighborhood, town, colonial, and even the intercolonial level. In the next chapter, I continue the story of the way these groups arranged themselves on the land in Andover, the significances of the social arrangements, and the changes in arrangements that soon began to occur.

Table 1. Backgrounds of 37 founding families of Andover:
24 Firstcomers; 13 Latecomers

FIRSTCOMERS: 1645–1646
in order of arrival in Andover as per the Faulkner List. The names in bold were the ten original Covenanters.

No	ORIG/OW	SHIP/DATE	PREV NE RES	AGE	NAME (as per List)	ORIG ACRES,N/S
01.	Stanton, WILTS	Mary&John 1635	Newbury	32	[Rev] John **Woodbridge** (left)	n/a N
02.	Horblng, LINCS	Winthrp Flt 1629	Camb; Ipswich	39	[Mr] Simon Bradstreet	20 N
03.	Andovr, HANTS	Confdnce 1638	Newbury	50	John Osgood	20 N
04.	Romsey, HANTS	Confdnce 1638	Newbury	31	Joseph **Parker**	10 N
05.	Suff? YORKS?	?	Rowley?	?	Richard **Barker**	07.N
06.	Cvershm, OXON	Confdnce 1638	Newbury	40	John Stevens	08 N
07.	HANTS? LANC?	James 1635	Newbury	43	Nicholas **Holt**	15 N > S
08.	Stanton, WILTS	Mary&John 1635	Newbury	30?	Benj Woodbridge(left)	08
09.	Basngstk, HANTS	Bevis 1638	Newbury	44	John **Frye**	08 N > S
10.	Kngsclre, HANTS	?	Newbury?	20	[Mr] Edmund **Faulkner**	06 N
11.	Bradstone ?SUFF ?	?	Salisbury ?	?	Robert **Barnard** (left)	05
12.	?WILTS	Bevis 1638	Newbury	21	Daniel Poor	04 N
13.	London? HANTS	Bevis 1638	Newbury	27	Nathan **Parker**	04 N
14.	Stanton, WILTS	?	Newbury	?	Henry Jaques (left)	05
15.	Scrooby, LINCS?	?	Rowley	?	John Aslett [or Aslebe]	07 N
16.	Andover, HANTS	Confdnce 1638	Newbury ?	?	Richard **Blake** (left)	?
17.	?WALES	?Mry & Jhn 1635.	Newbury	28	William Ballard	05 S
18.	Marlo,BUCKS; Lndn?	Confdnce 1638	Newbury	23	John Lovejoy	05 S
19.	WILTS?	?	Boston ?	?	Thomas Poor	04 ?
20.	BshpStfrd, HERTS	?	Roxbry; Cmbrdg?	28	George Abbot Sr	04 N > S
21.	SCOT	?	Nwbry; DovrNH	33	John Russ	04 ?
22.	SCOT	?	Lynn	30	Andrew Allen	05 S
23.	SCOT	?	Gloucester	66	Andrew Foster	05 S
24.	BshpStfrd, HERTS	?	Rxbry; Ipsw?	16?	Th [&Wm]Chandler	05 S

Who the Settlers Were: Summary Table 73

LATECOMERS: 1647+ (order of arrival uncertain)

NO	ORIG/OW	SHIP/DATE	PREV NE RES	AGE	NAME	ORIG ACRES/N or S End
25.	BshpStfrd, HERTS	?	Ipswich; Lynn	25	[Rev] Francis Dane	n/aN
26.	WALES ?	James 1635	Ipswich; Drac't	25?	Ralph Farnum	04 N
27.	Rowley YORKS	?	Rowley Mass	26	George Abbott Jr	04 N
28.	Hern Hill, KENT	James 1635	Ipswich,Rowley	39	John Johnson	04 N
29.	Skirbut, LINCS	Abigail 1628	Lynn	27	[Sgt] Henry Ingalls	? N
30.	Andover HANTS	Jonathan 1639	Braintree; Malden	36	Samuel Blanchard (Huguenot?)	? S
31.	Marlboro, WILTS	Mary&John 1634	Ipswich; Salsbury	28	Christopher Osgood	? S
32.	YORKS? NORFOLK?	?	Salem; Hamptn NH	34	John Marston	? N
33.	SCOT ?		Reading ?	32	Robert Russell	04 S
34.	?	Hercules 1634	Salem	33	Edward Phelps	? S
35.	?	?	Newbury ?	?	Joseph Wilson	? S
36.	?	?	?	35	Laurence Lacy	? N
37.	HOLLAND ?	?	Boston	37	[Mr] Andrew Peeters	? S.

Here is the key to the column heading abbreviations in table 1.[10]

NO = reference number. Woodbridge is given a number although he does not appear on the Faulkner list. Bradstreet is the first name. Ministers' land was not subject to the lot-drawing system.

ORIG/OW = Origin/Old world. All were from Great Britain (town and county given where known) with possible exceptions of Blanchard (30), who may have been a Huguenot, and Peeters (37), who may have been Dutch and/or most recently living in Holland.

SHIP/DATE = name of boat and date of arrival, for determining boat-group associations.

PREV NE RES = previous residence(s) in New England if known.

AGE = Self-explanatory.

NAME = shows also titles (Mr indicates gentry status), the ten Covenanters (bold), and those who left town very soon although none of this information is shown on the Faulkner List. Those marked (left) did not stay on, even though they had land and were on the Faulkner list.

ORIG ACRES/N or S End = original acres granted/North or South End, an indicator of relative initial wealth. N/S shows whether this family became associated with the North End or South End of town. Some switched Ends, or held divided property, and Barker became associated with Boxford (the area of Andover's dispute with Rowley; of which more later).

---

[10]Sources for this material are the Charlotte Helen Abbott genealogies, other family genealogies as noted, and local histories of Andover and surrounding towns as noted in the bibliography. Also see Greven 1964:chap. 1 and tables 1, 2, 4, and 5, pp. 91–109. I am indebted to M. Barker (personal communication 2004) for information that Richard Barker, whose origin has been a mystery, may have come from Holmes-on-Spaulding, Yorkshire. Barker family historians have also proposed Nayland-on-Stour, Suffolk, and County Kent as origins for their ancestor. Lack of definite information about a major Andover family like Barker leaves a big gap. However, the Barker family's cousin marriage frequencies are closer to the north England type than the East Anglia type. Barker apparently spent time in Rowley before Andover, and the Rowley company was from Yorkshire. thus I have listed Barker as from Yorkshire, with a question mark. See the Barker Family website at <http://www.rootsweb.com/~mecnewry/barker_brothers.htm>.

4

"Cochichawick Called Andover"
From Plantation to Town

1643: About this time two plantations began to be settled upon Merrimack, Pentuckett called Haverhill, and Cochichawick called Andover. (John Winthrop, Journal).

1654: ...there was a town founded about one or two mile distant from the place where the goodly river of Merrimeck receives her branches into her own body...the honored Mr Simon Bradstreet taking up his last settling there, hath been a great means to further the work, it being a place well fitted for the husbandmans hand, were it not that the remoteness of the place from Towns of trade bringeth some inconveniences upon the planters, who are enforced to carry their Corne far to market; this Town is called Andover, and hath good store of land...they soon gathered into a Church, having the revered Mr Whodbridg to instruct them in the wayes of Christ, till he returned to England, and since having called to office the reverend Mr Deynes...(Johnson, Wonder-Working Providence, chapter VII)

1660: Hard upon the River of Shashin where Merrimack receives this and the other branch into its body, is seated Andover, well stored with land and Cattle. (John Josselyn, Second Voyage to New-England)

By 1643, according to Winthrop, the plantations were under way at Pentuckett and Cochichawick (Haverhill and Andover), although there is uncertainty as to whether they were still in the planning stage or whether any of Ward and Woodbridge's company had in fact begun to live there. At least one family, the Tylers, was living there unofficially, unconnected to the Ward company. Whoever it was, there must have been some sort of permanent settlement at Andover, for in 1643 the General Court had established four shires or counties and ordered that all colony towns now come under the new county jurisdictions. The settlement of Cochichawick was listed among the eight towns that now came under Essex County (see Bailey1880:6–7; also Hurd 1888, chapter 1). By 1647, Andover had become the official name, although it was probably pronounced a bit differently from the way it is today. Bailey cites passages from the Bay Colony records of 1647 in which the Court is concerned about upkeep of the roads and bridges in the frontier towns. "For want of a bridge...especially in winter and in the springe when the waters are high, some travelers have been in great danger of drowninge [on] the common road to *Andivver* and Haverhill" (p. 55, emphasis added). The court clerk's spelling here, and elsewhere as *Andivir* (loc.cit), suggests that unlike today's residents, seventeenth-century townspeople stressed the first syllable of the name, without a long 'o' in the second.

Andover was mentioned by Winthrop and in at least two of the early documents relating to the Bay Colony (see the opening of this chapter). Edward Johnson wrote for London readers in 1654 of the "Providence of Sion's Saviour in New England," and told of conditions in Bay Colony towns. Andover, he said (chapter VII), though remote, is "a place well fitted" with an "honored leader," Simon Bradstreet. He added that the town was undergoing an unexpected change of ministers. John Josselyn seemed to think things were going well in 1660. In this chapter I will trace the early development of the town, pointing out the signs of fission that might have been missed by these passersby.

The period from 1643 to 1680 was a frontier period in the Bay Colony, a time of building, fusion, fission, and change in the outlying towns. Winthrop's ideals set forth in his shipboard sermon "Model of Christian Charitie" continued to guide the Colony to some degree; the tumult "at home" in England seemed far away as the civil war storm gathered and broke. With Cromwell's apparent victory, many returned. But in 1661 the colonists heard the news from across the sea of the final end of Cromwell and his Puritan republic and the restoration of the monarchy in England. The Crown, which had hardly been able to think about the far-away colonies, began to reassert authority over them. Finally in 1678, "all Male Persons" in the colonies sixteen or older were ordered to take an oath of allegiance to the Crown. In the 1670s, a series of Indian hostilities radically disrupted the colonies throughout New England. Andover as an outlying settlement was especially vulnerable. Several young men were attacked, killed, or kidnapped while working in their fields in the western part of town. (See Church's diary [Simpson and Simpson 1975] for a contemporary account of these hostilities, which became known as King Philip's War; see Lepore 1998 for a recent analysis.)

Throughout this time there were signs of the internal fission that, along with the inevitable town growth, would lead eventually to Andover's splitting. In this and the next two chapters I look at early Andover society from several perspectives. In this chapter, I explore Andover society during the frontier period, as the people of Ward's (now Woodbridge's) company started their plantation at Cochichawick. Incorporating as the town of Andover, they exchanged the Indian name for the name of their leading citizen's hometown in England. In chapter 5, I focus on marriage patterns in the early years and how they reflected divisions and alliances in the social structure among Andover families. In chapter 6, I return to the process of the town split as manifested in several town and regional cases and crises, including the witchcraft panic that swept through Andover as well as Salem in 1692. Wherever possible I look at the terms in the records used by the colonists to express and describe categories of social identity.

Frontier Andover

Scattered records illuminate the lives of people in Andover and the neighboring towns for the first thirty-five years of settlement. Birth, marriage, and death records for many of the founding families have been compiled in family histories, and there are court cases, Andover town meeting records, and tax records.[1] Tax records before 1679 have never been found, perhaps because they were kept in the home of Edmund Faulkner, the town clerk whose house was burned down by Indians in the 1670s. After 1679, tax records are fairly complete and provide a record over time of the changing economic ranking of the town's men and families, as well as an account of town growth as measured by numbers of *polls rated,* or people taxed, and what they paid from year to year. I make use of these various sorts of records in this and the following chapters.

The records of the frontier years until the coming of the Indian war in 1675 picture a period of intense construction and reconstruction, both material and social. The settlers were involved in negotiations (and ongoing relationships) with Indians. They had to explore the land and classify it as to its resource value, survey and assign lots, clear it, set boundaries, erect fences, and make roads. They built houses, shelters for their animals, a central meetinghouse, and a mill. They also had to build a house for their minister and his family and supply them with food, firewood, and a little money. They felled trees, sawed them up, planted fields and gardens, found pasturage, and learned how to fish, hunt, and forage in

---

[1]Tax records for Andover are stored in the original in the Town Hall and on microfilm at the Memorial Library in Andover. The Andover Historical Society holds typed transcriptions for several years of the tax records. I reordered the lists from highest to lowest taxpayers, and included them in appendix D.

their new environment. Specialists worked leather, made pottery from the clay pits, and developed the iron deposit and foundry, making and repairing metal tools and nails. They set up market days and locations for trade and barter with one another and people of neighboring towns.

People traveled about the region by foot, animal, or boat. Court records and diaries indicate that travel at the county and regional level was common; the towns were not as socially isolated from one another as is sometimes assumed. Accounts from later periods such as Madam Knight's diary of her journey from Boston to New York in 1702 (Knight 1935) and even the later journal of Kendall (1809) help in understanding what travel conditions were like in what is now one of the busiest traffic corridors in the United States. Andover residents traveled by foot or animal to Boston, Salem, Ipswich, and other towns to market, visit friends and family, or answer a summons to the quarterly court session. They fought, stole, sued, killed, helped, and cared for each other, as the court records show. All through this they married, gave birth, got sick, and died young, old, or middle-aged. Meanwhile, new families were arriving, many to join kinsmen already settled in Andover. All had to find, learn, or make their own place in the developing social order of the town.

At the outset the colonists had little choice but to reconstruct in the new setting some adaptation of the social structure brought from their home region. The society they came from had a three-part social structure, consisting of civil, ecclesiastical, and military orders, each order a hierarchy with its leadership role or set of roles. The Bay Colony, and a typical settlement within it, was built around these three orders as well. While New Englanders could not help but base their social order on these familiar elements from old England, they also transformed and adapted them, constructing amalgams of redefined old world and emerging new world categories. In common with David Allen (1981) and David Cressy (1987), I do not see in the records the wholesale abandonment of old world institutions and roles that earlier historians such as Sumner Powell proposed in his discussion of Sudbury (Powell 1963:142–143).

In the ecclesiastical order, the offices ranged from minister, deacon, and elder to *tything-man, sexton,* and *bell-ringer.* The military order had its ranks at colony and county level, each town as well with its local militia or *trainband,* as the men of each town organized, elected a captain and officers, and drilled on the town green. In the civil order of old England, town freemen had long elected their civil officers. In New England this continued. Freemen elected their representatives to the General Court, the grand jury, and the county quarterly courts, as well as selectmen, constables, and a host of other town officers, such as *fence viewer, pound keeper, hay warden,* and *surveyor.* But in New England, unlike in Old England, freeman status came to be defined in terms of church membership. Until this law was changed by protest of excluded colonists and order of the Restoration monarchy, only church members could be freemen, and thus only church members could vote.

The old inherited social ranking of gentry and commoners persisted in the Colony, but the amount of available land gave commoners a new footing such as would never have been available to them in old England. Furthermore, in the Puritan plan it was to be church membership that conferred certain rights and privileges, not birthright. thus a commoner might be a covenant member of a church where a man of gentry rank was not, and so the former status relations could be undermined by the new rules. Simon Bradstreet, who was Andover's gentry but who never signed the covenant, may have found himself and his family in this position.

The Plantation

Land was available in the Bay Colony in quantities unheard of in old England. Some four hundred square miles were granted to the new plantation at Andover. Colony law at first required that town centers be nucleated and that for safety and order, all homesteads must be within a mile of the meetinghouse. The Andover settlers laid out their first houselots, not in the geographic center of their tract but in the northeast corner of it (see maps 6 and 10). This decision resulted in difficulties later as the population dispersed into the western part of the tract. However, the reasons for the choice of the original site are clear. It was near a ford of the Merrimack, near the great lake, near an excellent location for common pasturage, and near the stream they had spotted as a good mill site. The settlers first selected the site for the meetinghouse, Reverend Woodbridge received his houselot near it, and each of the Firstcomers was allotted a number of acres for a houselot. Some multiple of the acreage of a man's first plot was then used to determine the amount he received in subsequent divisions of the rest of the common land.

The size of the first-allotted plots varied with men's initial wealth and status. The right-hand column of table 1, p. 72, shows this (with acreage figures adapted from Greven 1970:46). Original allotments ranged from twenty to four acres. Simon Bradstreet, gentleman and civic leader, started with a twenty-acre houselot, whereas Daniel Poor, a young, unmarried, newly freed indentured servant, got four acres. Yet gentry status was not enough to guarantee a larger allotment. John Osgood, classed as a yeoman but leader of the Southwesterner Newbury contingent, got twenty acres just as did Bradstreet. Edmund Faulkner, son of a cadet lineage of Hampshire gentry, but young and unmarried, got only six acres at first. Nicholas Holt was a tanner, a crucial but not a high-status specialty. He got an initial fifteen acres, the next highest allotment after Bradstreet and Osgood.

Most of those who received the initial small lots of four and five acres were not of the Newbury company or of Southwesterner background. They were the Hertfordshire men, the Scots, and the bondservants. Their lots were on the lower ground in the south section of town whereas the houselots of the Newbury families were on the more desirable higher ground to the north. Using table 1 in conjunction with maps 7 and 8 shows the initial layout of the town center.[2] Note that those Firstcomers who shared the Southwesterner/Newbury/Covenanter set of identities settled as neighbors in the north part of the original town center. Most of the Hertfordshire/Ipswich/non-Covenanter group, together with some of the Scots and those who had been or still were indentured servants, settled in the south part.

The early rule of the colony, that no one should live more than a certain distance from the town meeting house, could not be enforced for long. The central properties remained the desirable ones, but movement away from the town center was inevitable. Firstcomers passed on their original lots and homesteads usually to eldest sons, but as the Firstcomers' other sons began to marry and need their own homes, there was no room for them in the center. As Latecomers arrived, they were soon unable to obtain houselots within the specified one-mile distance. Further divisions of land were made, and before long the Bay Colony rescinded the one-mile rule as unworkable.

The town gave choice of lots in subsequent divisions on the basis of the order of arrival, and that order was used in later allotments. The town records for November 16, 1662, state

> It is ordered and granted that for every acre of houselot there shall be laid out to it twenty acres of upland to be taken up and *chosen the same way and order* that hath been used in the divisions of the land according to the time of mens [first] coming to the town. (Quoted in Greven 1970:57, my emphasis)

Fortunately, as was mentioned in chapter 2, that list survives, known as the list of Freehoulders or Faulkner's list.

---

[2]Adapted from the town center houselot reconstructions of the late Forbes Rockwell, a resident of North Andover.

At first the town followed the open-field system, a practice Greven attributes to the regional custom of the Southwesterners who dominated the town (1970:43–44). In the open-field system each householder owned sections of the various kinds of landform: upland, lowland, swampland, and so on, rather than large consolidated holdings, and the town maintained a common pasturage for everyone's animals. Later, however, men began to sell and exchange their holdings so as to acquire single enclosable properties.

The records show that within fifteen years after incorporation, a drift of residences was under way to the south and west towards the Shawsheen River from the original town center, despite the town's attempt to stop it. At the town meeting of 1660 the selectmen voted a stiff fine of twenty shillings per month for anyone living elsewhere than on approved homestead lots. They said that a man could "put up a shedd" on his outlying lands, but that no one should "make it his constant abode" (ATR March 1660; see Greven's discussion 1970:54–56; 60ff.).

Features of the Town Center

The choice of location of the town center was originally influenced by the settlers' orientation towards local water resources. This location established what would become the central place.[3] The colonists would not start a settlement without having proximity to fresh-water springs, a primary requirement. Next in importance was a good millstream. They also looked for high ground for house lots and safe pasturage for animals. Andover's natural resources met all these requirements and offered even more. Map 7 shows the basic landform and waterways of what became the central part of town.

Thanks to the care of the North Andover Historical Society, nothing has been built on what was the old center green (see cover photograph). Today it is still possible to walk over it and imagine something of how the settlers must have seen this particular piece of land and chosen it as especially suited for the town center. Two low ridges run north to south, rising slightly at the northern end, flanking a long, shallow valley. Down the middle of this valley runs a little stream that disappears here and there and wells up later from underground. As map 8 shows, the first house lots were laid out in strips along the ridges on each side. The homes of the

---

[3]The concept of central place (Binford 1982) and Paynter's discussion of the interpretation of settlement patterns in historical archaeology (Paynter 1982) have been a source of insight into how to look at the layout of the old part of the town of Andover.

gentlemen, Bradstreet and Faulkner, were located towards the north, at the higher ends of the ridges. Around them were the house lots of the other Covenanter families. Although no vestiges of any of the first meetinghouses remain, they must have stood near the old town cemetery, which is still there as is the parsonage of 1704. A few of the early winged-skull slate headstones still survive in the cemetery.

The first surviving record of an Andover town meeting is from March 1656. That meeting was held at the house of John Stevens, not in a meetinghouse, though no record exists of why the meeting was held there. Maybe Stevens' house was warmer in March. Or, the settlers may have been in the process of building a new, larger meetinghouse, as there is on record that there was a new meetinghouse by 1661. What is significant about the account of the meeting at Stevens' house is the insight given into the initial social identities at Andover. This account contains the first use I found of the category *firstcomer*, referring to those who had contributed labor and money to the construction of the original common buildings. The selectmen ordered

> ...that all first comers of inhabitants that have been at the charge of purchasing the plantation and building *the minister's house, the mill and meeting house*...are allowed an acre and a half to every acre houselot of low and swamp land, and every other inhabitant that have been at the charge of building the meeting house and mill is to be allowed one acre to every houselot...(ATR 1661; in Bailey 1880:410–411, emphasis added)

Firstcomers, then, were involved in certain common projects: the purchase of a lot in the plantation in the first place, then the joint construction of three buildings of central importance, the minister's house, the mill, and the meetinghouse. The record says that "other inhabitants" had helped only with the meetinghouse and mill (suggesting that the minister's house was the first collective project). Those who had contributed to only two of the three communal projects received less in the reward of extra acreage. (The location of these community projects, and also the inns or public houses, discussed below, may be seen on map 7.)

The minister's house

First priority for a plantation was provision of a home for the minister's family, and every man owed some of his time and labor to this task above his own interests.[4] Townsmen also committed to supplying the minister with a load of firewood each year. A man could be fined for failure to

---

[4]See Hall 1972 for a full-scale study of the New England ministry, although he does not give as much emphasis to the social as he does to the intellectual history of it.

supply wood or for supplying poor wood. Each covenanting community was to work out an agreement with its minister for his support. The *rates* (taxes) for the support of the minister and his family were levied on the basis of a man's landholdings. A man could pay in both money and grain, as the amount of available money in the colony was variable. The job of the constable was to collect the rates and submit a signed list of the ratepayers and the rate paid each year. All landholders, whether church members or not, were required to contribute to the support of the minister. When members of a church-town were at odds with the minister, these obligations to him grew onerous, even more so to those who were not covenanting church members.

The mill

We do not have clear information on how many mills and which sort operated in Andover at any one time.[5] Simon Bradstreet is "said to have built the first saw-mill" in 1644 (but see Bailey 1880:12, 574, who could find no source in the records for this tradition). Whether or not it was an undertaking of Bradstreet's, a sawmill was the first necessity in order for settlers to proceed with building anything else. Andover's mill, located near the ford across the Merrimack, and near the entrance to the tributary stream Cochichawick would have made water transport for the logs and boards easier. Settlers bringing their goods from Newbury up the river could go to the docks at Haverhill, the upper navigation point. At that point they crossed the river, probably at "Broad Ford" (later Bradford), or went around the bend of the Merrimack to the new landing and mill site near the mouth of the Cochichawick. They could then get their household goods and lumber the short distance down to the new town center either by the Cochichawick River or overland. Maps 5 and 7 show these relationships.

Bradstreet, if the mill owner, doubtless did not do the actual building or running of it himself, so the question arises: Whom did he employ? Who were his people in the company? He and his wife were of the Lincolnshire contingent, but they had no other "countrymen" with them in Andover. Bradstreet was, however, brother-in-law to the minister. Their wives were sisters. He had also brought several servants, and he could count people from the Newbury group in his wider circle of kindred. Firstcomer Joseph Parker who had previously been at Newbury, was Andover's first miller, mentioned in a surviving record as having left his "Corne-mill on the Cochichawick" valued at twenty pounds to his son in 1678 (in Bailey, p.

[5] See Anthony Wallace's description of Rockdale (1978) for an illuminating description of how water mills worked, though from a later time in American history.

574). Parker was also a cousin of first minister John Woodbridge, in turn Bradstreet's brother-in-law. Bradstreet may have hired him to supervise and build the sawmill. Parker received rights to the millrace at the other end of the Cochichawick, near its flow out of the Great Lake (map 7). This site was probably where the grainmill was located. The location was near the town center and women and children could more easily and safely carry their household grain there to be milled.[6]

The record of mill licenses granted in town provides a clue to town growth, as the town needed more mills as the population grew. In 1664, the selectmen granted free access to the timber on the west side of the Shawsheen to anyone who would build a sawmill or a cornmill there, evidence that there was activity in that part of the town but not that there was a village yet, for there is no record that anyone took up the selectmen's offer. It was apparently hard to persuade permanent settlers to go to that location, no doubt because of the genuine danger posed by Indians. The need for millers grew so great that by 1682, the selectmen were willing to offer twenty acres of land and the full privileges of a townsman to anyone willing to set up on the Shawsheen any of the three basic mills: gristmill, fullingmill, or sawmill. In 1688, Joseph and John, two sons of Firstcomer William Ballard, took up this offer. The mill system they erected remained in place for the next two hundred years, and the hamlet around it is still called Ballardvale (Abbot 1829:50, Bailey 1880:578. See also Shawsheen River on map 10).

Other second-generation sons also were establishing themselves on the outskirts of town. For the first time (on record) in 1686, permissions were granted to erect mills on the two lesser streams of Andover, to Henry Ingalls, Junior "to set up a saw-mill on Moskito Brook and to Henry Holt to set up a saw-mill on Ladle [Little?] Meadow Brook." During the 1690s the records contain notices of at least four more licenses granted to erect mills on the town's main streams (in Bailey 1880:574–575). The growth in the number of mills indicates the growth in population to support them, and the fact that millers were building even on the small streams suggests a steady dispersal away from the town center.

---

[6]Until the fields at Andover were cleared and producing, the residents had to get their grain at the coastal markets and bring it up the river. But by 1653, less than ten years after the first clearings at Andover, there was enough grain being grown there to take to the markets at Salem and Boston for barter and sale. Greven found that the account books of merchant Thomas Corwin of Salem for this period show Andover residents paying him in what was called country pay, that is, wheat, rye, or Indian corn (Greven 1970:68).

The meetinghouse

The meetinghouse remained the symbol of the town center. In the church-towns of the early Bay colony, the meetinghouse was a practical, symbolic, and architectural center of all that united the settlers. It served as a spatial focus, a place of meeting for the various orders of life: ecclesiastical, civil, and military. The people met there for worship and for their rites of passage, for schooling and for town business, and for protection or muster in case of threat. At first, seating in meetinghouses was not as formally organized as it later became, according to Winslow's study of the New England meetinghouse (1952). Gradually, carefully controlled seating arrangements were worked out in a process called "dignifying the pews" and "seating the meeting-house," and the results reflected status in the new social order. The seating was worked out according to a system of reckoning rank that grew ever more elaborate with the passing years until it reached rococo-like proportions (see texts in appendix B detailing the criteria for seating the meeting house in the churches at nearby Beverly and Tewksbury). Some of those assigned to work out the seating of the meetinghouse are on record as protesting the assignment as it was "a fruitful source of jealousies and hard feelings," says Bailey. Dudley Bradstreet is on record as having "protested against being compelled to serve in seating the meeting-house" but even he protested apparently to no avail (in Bailey 1880: 412).

The approximate location of Andover's first meetinghouse can almost certainly be established since, as in England, it was the custom to use the land beside it for the graveyard. The early graveyard of Andover is extant, though with many missing and broken headstones, and from its vantage point we can see how the layout of the original homesteads might have been in relation to it. One larger meetinghouse was built sometime in the 1660s according to the records, but until the parish split in 1710 only one meetinghouse for Andover existed, still located in that same area around the old town center. The meetinghouse was simultaneously a place of unity and safety and a place of bitter contention as well.

The ordinary

In addition to the buildings mentioned by the selectmen in the passage above—minister's house, mill, and meetinghouse—there was another type of important communal gathering place in town, one that also could and did cause controversy in the town. That building was the public house, or the term more commonly used in the seventeenth century, the *ordinary,* which served as the colonial tavern and sometimes inn.

The public house has had a long history and particular place in English village life where the town "pub" still plays quite a different role in neighborhood life than does the American "bar." In early New England, the public house or ordinary quickly rose to the level of importance it held in the towns of the old country.[7] Licensing and other matters relating to ordinaries and the regulation of liquor frequently took the time of the General Court, the quarterly courts, and local civil bodies. Alcohol was no less volatile in the new world than in the old, and an added problem was its effect on Indians. Soon the Court forbade the sale of liquor to Indians and struggled to arrive at a satisfactory policy for issuing licenses to the towns. The Court itself required that towns have public houses and allotted each town a certain number of licenses. A public house was at first an adjunct to someone's home, a place for news, refreshment, and entertainment for townspeople and travelers alike. Only those who were believed to be responsible citizens received licenses. No doubt they were prized as it became clear that tavern-keeping was going to be one of the most lucrative businesses in the colony.

Andover was allotted two ordinary licenses and a retail license (see Bailey 1880:64ff. for the following material regarding taverns and licenses). Retail licenses permitted the owner to sell liquor not to be consumed on the premises. The first license in Andover was granted in 1648 to Mr. Edmund Faulkner, listed as a "vintner," the only other member of the gentry besides Bradstreet and later the town clerk. Selectman John Osgood held the other ordinary license, and Deacon Frye held the retail license. However, all three of these men were part of the Southwesterner/Newbury group of Covenanters, and they all lived near one another in the north part of the town. Note the location of their lots on map 8, especially Faulkner's house, near the conjunction of roads coming into Andover from the north bringing the Haverhill and Newbury traffic.

The Court's allocation of licenses in this way, however, meant that there was no public house in the south end of town to serve either the neighborhood people or the growing volume of traffic passing through that end on the Ipswich-Billerica road. This situation added to the tensions between the two ends. Travelers passing through the south end had to go about a mile and a half to the north end of town, to Osgood's or to

---

[7]Since Field (1897) surprisingly little has been written on the role of the pub or ordinary in colonial New England, or on the social role generally of liquor (except for its effect on Indians). See, however, a treatment of the role of the two pubs in a contemporary English village and how they developed in relationship to the distinct sociogeography of their two sets of patrons (Hunt and Satterlee 1986).

Faulkner's, if they wanted to find refreshment or lodging in Andover. Many travelers would stop at the houses of those who lived beside the road in the south to ask for what they wanted, food or drink for themselves and water for their horses. While it was right to show hospitality to travelers, it could also become a burden, and so the residents of the south end chafed under the need for an ordinary in their own area.

The licenses were firmly held by the North Enders, who for some reason made no effort to accommodate the south. It was not long before a public house appeared in the south part of town. It was in the home of William Chandler (see map 7). The North Enders claimed he had no license; he claimed he did. Eventually, controversy erupted over Chandler's house and his suitability to be a license-holder. The issue swept up the town in a flurry of petitions and counter-petitions. The conflict engendered by it will be followed further in chapter 6. At this point it is sufficient to note that it was an issue that both contributed to and reflected the fissioning of the town, north and south, and that the division over this situation followed the same lines of social identity that have been previously noted, between Southwesterner and Hertford groups.

Andover in the Regional Setting

The insights of Carol Smith in her classic *Regional Analysis* (1976) pointed many anthropologists toward the importance of the relationships of people and social units in a region, countering a preoccupation with village level work. Although the town of Andover is in focus in this book, the importance of its regional relationships should also be emphasized. As discussed earlier, Andover and Haverhill were established together by groups originally associated with the same company organized by Nathaniel Ward. Ward expected to go to Haverhill, while his son John would go to Andover. Since in the end Ward was unable to go to Haverhill as he planned, his son took his place as the first minister there, and another young minister, John Woodbridge, Bradstreet's brother-in-law, was recruited to the Andover post. The first plan suggests that Haverhill was expected to be the more important settlement, if the senior Ward was going to go there. Perhaps its location at the upper navigation point on the river Merrimack meant it would likely develop as a major colony shipbuilding port.

Haverhill and Andover remained closely linked. When leading families of Andover such as the Osgoods and Aslebes looked for suitable matches for their children, they approached their opposite numbers in nearby towns with which they had a suitable (to them) connection, such as Haverhill. The new settlements to the west of Andover, Billerica and Chelmsford were closer geographically than Haverhill across the river, but Andover's leading families did not make any matches with Chelmsford or Billerica during these first seventy years (see Hazen's genealogies, 1883). The settlers in those rough outposts may have been considered what Ward had earlier called "the meaner sort." Nor did Andover's Covenanters seem inclined to court the Yorkshire people of neighboring Rowley. They went to Haverhill or back to the established coastal settlements where the other Southwesterners were to be found (see Chase 1861 and Clement 1927 for the classic accounts of early Haverhill, including genealogies).

Another regional issue that had become a colony-wide concern and source of conflict was road maintenance. The Court periodically appointed committees of men from several towns to see to the laying out of a better set of "common high ways." Although settlements like Andover and Haverhill had good water and wintertime ice transportation via the rivers, the problems of land transportation occupied the attention of the town leaders at one town meeting after another. In 1647, soon after incorporation, Andover appointed men to lay out the roads that would connect it with its neighboring towns to the south and east. In 1648, the town was called before the Court for not getting its own roads and bridges fixed as required. Getting the townsmen to do the work of road building was apparently not easy. In 1661, the surveyors of Andover were authorized to call up every male over sixteen for road work on three days' notice, with a fine of four shillings a day to be levied on those who did not show up (Bailey 1880:55–56).

The maintenance of the road to Salem was an especially difficult issue. Salem was the chief market town and port before Boston grew, and it was the site of the Court. In 1671, the selectmen of Salem petitioned the Court, complaining that their town's assignment of work in a new road-building endeavor was unequal in that they would have over "an hundred rods" of meadow and swamp, "some of it very deep," to turn into road. No wonder some preferred to pay their fines. The Salem men said that in consultation with the men of Andover they had come up with a different route, and they begged the Court's permission to lay out this alternative. But in 1688, it was still very difficult to "get a Cart over the road to Salem." Andover petitioned the Court to do something about the condition of the Salem road, calling on "the established law, that the country allows us the nearest and best way to every town." The Andover selectmen said that it was unfair to the "inland Townes" that had to depend on carts for transportation to market, to let other towns get away with poor road maintenance in their areas (in Bailey 1880:57–58).

As early as 1649, Andover had been presented before the county court for "want of settled weights and measures," definitely showing that the town and region had already developed markets. Evidence shows that Andover itself became a regional center for the sale of fish from its abundant supplies. In 1681 the selectmen granted to three of their own number the rights to catch fish by weir at the mouth of the Shawsheen and permission to sell their catch, provided they sell to "Inhabitants of ye town" first. But Andover probably continued to be dependent for its larger market outlet on Salem. In the year 1693, for the first time in the surviving records, an office "clerk of the market" is listed among the town offices (in Bailey 1880:140, 144, 153), although this does not mean that there had not been such an officer before.

The isolation of all these frontier towns, however, became a problem, especially as the Indian hostilities began to mount. The rise of the county militias also drew together the inland regional towns. Meanwhile, political growth and change in the colony meant that men like Simon Bradstreet, who were both civil and military leaders at the colony level, found they needed to be nearer the central political and court life of the colony on the coast. Bradstreet found it difficult to lead from Andover under the inland travel conditions. After his wife's death in 1672 he soon moved back to the center of things at Salem.

Growth and Fission: North and South Ends Emerge

Even in the early stages of Andover, two ends of the town were emerging that reflected the pre-existing social relationships, specifically the social hierarchy between and within the companies that started the original settlement. The North and South Ends contained the nucleus of the social clusters that became the precincts and then the parishes. Most important, the old division present from before the beginning of the town in its English origins continued to show its strength in settlement, land transactions, and subsequent social alignments. These divisions were first between the Covenanters and the others. In turn, Covenanter solidarity traced back to older pre-emigration regional ties.

New world categories began to overlay those of the old world in the context of Andover, while continuing to underlie old world forms of social structure and identity. For example, Covenanters in Andover were starting to take on the role of gentry. Southwesterners or "Southton men" were slowly shedding that English identity for that of *North Enders*. However, apparent exceptions to the patterns characteristic of these social categories existed as well. Nicholas Holt, for example, was listed as a Southwesterner and as a Covenanter, but he and his family followed a very different pattern of settlement and marriage from the other Southwesterners. Sure enough, a closer look at the information about Holt shows that he may not have been a native Southwesterner to begin with, but from farther north in England, perhaps Lancashire, although as Holt family historian Durrie cautioned, this is not established (Durrie 1864, reprinted at www. holt.org, Holt Family History Website). In any case, Holt moved away from the Southwesterner enclave quite soon to establish his own territory on Holt's Hill (see map 10), and Holt family marriage patterns definitely are unlike the Southwesterners, especially in the marriage of cousins. The Holt variation highlights the Southwesterner pattern.

The 1679 list of rates (taxes) collected for the support of the minister is the first available information on economic status in the emerging two ends of Andover. Earlier rates lists have disappeared. The 1679 list is really made up of two lists, in two different handwritings. They are labeled the North and the South "Ends of Towne," and each list is signed by the constable from each end whose job it was to collect the taxes, add up the totals, and present it all to the selectmen. Although there are no earlier rates lists, there is other evidence that shows that there was already a gradual movement towards this dual division in the civil order. Lists elsewhere tell who held town offices in earlier years. It appears that as early as 1669 fence-viewers and surveyors were appointed from time to time for each of what were earlier called the north and south "parts" of town. From 1676 on, there was a regular appointment of two constables, one from each end (in Bailey 1880:137–138; see also Kent (1981) for a good background on the role of the constable in English towns).

Clearly the town had some basis for division, but what? In Philip Greven's view, it was primarily population pressure that had pushed these two ends of town into the territories that would eventually become the North and South Parishes when the parish split occurred in 1710 (Greven 1970:56). He took the South End list of 1679 as an indication that over half of the residents of Andover were already living on the Shawsheen River, some seven or eight miles away from the meetinghouse. However, the South End and the South Parish were not the same. Andover resident Forbes Rockwell's reconstruction of land holdings and transfers in the old part of town for the first hundred years demonstrates that the "North and South Ends" on the 1679 lists were still the two ends of what became eventually the North Parish. With later expansion, however, certain South End families did move away towards the Shawsheen and became the nucleus of the later South Parish.

Settlement and Dispersal

Two sequential maps clarify this picture. Adapted from the Rockwell reconstructions, they show changing land holdings in the old town center.[8] Map 8 shows the initial layout of household lots in 1646. Note again the distinction between Covenanters and other Firstcomers who were not Covenanters. Almost all in the Covenanter category were also linked by prior residence in Newbury and, before that, association with the two southwestern English counties, Wiltshire and Hampshire.

Nine lots are shown, since Richard Blake, one of the ten Covenanters, did not stay in Andover for long. Except for Nathan Parker's, the Covenanter lots are contiguous and clustered together in the north end of the center. Parker had come to the colony as one of John Stevens' bondservants, according to Greven (1964:6), and he was a young single man who remained unmarried until 1648. This seems to explain his location next to Stevens' lot, and away from his brother and the more mature family men who made up the bulk of the Covenanters. Stevens himself was one of the category exceptions. Although he had been with the Newbury group, he was neither a Covenanter nor a Southwesterner, but he was one of the top taxpayers. Stevens may have been one of those in the Rowley meeting back in 1644 who objected to being asked to covenant again (see pp. 66–67). Stevens and Richard Barker, neither of them Southwesterners, both established their home territories to the north of the North End and their families became closely related. In chapter 6, I recount Stevens' appearance in a court case, the outcome of which cost him his position as leader of the town militia.

The location of lots that belonged to those who were Firstcomers but not Covenanters shows that most of the people in that category lived from the beginning in what was the South End. Greven's discussion of the residents of the two ends does not bring out this aspect of the social composition (1970:139–141). Maps 8 and 9 shows the dispersal of non-Covenanter families from the town center. Marriage and court records now augment the maps and tax records for a deeper understanding of the relationships among

---

[8] A map is not yet available comparable to the Rockwell maps, showing the changing land holdings in the area to the north of the old town center. When the Andover Historical Society's project of mapping land holdings in the South Parish are completed, it will be possible to look again at the marriage and tax records with new insight.

the various groups. Next I look at the situation in both ends of town in the year 1679, the baseline tax record year (appendix D).

The North End

Town center lot ownership in 1679 shows important changes from the 1640 layout. Simon Bradstreet had remarried by that time and moved away in order to be in Salem, the political center of Essex County. His son Dudley remained on the Andover homestead in the role of town gentry. The Bradstreet lot in 1679 now included the lot of former neighbors Robert Barnard and Richard Sutton. Bailey (1880:34) cites court records that Sutton left town after quarrels with the elder Bradstreet (after which Bradstreet somehow acquired his lot). Barnard a cousin of Andover's second minister, did not stay in town but early on sold his lot and joined the group moving to the island of Nantucket (Abbott n.d.:Barnard). Much buying, selling, and exchanging had gone on around the town center. The lots in general had become larger, and fewer people owned land there.

Summarizing the changes: those who now owned town center lots were the Covenanters, their sons, or their sons-in-law (except for Bradstreet, who though a leader was never an Andover Covenanter). Most of the Covenanters were also Southwesterners, and they were also part of the former Parker Company at Newbury. Other than Bradstreet, of the non-Covenanters only the family of John Stevens had established and maintained itself in the center. Stevens, originally from Oxfordshire, was neither a Southwesterner nor a Covenanter, but he had traveled and settled at first with the Southwesterners at Newbury.

As for the South End of town, the non-Covenanter Firstcomers of Hertfordshire owning lots had moved there. This was perhaps through double marriage alliances with Covenanter Richard Barker, whose background is unknown but who also does not fit the Covenanter pattern. The Barker and Stevens families, as the odd ones in the north, established a pattern of marriage between themselves that continued well into the nineteenth century.

The most noteworthy change is that the non-Covenanter Firstcomers who did stay in the old center acquired a sort of Covenanter status in the next best way: they married daughters of John Osgood, the First Covenanter. This was the case with Aslebe and Poor. Osgood had left his entire estate to his eldest son, a rare instance of primogeniture in this time of increase in the practice of partible inheritance (according to Greven, who made a close study of wills and inheritance in Andover, (1970:60–62, fn. 25). But Osgood's action insured that his family's estate and position in the town center would not be dispersed. John Marston and

Henry Ingalls, Latecomer men who also appear as landowners in the old center at this point, also married Osgood daughters. How they acquired the land is not clear. These four men, Aslebe, Poor, Marston, and Ingalls, were thus all brothers-in-law to each other and to John Osgood Junior, now heir to his father's lands and position. According to the tax record, Osgood was now the town's wealthiest man and his four brothers-in-law were among the other top taxpayers. The succeeding generation of the remaining Covenanter families and those who had intermarried with them became the social and economic core of the North End.

The South End

Only one Covenanter, Nicholas Holt, sold his lot and moved away, leaving the community of the other Covenanters. Holt left the North End altogether, as maps 8 and 9 show. Holt's role seems to have been a key one as a broker family. Socially and territorially, he occupied a pivotal place in the emergence first of the South End and later the South Parish. Holt, married four times, had ultimately seventeen children and stepchildren to provide for. He led the move south out of the town center to that part of his property still called Holt Hill. His outlying holdings centered around Holt Hill, on the border between what later became the Farnum and Holt school districts. (See A Plan of Andover in 1795, reprinted in Mofford 2004:48–49, for the school district names.)

It seems that Holt himself moved to the hill sometime in the 1670s. In 1675, the town ordered that his land be surveyed and the bounds "stated and New Marked." Bailey, taking a perceptive look at the language of the surveyor's report, points out the reference to a black oak standing near the "highway going *up* to his house" and reckons the report to provide good evidence that Holt must have been living up on his hill at the time (in Bailey 1880:96). If so, then he must have been one of the first townsmen to move so far out of town, and was the only one of the Covenanters to do so.

Holt was strongly allied through his children's marriages to a Latecomer family, the Farnums from Ipswich. These families had long connections. The Farnums probably of Welsh background (Abbott n.d.:Farnum) had come with the Holts to the colony on the same boat, and their presence in Andover seems due to their Holt connections there. Holt ultimately married four of his children to four of Ralph Farnum's. Marriages between the children of these four couples in the next two generations were so frequent that they give the Holt and Farnum families the highest percentages of cousin marriage in all of Andover (see table 4, chapter 5).

In general, however, and except for Bradstreet and Stevens, it was the non-Covenanters who left the old town center. Following Holt, Thomas Chandler, George Abbot, William Ballard, and Christopher Osgood spearheaded the move towards the Shawsheen. Map 9 shows that these men no longer have holdings in the town center. Bailey thinks it was at about this same time as Holt made his move (in Bailey 1880:95–96). These four men and Edward Phelps, a Chandler son-in-law, were the highest taxpayers in the South End in 1679. Two different and separate family clusters formed the basis of this group. One was the old Dane-Chandler-Abbot group from Hertfordshire, part of that set of families and single young men who had followed the Reverend John Norton to Massachusetts. This group was now in its second-generation form in the colonial society. Dane, one of Harvard's new young graduates, was Andover's minister in the North End in the parsonage. His brother's daughter was also now in Andover, married to Dane's stepbrother (and the girl's step uncle) William Chandler. Abbot and the Chandlers were also brothers-in-law as well as step-kin. They were beginning to incorporate another family through marriage: the Ballards. Phelps' children were also married to children of Chandler and Ballard. This group of tightly intermarried families formed one South End cluster (Abbott n.d.:Dane; Chandler).

The other South End cluster centered around Christopher Osgood. His group steadily rose to prominence over Chandler's group, or rather in tandem with them. Christopher Osgood's relationship to John Osgood of the North End is an intriguing unknown, but the two men and their descendants clearly ought not to be counted under the same surname, as Abbot (1829:19), Greven (1970:219), and others have done. Greven persistently counted the two Osgood families as one (see, for example p. 140), thus obscuring their very real differences and roles in Andover. In fact, the difference between the two Osgood families and their roles in early Andover is one of the clearest facts to emerge from a study of their marriage histories and other records. (The same can be said for the two Abbot/Abbot families, also counted as one by Greven.)

Christopher Osgood had come to Andover as a boy, stepson of Thomas Rowell, a miller. Rowell had moved to Andover sometime in the early 1650s with his wife and her children by her first two marriages. One of her sons was Christopher. But Rowell died not long after the move. His widow, Christopher's mother, soon remarried and moved away, but her older children by her former marriages stayed in Andover. The oldest daughter married John Lovejoy, Rowell's neighbor in the South End. The second daughter married a son of John Russ, one of the Scotsmen also living in the South End. His sisters probably looked after young Christopher, only about twelve years old, until he was ready to make his own way. He lived in the South End from the time of his arrival in Andover and his connections remained strong with the other South End families. He married in 1664 at the age of twenty-one and had his first child the next year, the first of four marriages and fifteen children. The Osgood connection that Greven reports for Mary Allen (1970:219) is almost certainly with the Christopher Osgood family of the South End, not the John Osgood family of the North End, if C. H. Abbott's research is reliable (Abbott n.d.: Osgood [Christopher]). Christopher Osgood's children continued marriage connections started by his older sisters with the Russ and the Lovejoy families. These were families of Scots and indentured servants, families with whom John Osgood's family never married.

Christopher Osgood's rise to the top of the South End and later the Parish, can be marked in the civil order, where he finally was elected Representative to the general court, in the military order, where he finally was promoted to militia captain, and in the economic order, where he came to be among the top taxpayers in the South End. Like Holt's, his was an exceptional career. He fit none of the social categories when he arrived in Andover as a boy with his mother and stepfather, and the pattern he followed was eclectic. I think of his role and that of Nicholas Holt in terms of social brokers, families who nevertheless were not considered of highest rank or at the social center. But through marriage, they integrated the more peripheral families such as the Scots and other Old Britons into the larger network.

What the Tax Lists Show: Summary Table

Table 2 presents a summary of information from the tax tables in appendix D. Consult appendix D to see the names of taxpayers and how their places on the lists dipped and rose from year to year. Here I have summarized and reordered the columns to show how taxpaying changed in the two Ends of Andover at intervals over the years 1679 to 1716. I wanted to track and compare variations over time in numbers of payers and comparative wealth in the two parts of town.

Table 2. Taxpaying in Andover: North and South Ends
At Intervals From 1679 To 1716

	NORTH END				SOUTH END			
YEAR:	#P	#R	AV	RANGE	#P	#R	AV	RANGE
1679	39	27	6.01	17.09/1.06	47	37	5.06	11.01/ 1.00
1684	54	37	3.09	10.10/ .06	57	40	3.11	8.11/ 1.05
1690	63	34	6.03	17.01/ 1.10	55	31	6.08	16.09/ 3.00
1693	83	42	3.04	9.07 / .10	69	42	3.08	7.11/ 1.00
1699	67	43	4.06	9.00/ .04	77	45	4.05	10.06/ 1.01
1707	84	43	2.06	6.05/ .03	97	42	2.06	5.11/ .10
1716	110	79	17.08	£2.3.03/ 5.00	101	68	14.10	£2.0.06/2.09

(#p) number of payers
(#r) number of ranks
average (av) and
range (in shillings and pence)
(Source: Town of Andover Tax records: Microfilm, Memorial Library, Andover, Massachusetts)

Column #P shows the total number of payers on record for each year. Column #R "number of ranks" shows the number of different ranks of taxes paid. The next column AV shows the average tax rate. The last column shows the range, highest and lowest tax amounts paid in that End for that year. For instance, in 1679 in the North End there were thirty-nine taxpayers (but there was a range of only twenty-seven different rates paid) . The average in shillings and pence of the 27 rates was 6.01, with a range from 17.09, the highest tax paid, to 1.06, the lowest. The changing ratio of payers to ranks gives some idea of the spread of economic wealth in the community. If there were 50 payers, and 45 ranks, this means the assessor (for whatever reasons) would have been making quite fine distinctions about men's relative wealth in assessing. If on the other hand, there were 50 payers and 20 ranks, the assessor would have been placing more families in the same tax rank, suggesting less socioeconomic distinctions in that section of the town. Note that in 1693, the year after the witchcraft crisis, a sharp drop occurred in the average and the range of taxes paid in both Ends. It was a year of lower rates for everyone.

The table shows the increase in wealth and in numbers of taxpayers —and therefore voters—in the South End in 1699. This finally gave it enough power in 1707 to elect a set of South Enders as selectmen for the first time. This move in turn made it possible for the South to petition the General Court for independent parish status, against the wishes of the North. Note that the North End in 1716 seemed to reassert itself in wealth and numbers. The present research does not extend to this period and beyond, intriguing though the trend is. Perhaps the North Enders under Parson Barnard had found a way to recover from their season of being made "the lesser part" (see his letter, appendix C).

This period of the emergence of the two Ends looks rather like a cell moving towards division, as Andover residents dispersed from the original settlement and began to form another nucleus or center next to the original. Fission followed some predictable lines. In the old center, the Southwesterner-Covenanters, led by the John Osgood family, had intermarried and consolidated their control over center lands and town offices. However, when the minister, Southwesterner Woodbridge, left so soon, they no longer controlled the ministry. The new minister, Dane, came from the Hertfordshire contingent. Although Dane himself and his family continued to live in the parsonage beside the church in the North End, all the other Hertfordshire families, all related to him, were the nucleus of the emerging South End.

As for the original Lincolnshire gentry, Dudley Bradstreet continued to hold the social and military power his father had left him, but the Bradstreet family did not continue in Andover after the witchcraft crisis of the 1690s. The family came under accusation and they left; Bradstreet influence essentially waned in Andover after that time. The Barker and Stevens families, leading families economically but never part of the Southwesterner group, had begun to intermarry and form another bloc in the North End. They would provide the connection to Andover's third minister, Thomas Barnard, through their sojourn with the Southwesterners in Newbury.

Many Firstcomers who were neither Covenanters nor part of the Newbury-Southwesterner subcompany made their way from the South End into the new lands to the south and west of town. None of this was accomplished without considerable stress along the way, some of which found its way into the records and much more of which certainly did not. The settlers not only endured conflict and division within their own ranks, but also attack by Indians from without. However, none of what they experienced in the opening years of their life together in Andover compared to the severity of the trauma they would undergo in the next fifteen years. I will return to that story and the process of town fissioning in chapter 6. In the next chapter I look more closely at some patterns of marriage in Andover's families, and how these rejected both former and emerging social identities.

5

"A Motion of Marriage"
Marriage and Alliance in Early Andover

Deposition of Mr Simon Bradstreet, 1675: When Mr Jonathan Wade of Ipswich came first to my house at Andover in the year 1672 to make a motion of marriage betwixt his son Nathaniel and my daughter Mercy, he freely of himself told me what he would give to his son vz one half of his Farm at Mistick and one third p't of his land in England when he died....I was willing to accept of his offer, or at least said nothing against it...After he came home he told several of my Friends & others that he had offered to give his son better than one thousand pounds and I would not take it. (Essex County Court Records, 1675) [1]

Few people today think of their marriages in terms of alliances that have been established between families, so in that respect, the past really is a foreign country to us. Marriages in early New England as in old England were usually worked out (if not strictly arranged) through a series of negotiations between families, formally initiated by one family's "motion of marriage." We get a glimpse into this above, as Simon Bradstreet describes Jonathan Wade's initiative as part of a court case where the two fathers were at odds about the agreement. Marriages constituted alliances not only between the two families, but also as extended to clusters of related families that made up the larger social categories. Wade and Bradstreet were among the wealthiest men not only in the Bay Colony but also in wider New England. Concern for their estates and reputations as well as their children's marriages may explain Bradstreet's seemingly prickly tone in the deposition cited above ("I was willing to accept of his offer, or at least said nothing against it..."). The marriage negotiations

---
[1] ECQCR vol. xliii: 66; in Bailey 1880:76.

and resulting alliances of men in this class affected their extended families and their properties in the wider Bay Colony, in neighboring Connecticut, and even those back in England. As it turned out, these fathers did work out their differences and Nathaniel Wade and Mercy Bradstreet married and settled in Connecticut Colony later that year.

However negotiated, whether between families of high, middling, or low status, the marriages made by the second and third generations in Massachusetts were forming the social bedrock of the new colonial society for several generations to follow. In some cases, marriages in the colony carried on premigration alliances between families who also continued to intermarry generation after generation in the new world. Such ongoing marriage ties between families formed what Dumont (1984) terms "valued affinities" (affinity in the anthropological sense of an in-law relationship). Many families in the founding generation brought their valued affinities to the colony along with their other sets of social relationships from the old country. Thus Bradstreet's own marriage had taken place in Lincolnshire to Anne Dudley, daughter of Thomas Dudley, his former guardian and patron, and it had established a permanent connection between his family and the Dudley family. Both men had served under the Earl of Lincoln, Dudley over Bradstreet in the hierarchy. This relationship was perpetuated in the next generation in Massachusetts when Bradstreet's' daughter married her cousin, a grandson of the now Governor Dudley.

The higher a family's position in the social structure, the greater the potential scope and import of its members' marriages, although, at the same time, the smaller the pool of potential spouses for the children. When James I of England tried to negotiate a marriage in 1621 between his son Charles and the Catholic "daughter of Spain," many in the growing Puritan Parliament objected fiercely and called instead for war with Spain. James was outraged but forced to drop his suit (especially when it was reported that Maria said she would rather go into a nunnery than marry Charles [Willson 1967:375; Fleming 1973]). But the marriages of families in power at lower nodes in the hierarchy also excited interest and opinion in their sphere of influence and affected those around them. The prototype incident cited at the close of chapter 2 showed how the two Bay Colony leaders, Winthrop and Dudley, reconciled after a history of quarreling and like two tribal patriarchs arranged a marriage between their eldest children. In customary seventeenth-century English kinship terminology usage, a man called his child's spouse's father "brother." These men named two great rocks on Winthrop's property in Concord "Two Brothers" to commemorate their reconciliation and the new relationship established through this alliance. The site can still be visited today in the State Forest at Concord.

Winthrop and Dudley well understood that their children's marriage, whatever its financial and reproductive outcome might be, would have symbolic power for the rest of the society as well. The ebb and flow of conflict between these two men from the outset had strained the loyalties of their respective Suffolk and Lincolnshire companies, and to some extent the whole colony had become divided behind them. Thus this early Winthrop-Dudley marriage alliance was to stand as a "model of Christian charity," not only for the two nuclear families or even the extended families of which they were a part, but for the two regional contingents they represented and thus for the whole Bay Company as well.[2]

Marriage in Andover

Marriage patterns in Andover provide a unique kind of information about individual and family strategizing—planning and choice—as well as out come, with relationship to social identity and hierarchy in the town. Andover's patterns reveal, not surprisingly, that marriages of the second generation, children for the most part actually born in the colony, continued many of the old alliances of their parents. But as the first generation of those who had grown up in English ways passed from the scene, as events in the new world overtook them and their children, memories and loyalties from the old world faded. By the third generation, marriage choices and alliances in Andover and the regions around began both to reflect and to build the new identities of the new world.

My treatment of marriage in Andover is divided into two sections, one in this chapter and one in the final chapter. In the final chapter I will look at the marriages of particular families as one of several facets of life in Andover, affected after the town had endured the witchcraft crisis and the parish split. In this chapter I explore marriage patterns before that traumatic time. Greven also took the marriage records of Andover and used the categories of historical demography to analyze marriage in Andover. I will suggest that Andover's marriages can best be understood if explored not only in terms of demographic categories but also in terms of townspeople's emic categories. Andover people's marriage patterns seem

---

[2]"A Model of Christian Charity" was the title of Winthrop's famous sermon on board the Arbella on the voyage to Massachusetts, and it was the ideological touchstone for the committed Puritans. It has been reprinted in many sources, for instance, Vaughan (1972).

definitely affected by contingencies and changed relationships underlying the process of town fission with its acute episode of the witchcraft crisis.

Although in the 1970s and 1980s colonial historians increased their interest in how British local culture and society had affected the formation of colonial societies, they did not widely explore themes of kinship and marriage. Little is known either about regional variation in this domain in seventeenth-century Britain itself, let alone how the new colonial situations might have unfolded in relation to such variation. Cressy (1986:chap. 11) reviewed sources of information about kinship in New England and remarked that kinship "is one of the great unexplored areas of early modern social history" (p. 274). So there is no body of background work (that I know of) on regional marriage patterns in Britain which could shed light on the colonial situation, as has been done for land tenure and use.[3] This limited study of one town, Andover, suggests that there were clear differences relating to what the colonists called country and blood, each other's regional and ethnic backgrounds. But more studies are needed of seventeenth-century marriage patterns in both Britain and various parts of New England.

So far in this study I have traced the ties of patronage, friendship, and kinship in the clusters of persons and families that gathered around Nathaniel Ward to form a company for the purpose of planting Andover and Haverhill. In some cases substantial information is available about origins in Britain. In other cases only a general indication of ethnic or regional background is available, and in other cases nothing is known. Genealogical records, some more complete than others, exist for thirty of these founding families of Andover. For each of these thirty, I followed the marriage histories for three generations, the founder couples being counted as the first generation. Of these sixty people, there is background information for fifty-two. The second and third generations are their known and recorded children and grandchildren, 1,109 total. Altogether then, there were 1,161 persons whose marriage histories are included here, 614 males and 547 females.

I analyze the marriages of the Andover founders, their children, and their grandchildren in terms of both old and new world social identities, that is, in terms of their regional and ethnic backgrounds in Britain, and their emerging identities, such as Covenanter, in the new colony. I will explore endogamous and exogamous marriage patterns in relation to kinship, ethnic group, economic and social status, and territorial units both

---

[3]However, see Smout (1981) and Molloy (1986) for studies of Scottish marriage. The study by Farber of post-revolutionary Salem is one of the few studies in New England history that pays close attention to kinship and marriage (1972:chap. 4).

above and below the village level. That is, did people tend to choose their spouses from inside their ethnic or village categories (endogamy) or outside them (exogamy)? Furthermore, I trace marriage choices using not only such etic terms, but also emic social category terms drawn from the settlers' own identity terms, which have already been discussed in other contexts. That is, did people tend to marry those of their own *blood*, or *country*, or *company*?

Briefly, I found that ethnic and regional background factors among groups in Andover did in fact relate to initial variation in marriage patterns, just as they did in such matters as residence, political leadership, and land use. Marriage choice patterns also changed in that the emerging social identities of the new world gradually superseded old world patterns but did not obliterate them.

Marriage and Social Location

I use the expression "social location of a marriage" to refer to the concept that certain families, certain lineages, and certain slots in the birth order in a society based on social rank can and should be given an importance in one's analysis that matches the emic view of the import of that marriage as a match (or mismatch). The marriages of Governor Winthrop's children, especially of his eldest son and daughter, for example, were marriages of key social location in the Bay Colony and in English Puritan gentry society as well. But each local social microcosm up and down a hierarchy had its ranking of families and sets of key social locations, the intersection of birth order of children in the family, and the social standings of the families involved in the marriage.

Several marriages of key social location took place in the matrix of New England colonial society. An upper-level gentry marriage, such as that negotiated by Bradstreet and Ward, concerned the whole colony. It was customary that gentry married gentry and especially the eldest children of gentry should marry their matches. Birth order mattered, so that marriages of a family's eldest son and daughter were in important social locations. Younger gentry children might make matches beneath them, but they served as rungs on the social ladder whereby the eldest children of up-and-coming families of lower rank could climb up. The marriages made by eldest children, however, were the ones that both indicated and maintained the family's social status. It was significant that the prototype alliance of reconciliation described earlier (chapter 2) between the Winthrop and Dudley families involved their eldest children.

One can try to see the marriages in a research population this way, emically, as closely as possible in terms of the people's own social categories. On the other hand, one can look at marriage as Greven did as "mate selection" in a group of people imagined as a homogeneous population of so many males and so many females of marriageable age marrying in or out of town (see, for example his tables pp. 207–211). Such an approach can reveal patterns and trends in its behavior that the research population itself never thought of. An emic approach, however, aims to illuminate the concerns and strategies of the people themselves when it came to marriage.

My main purpose in this chapter is to show marriage variation in terms of status or social locations among families in the world of Andover and the wider colony. I also want to show variation in the frequency and distribution of cousin marriages among the Andover families. Cousin marriage frequencies turn out to be not a function of social location, but are a strong marker of British background *country* and *blood* affinities. Colonists who came from certain regions in Britain sometimes married their kin; those from other regions never did. Table 4 (p. 118) shows comparative kin endogamy, that is, a family's tendency to marry relatives, in this case at the cousin level. Families can be compared with those from other regional backgrounds. It also will provide future family historians with a basis for comparison of Andover's with those of other towns. I stress, parenthetically, that readers need not feel uncomfortable about cousin marriages in their family history. Research of Ottenheimer (1996) and others have helped to correct earlier views arising out of the eugenics movement. Several states have changed their laws in light of this research.

Marriage and demographic categories

In his dissertation (1964), Greven included much valuable material about the British origins of the Andover settlers and their previous associations, which I have drawn upon for this study. However, in his book (1970) he omitted most of this information except as it bears on the issue of open- or closed-field agricultural systems, regionally based practices the colonists brought from England. Given his focus on land, Greven did not follow up the possibility that variation in Andover family marriage patterns as well as agricultural patterns might relate to old world regional backgrounds as well.

Greven took as his "overarching concern" the history of the family in colonial Andover, seen in terms of generational change (1970:12–16). In doing this, he says, he was trying to move away from approaches that took the "household" as the research unit. However, problems arise as well from taking the generation as a research unit. It was not an emic unit used by New Englanders reckoning their genealogies until later (Abbot 1971; also see the concern voiced by Demos 1970:xiii–xiv). Thus the generation is a problematical unit for following family history in early New England. Persons may be in the same generation genealogically but at very different stages in age and station of life, as when sibling-sets span, as they do, twenty-five or thirty years from eldest to youngest child. Furthermore, Greven used such categories as "family" and "kindred" without clarifying social context other than that they all lived in the same community. In the colonial towns like Andover, the families must be seen in some rank order to interpret their actions, especially the actions (including language) relating to the hierarchical social distinctions important to this society.

The kindred (or extended kin group) that Greven used as a unit is also a difficult group to bound and define. It is more of a folk or native category than an analytic one (as in "Let goods and kindred go," a line the colonists may have sung from the contemporary English translation of Luther's hymn "A Mighty Fortress"). Nor is kindred a term that was used much in their writings by the colonists. In any case, it does not carry over well into a social science definition. A kindred is usually reckoned from the perspective of a central Ego, but who is to be the Ego here, the senior male? Where do the boundaries of Ego's kindred end? If difficult to bound, then it will be very difficult to count, and thus the notion of kindred does not lend itself easily to quantification, the approach Greven wanted to use.

Greven's problem with the shifting nature of kindred boundaries, made it difficult for him to classify people and families in Andover. Since he could not actually count people in terms of a "kindred," what was he counting? Greven's summary below of the social composition of Andover in the early 1700s, the time of the parish split, seems to be merely a count of the men who have the same surnames on the tax lists, listed in alphabetical order.

> ...family groups often concentrated together in particular areas of the town. The Abbots, Ballards, Blanchards, Chandlers, Holts, and Lovejoys, for instance, were largely concentrated in the South Parish, whereas the Barker, Farnum, Foster, Frye, Ingalls, Osgood, and Stevens families were concentrated in the North Parish. Some families obviously had been more prolific than others, with the result that more of them lived together in Andover. In 1705, for example, there were sixteen Abbot men taxed in Andover...There were large groups of Chandlers, Farnums, Fosters, Holts, Johnsons, Osgoods, and Stevenses. Other families usually had between four and ten

men residing in the town and paying taxes, and often they were connected by marriage and kinship to many other families in the town as well. A few families failed to flourish and died out, including the Bradstreets and Aslebees, or barely maintained the family name in town, like the Russes, Allens, and Tylers. (Greven 1970:139–141)

Here Greven was counting surnames and listing them in alphabetical order rather than working with the actual on-the-ground differences in the population. He was not the first Andover researcher to be misled by reliance on surnames both here and in his count of the number of "males on tax lists by families" (Greven 1970:140). Several significant misunderstandings about the composition of families in Andover and the two Ends arise from this approach, bringing out the importance of doing detailed genealogical comparison with dated tax lists. For example, the "sixteen Abbot men" on the 1705 tax list, mentioned above by Greven, were from at least two distinct extended families, although they were possibly distantly related.[4] One was a Latecomer North End family that remained there and intermarried with other North Enders. The other was a Firstcomer family that remained allied with the South End in location and marriage patterns. There were also at least two separate Foster families, but they were also counted as one by Greven because of the similar surname (Charlotte Helen Abbott says perhaps four Foster families, Abbott n.d.: Foster Families of Andover). One was a Firstcomer family that became a South End family. The North Parish Fosters mentioned by Greven in the text above were Latecomers. Although both were Scottish, and possibly distantly related, the distinctions between them are crucial in sorting out the role of the two families in the witchcraft crisis.

Two separate Osgood families also lived in town, as has been pointed out already. In the case of the Osgoods, it is particularly important not to lump them together. Not only was there one Osgood family in each parish, but also the heads of these two families came to be the leaders of the two parishes. The founders may have been distantly related; their families both came from the southwest region of England (see table 1, p. 72). But family genealogists have never found a connection. The marriage records of their children and grandchildren reveal that the two families drew from completely different social circles for their marriages for at least the first three generations. To count them together is to obscure a major

---

[4]One was a South End family (the founder from the East Midlands county of Hertfordshire), and the other was a North End family (the founder probably from Yorkshire in the north of England). They gradually, if inconsistently, distinguished themselves from each other by different spellings, Abbot and Abbott, respectively. The double t may have even represented orthographically a perceived difference in pronunciation of the final consonant by settlers from different regions.

internal social difference in early Andover. In his dissertation, Greven did note that the two Osgoods, John and Christopher, were probably not at all closely related (Greven 1964:45, fn. 84). Yet in his book he chose to count all Osgoods as if they were one family, whereas the very difference between the two Osgood men constituted one of the major social dynamics in the town.

Marriage and emic categories

Greven looked at marriage in Andover from a number of perspectives, including generational differences in marriage patterns, changing ages of women and men at marriage, and residential origins of marriage partners, whether they came from Andover or elsewhere. His treatment of marriage is discussed in two parts, here and in chapter 7. Here I focus especially on his interest in the residential origin of spouses, or what I will refer to as town exogamy and endogamy (Greven 1970:122–123, 210–211).

Greven charted all known marriages at three time periods from 1650 to 1749. He found significant shifts during these periods in the frequency with which women were tending to marry men from inside or outside Andover. He wondered why and relates it to demographic categories. But he does not press his findings to the question of *which* families of the population, sociologically considered, were marrying in or out of town, or to their emic categories, such as rank, regionality, or factions within the population. In the following section, I look at the question of marriage and at the results obtained with the same population when exogamous and endogamous boundaries are defined differently, in terms of such native social categories and internal variation.

In chapter 7, when I look at marriage in Andover after the witchcraft crisis and the parish split, I will return to Greven's problem, variation across time in village endogamy and exogamy, and the problem of classification itself.

Concepts of exogamy and endogamy have long been standard points of departure in anthropology from which to generate a series of social maps. A marriage may be counted as endogamous "marrying in" with respect to one category and exogamous "marrying out" with regard to another. If, for example, we read that a certain society practiced kin exogamy and village endogamy we would know they married people outside their kin group but inside their town. It is legitimate for an analyst of marriage to count and map marriages in terms of introduced etic categories, or of emic ones derived from an understanding of the natives' marriage rules, or both. However, these approaches and the relation between them need to be made clear. Simply to take the set of marriages made by people from a given town and count and label them on the basis of whether spouses came from in or out of town does tell us something. However, without more clarification of the social context, this approach can obscure the very thing that helps to make sense of the resulting figures.

Here is where Greven's discussion of the residential origins of Andover spouses overlooked key issues, and where I think an emic view illuminates them. For example, in Greven's undifferentiated count of "village exogamy," that is, Andover children who married out of town, Simon Bradstreet's children would all be counted among them. However, Bradstreet was of the gentry. The only other member of the gentry in Andover was the young Edmund Faulkner, although he was not of the same status as Bradstreet. His children were too young for Bradstreet's anyway. But gentry customarily married gentry, and Bradstreet's children were married to members of families at their social and age level from towns all around the colony. So, one could chart and count the Bradstreet marriages at one level in terms of village exogamy. But at another level they should be counted in terms of gentry endogamy. Both levels tell us something, but one tells us more about colonial society from the natives' point of view, as they saw their choices.

I look at the Andover marriages in terms of a set of concentric circles that aim to bring etic, investigator's categories (exogamy, endogamy), to bear on emic, native terms. These circles widen outwardly from the perspective of various exogamy categories, and narrow inwardly from the perspective of endogamy. Family, old world regional background, "End" of town, and social status within both the end and the town are some of the categories that mattered to Andoverites in relation to endogamous and exogamous marriage choices. Although there are missing and incomplete records, enough data is available to show whether the marriages of the founding, second, and third generations at Andover tended to be with other Andover families, or with outsiders, and if with outsiders, whether the couple stayed or left Andover. One can identify the families who intermarried frequently (cousin marriage, the innermost circle); those whose members almost always married within their End of the village; those who sometimes married into the other End; those who frequently married outside the village, yet within Essex county or the region north of Boston; and those who established inter-county, inter-colony, and even trans-Atlantic alliances back in England. Using background information and tax lists, these circles of endogamous and exogamous marriage can be correlated with country, blood, and people's ways of reckoning social status.

Old and New Social Identities in Andover Marriage Patterns

To review, my approach in this research has been to derive units of analysis from the colonial literary texts, treating them as emic categories of social identity with which to identify and follow specific groups and people through various kinds of actions and events. In the following section I look at a key domain, marriage choice, in terms of both old and new kinds of social identities familiar to the settlers.

No constraints existed on early New Englanders to marry either in or out of one's town, nor was there any fixed rule of residence. Generally, marriage should be suitable to one's social status. But there were legal issues concerning marriage with kin, specifically first cousins, and with the brother or sister of a deceased spouse. The Church of England had not forbidden the marriage of people in either of these relationships, because the Scripture did not forbid them, but different regions of England nevertheless had developed different patterns with regard to them. A fascinating debate took place in the Bay Colony as to what should be done about kin marriage, especially whether first cousin marriage should be permitted. Perhaps more than any other kind of data that can be generated from the records of Andover, the data concerning frequency and distribution of cousin marriage reveals both the differences and persistent patterns carried over from British regional and ethnic background. A social map can be drawn on the basis of kin endogamy showing the frequency distribution of cousin marriages across the range of families, from those who never had a marriage between cousins to those with the highest percentages.

Gentry ("persons of quality; the better sort") and commoner ("the meaner sort") were old world categories that initially came to the Bay Colony intact. As we have seen the few members of minor nobility, such as Sir Isaac Johnson and Lady Arbella who came with the Winthrop fleet, soon died or departed. With no one left above the gentry in rank, as there would have been in Britain, the gentry became the top echelon in the colony. In 1634, the new colonial elites like the Dudleys and Winthrops had been living in fairly close proximity in the settlements around Boston Harbor. Forty years later, according to the deposition of Simon Bradstreet's that heads this chapter, in the expanding colony of the 1670s gentry families even in frontier towns like Andover looked to other gentry for their children's marriage partners. In fact, the alliance network was not only at the regional, but also at the intercolonial level, as Massachusetts gentry families like the Bradstreets sought to marry with Connecticut gentry families like the Wades. The further details of the Wade-Bradstreet case show that not only the immediate families but also others in the larger clusters of kin and non-kin around them were affected by these negotiations.[5]

The marriage histories of the two gentry families of Andover, Bradstreet and Faulkner, can be usefully compared. The Bradstreet family as a whole had the most widespread network of marriage alliances of any Andover family. None of Simon Bradstreet's children married into Andover. But they did marry into other leading political and ministerial families of or near Bradstreet's rank within the Bay Colony. Thus they are better understood as practicing elite endogamy as well as town exogamy.

Edmund Faulkner, cadet (youngest) son of a Hampshire gentleman, was young and unmarried when he came to Andover. Note that even so he was given an important role to play, alongside the pastor Woodbridge, in the negotiations for the land. Faulkner went on to become a prominent citizen as licensed innkeeper and as town clerk, a post he held for many years. His children were not ready to marry until the 1660s and 1670s. But Faulkner did not follow the Bradstreet's pattern of marrying his children out of Andover with other regional gentry. Instead he married them to Andover people. He did, however, follow the practice of marrying with new elites within the town. His eldest son married the daughter of Francis Dane, the minister, which would have been a marriage of key social location (as were all marriages of ministers' children).[6]

A number of new social categories within the population resulted from the exigencies of the new world situation, and this had lingering effects in determining internal social divisions later. I discuss them here as the results of tracing and separating the families on the Faulkner "List of Freeholders" into Firstcomers and Latecomers. In table 1, page 72, I listed the Latecomers' backgrounds. In the next set of tables I treat those with the same regional background as a category in order to contrast them with the Firstcomers.

Within the Firstcomers were the group of Covenanters, and their marriage data that will be explored in depth in this next section. Most of these men and families had been together at Newbury before Andover and before that briefly in Ipswich. With the exceptions noted, they were almost all from the southwest region, many from Hampshire County in particular and some from Wiltshire. All were part of the Woodbridge/Parker

---

[5]Dowries had grown to be considerable and were subject to dispute. For an analysis of the case between Wade and Bradstreet from which the excerpt at the beginning of chapter 5 is taken, see Greven 1970:79–80. See also the debate between Slater (1976, 1980) and Mendelson (1980) about gentry marriage in England.

[6]In the words of Campbell (1890 ch. ix), the ministry became to New England what the House of Lords was to old England.

company. The Wiltshire people left Andover fairly soon, so that the remaining Covenanter families were Hampshire people. Here I will contrast their second-generation marriages. Their initial land holdings show that they were for the most part the richest of the Firstcomers, except for Bradstreet and Stevens who were not among the Covenanters. Of the ten Andover Covenanters, one did not stay in Andover.[7]

One Covenanter, Richard Barker, has always been a puzzle to town genealogists. His family's marriage pattern is very different from the rest, suggesting that, although he traveled with the Southwesterner/Newbury company, he was not from the southwest originally. Recently, Barker genealogists have placed ancestor Richard's origin in Nayland, Suffolk, which would indeed explain the differences (Barker 2004). Yet others have him coming from Yorkshire or from Kent. The same confusion applies to another Covenanter, Nicholas Holt. Although he is listed as coming from Hampshire, his family's marriage pattern is so different from that of other Southwesterners that the claim by some Holt genealogists that he was not originally from there seems substantiated. They place him as from Lancaster in Britain, a more northerly origin that fits with the Holt family marriage pattern.[8]

The non-Covenanters who were among the Firstcomers included a small Hampshire contingent and the Scots, but otherwise they were from scattered locations both in residence prior to Andover and in English background. Tables 3c and 3d show that initially these two groups were about equal in numbers. But the Covenanters were on the average older than the non-Covenanters, and most of them were already married, a factor that must be considered in light of the finding shown on the next set of tables, that Covenanter families tended to marry out of town. This first cohort of Covenanter children were on average older than the children of the non-Covenanters, thus without a choice of spouses of the right age from Andover.

---

[7]That man was Richard Blake, who may have been related to the Blakes of Gloucester who were at this time moving into the area that would become Topsfield. On the other hand, his name may have been Black. If he had a Gloucester connection, he may have been the link that brought Andrew and Ann Foster, previously of Gloucester, into the Firstcomer group. See Greven (1964:13) and Perley (1880) for information about the Blakes of Gloucester and the Blacks, a Scottish family of Boxford (Black 1968). According to Perley, the Blakes and Blacks may have been the same family, confused by clerks' handwriting (Perley 1880).

[8]Another example of genealogists' trials: Some genealogists say that William Ballard who sailed on the *James* in 1635 is "William Ballard of Lynn," who was not the father of Sarah Ballard, wife of Henry Holt. The father of Sarah Ballard, wife of Henry Holt, is William Ballard of Andover, who came on the *Mary and John* in 1634. Online: <http//dgmweb.net/genealogy/7/Nroots/FGS/HenryHolt-SarahBallard.htm/>.

The problems with Holt and Barker origins have been discussed above, but their family marriage histories may be a previously unexamined source of indirect evidence toward a solution to this problem. Certainly, they are very different from those of the other Covenanters. On the basis of this indirect evidence for purposes of this research I will classify them as from elsewhere than the Southeast.

Marriage in the Second Generation: Covenanters and non-Covenanters

The lack of firm knowledge about certain key families' origins, and the small numbers involved in this population, mean that it is not possible to make claims of statistical significance here. Rather, the findings suggest trends to be explored for marriage patterns in a study of a larger sample of towns.

To review, within the group of Andover's Covenanters were those who came from the southwestern counties of England and the others who came from elsewhere. The two families I am classifying as "other" within the Covenanter group, Holt and Barker, had a high percentage of close-kin marriages, quite unlike the Covenanters from the southwest. When they are not included in the Covenanter group because of their high rates of close kin-endogamy, the town-exogamy rate of Covenanter marriages rises even more strikingly in comparison with the rest of Firstcomer families.

Tables 3a–d show six ways of breaking down the frequency and distribution of marriages of the sons and daughters of the second generation at Andover, in terms of village exogamy and endogamy. There are 225 children in this second generation whose spouses could be determined. The percentages of exogamous and endogamous marriages are further shown in terms of selected smaller subsets of families within Andover.

These tables show that while town endogamy (taking a spouse from within the town) was more frequent in the second generation of the settlers as a whole, town *exogamy* characterized the marriages of the Covenanters' children. As the new elites, Covenanters may have been following the common pattern of elite out-marriage to their social equals or families with whom they had traveled in other towns. On the other hand, as Covenanters were a bit older, their children may not have been the right age for marriage with the non-Covenanters. But in addition to the age factor, there is strong evidence that regional and ethnic background factors overrode the factor of Covenanter status. The Covenanter families that did not come from the southwest of England had different marriage patterns from those that did.

Table 3-a. Town exogamy and endogamy, all families
(n = 32)

	Exogamy	Endogamy	Total
Sons	37	72	109
Daughters	45	71	116
Total	82	143	225
Percent	36%	64%	100%

n = number of families

This first table, 3-a, shows second-generation marriages of thirty-two families in the research population (Barnard and Lacy are included here, although they drop out for third-generation). These families had a known 264 children, an average of over eight children per family. Of the 264, the marriages of 225 could be traced, 82 married out, 143 married in. Notice that more daughters than sons are known to have married out of town, exogamously. Almost two-thirds of the second generation children (64 percent) married endogamously, within Andover, thus the nearly even numbers of sons (72) and daughters (71). The following tables show subsets within this basic group.

Table 3-b. Town exogamy and endogamy: Firstcomers and Latecomers compared

Firstcomers (n = 21, including minister)				Latecomers (n = 11)			
	Exogamy	Endogamy	Total		Exogamy	Endogamy	Total
Sons	24	43	67	Sons	13	29	42
Daughters	37	34	71	Daughters	9	36	45
Total	61	77	138	Total	22	65	87
Percent	44%	56%	100%	Percent	25%	75%	100%

The thirty-two families are made up of at least two groups. One group, the Firstcomers, is the emic category, named in the Faulkner List (see chapter 1 for the list). How are the twenty-one families of Firstcomers in the table above derived? Of the twenty-three on Faulkner's List, three never actually stayed on and raised families in Andover. The other twenty remained and are well documented. The first minister, John Woodbridge, who headed the Firstcomers, has also been included, making twenty-one. Woodbridge, although he came to town with the others in the beginning, was not on the Faulkner List because he did not have to draw lots for his land but was given it by virtue of his status. The Latecomers were those who came after the twenty-three families. Of the Latecomers, I have chosen eleven of the first wave of families in that category who were in Andover before 1655 and for whom there is good documentation.

Table 3-b shows that, although town endogamy predominated among both Firstcomer and Latecomer children, the percentage of Latecomers marrying endogamously was considerably higher (75 percent) than it was for Firstcomer children (25 percent). In fact, it is the Latecomers' marriages that give the figures for the total population in table 3-a their endogamous weight.

Next, in table 3-c, I look at a key contrast within the Firstcomer group itself, the Covenanters and non-Covenanters.

Table 3-c. Covenanters and non-Covenanters compared

	Covenanters (n=9)				Non-Covenanters (n=12)		
	Exogamy	Endogamy	Total		Exogamy	Endogamy	Total
Sons	16	14	30	Sons	10	31	41
Daughters	17	11	28	Daughters	21	26	47
Total	33	25	58	Total	31	57	88
Percent	57%	43%	100%	Percent	35%	65%	100%

Table 3-c shows a significant breakdown within the Firstcomers group, again using categories important to the colonists themselves, in this case the covenant. The marriages of the fifty-eight children of the nine covenant Firstcomers who stayed in Andover are shown on the left, compared with those of the eighty-eight children of the non-covenant Firstcomers on the right. Note again that Covenanter and Latecomer were *emic* categories for the colonists.

The import of the series of findings so far in this series of tables is this: while as a whole the second-generation children were much more likely to marry endogamously, those of the Firstcomers were more likely to marry exogamously. Table 3-c shows that the children of the Covenanter families, the inner circle of the Firstcomers, were even more likely to marry out than the rest of the Firstcomers (57% to 35%). How can this be explained? One cannot be sure, yet it is startling to see different marriage patterns emerge so clearly from the data when emic categories are used. Similar close studies of marriages in other towns would be needed to proceed to a conclusion. However, I list below possible explanations.

As mentioned above, in the early days at Andover, the Covenanter children may have been in a different age cohort than other children, since their parents were on the whole older than the rest of the Firstcomers. So their children were a little too old to find mates from within the new town. This would be the closest to a straight demographic explanation.

Or, Covenanter status may have become the new criteria for elite identity. Just as Simon Bradstreet's children married their peers in other towns, so the Covenanters began to do. If in fact the Covenanter families were emerging as the town elites during this period, these findings are to be expected, given what we already know of elite regional marriage patterns.

Or, the key factor may have been that of home region. Covenanters, being Southwesterners, preferred marrying with other Southwesterner families in the colony, maintaining in the early days those old British *regional* loyalties.

A further breakdown remains to be examined among the Covenanters themselves. Here we separate out an old world category—region, or *country,* from the new world category of Covenanter. Although the results are suggestive, no claims can be made for their significance because of the small sample size.

However, among the Covenanters were the two families discussed above, Holt and Barker, whose regional identities were probably not southwestern. As for Barker, although his place of origin is not known for sure, family genealogists have never linked him with the southwestern counties. Suffolk, Yorkshire, and Kent are the three possibilities proposed for Barker. Although Holt is known to have been in Romsey, Hampshire, and sailed with Southwesterners, a strong family tradition places the seat of the Holt family in Lancashire, to the north (Durrie 1864). Certainly, the marriage patterns of these two families show differences from those of the other Covenanters. Especially significant was their propensity to marry cousins, which Southwesterners almost never did. Furthermore, Holt did not stay in the North End of Andover with the other Covenanters, but early took the lead in the move into the south part of town onto what is still known as Holt Hill. The Barkers remained in the North End, but formed a territorial enclave north of the lake (map 6). This enclave was at first made up of themselves and the neighboring Stevens family, a non-Covenanting family. The Barker and Stevens families grew closely related, with a pattern of marriage, and then cousin marriage, continuing through several generations.

Table 3-d. Marriages of the southwestern Covenanters
minus Holt and Barker families
(families = 7; persons = 41)

	Exogamy	Endogamy	Total
Sons	13	7	20
Daughters	16	5	21
Total	29	12	41
Percent	71%	29%	100%

Table 3-d shows that without the Holt and Barker families, Covenanter town exogamy jumps from 57 to 71 percent. The number of endogamous marriages drops from 25 or 43 percent (in table 3-c) to 12 or 29 percent. Thus Holt and Barker cousin marriages accounted for over half of the second-generation endogamous marriages in the Covenanter group.

These findings reflect the tendency for the Southwesterners in general to make exogamous marriages outside the circle not only of town but also of kin. I will propose a possible explanation for this in the next section. As for the Holts and Barkers, many of their endogamous marriages are perhaps better understood not as cases of *town* endogamy, but of preferential *kin* endogamy, since both families were among those with highest percentages of cousin marriages (see table 4).

Cousin Marriage and British Regional Backgrounds

In evaluating the findings above, the question arises: What else about marriage did different British regional background affect? One possibility is rates of marriage with kin, that is, cousins. Marriage with kin closer than that was forbidden by all, but there was variation in the cousin marriage law from region to region in Britain. What habits might the people of different regions of Britain have brought with them? What happened when people with different customs were mixed together in the colonies and had to work out new laws?

Certain marriage "rules" in seventeenth-century Britain were in a state of flux. In England there was ongoing debate over forbidden degrees of kinship in marriage, and the colonists carried the issues with them to Massachusetts. There were two decisions about marriage law facing the colony leaders. One concerned the affinal (in-law) ties, in particular whether one could marry a deceased spouse's sister or brother. This practice was sometimes called "levirate marriage" by those who favored allowing it, thus invoking by the name biblical sanction. However, the term was not really accurate because it was unlike the biblical levirate, where a man was *expected* to marry his deceased brother's widow. Marriage to a deceased spouse's sibling was a different matter, and debate over it had been going on in England especially since the time of one of the marriages of Henry VIII to his deceased wife's sister. The other issue concerned the marriage of first cousins, commonly called *cousins-german* or *cousins-germane* in the seventeenth century. (See Hall [1650] and Turner [1682a and 1682b] for contemporary discussions of the issues from the English perspective. See also Denison's autobiography, Slade 1892.)

In time the members of the General Court in Massachusetts had to make a decision regarding these two dilemmas regardless of what the home country did. They forbade affinal marriage, that is, with a deceased spouse's sibling. However, they decided to permit cousin marriage, since there was no biblical proscription against it and in fact there were several examples of it among the Hebrew patriarchs (Sewall 1973 [1695]:349; Mather 1695). How much the cousin marriage ruling immediately affected the colonists in terms of changing the beliefs and habits they brought from their regional culture is difficult to know. Regional attitudes and practices in Britain certainly varied. Andover marriage records show that the Holts and Barkers were more likely to practice cousin marriage than the Southwesterner families. The Scots and Borderers in Andover were also among those who married their cousins more frequently compared to people from other regions. Ballard, although said to be a Welsh name, is listed by some Ballard genealogists as from East Anglia (Suffolk). This discussion can be seen at the Ballard family history online at < http://freepages.genealogy.rootsweb.com/~wertin/ballard.html >.

Table 4 displays three-generation family marriage histories of Andover families, sorted by British regional and ethnic background and close-kin marriage (CKM) frequencies. Included under "close kin" for purposes of this table are first cousins, second cousins, first cousins once removed, and in certain cases step-cousins.

Table 4 shows that the Southwesterners and the East Anglians were least likely to marry kin. The Southwesterners are identified by their county abbreviation, Wilts (Wiltshire) and Hants (Hampshire). Two apparent exceptions are the Faulkner and Holt families, numbers 2 and 3 on the chart. Holt probably originated from elsewhere than the southwest as has been discussed. I will take up the question of the exceptional Faulkner situation in the section on marriage in chapter 7. Faulkner was definitely a Southwesterner in origin, but the difference between his and other southwestern family marriages is best understood, I will maintain, with reference to the traumatic history of the Faulkners and their Dane relatives, with whom they tended to marry for several generations.

Table 4. Close-Kin marriage (CKM), generations II And III, and regional origin

	Name	%M/B	#M	#CKM	%CKM	Place of Origin	Region
01.	FOSTER	76.0	19	5	26.3	? SCOT.	NB
02.	FAULKNER	73.9	17	4	23.5	Kngsclear HANTS	SW
03.	HOLT	83.1	59	13	22.0	Romsey. HANTS; LANC?	NB?
04.	ABBOT	76.9	70	15	21.4	B'ps-Stort. HERTS	EM
05.	ALLEN	57.5	19	4	21.0	? SCOT	NB
06.	FARNUM	78.8	56	11	19.6	? LEICESTER	EM
07.	ABBOTT	70.1	65	10	15.3	Rowley. YORKS	NB
08.	STEVENS	57.8	33	5	15.1	Caversham, OXF	CL
09.	INGALLS	53.8	35	5	14.2	Skirbet. LINCS.	EM
10.	LOVEJOY	81.8	63	9	14.2	Marlow BUCKS	CL
11.	BARKER	73.1	68	8	13.3	YORKS or SUFF ?	EA
12.	POOR	59.7	55	5	12.7	B'ps stoke HANTS	SW
13.	RUSS	81.8	18	2	11.1	? SCOT	NB
14.	DANE	63.0	29	3	10.3	B'ps-Stort. HERTS	EM
15.	RUSSELL	78.3	58	7	10.3	? SCOT	NB
16.	BALLARD	70.6	41	4	09.7	? WALES?.	WA
17.	CHANDLER	83.0	59	5	08.4	B'ps-Stort. HERTS	EM
18.	PEETERS	77.7	25	2	08.0	HOLLAND?	CE?
19.	BLANCHARD	68.0	34	2	05.8	Andover, HANTS	SW
20.	WOODBRDGE	54.2	19	1	05.2	Stanton. WILTS	SW
21.	PARKER, N	66.6	24	1	04.1	Romsey. HANTS	SW
22.	FRYE	70.2	26	1	03.8	Basing. HANTS	SW
23.	JOHNSON	62.5	30	1	03.3	Hern Hill KENT	EA
24.	BRDSTREET	58.3	35	1	02.8	Horbling LINCS	EA
25.	OSGOOD, J	61.3	27	0	.0	Andover, HANTS	SW
26.	PARKER, J	46.4	13	0	.0	Romsey. HANTS	SW
27.	ASLEBE	70.8	17	0	.0	Scrooby LINCS ?	EA
28.	OSGOOD, C	73.2	52	0	.0	Marlboro WILTS	SW
29.	PHELPS	61.7	21	0	.0	? WALES ?	WA?
30.	MARSTON	62.8	22	0	.0	? NORFOLK	EA
	Totals		1,109	124			

Arranged to show highest-to-lowest percentage by families,
and including region of origin in Britain where known
%M/B = % marriages per births; #M = no. marriages; #CKM = no. close kin marriages; %CKM = pct. CKM to total marriages.
Regional designations as follows:
(NB = North Britain incl.Scotland; SW = Southwest; CL = Central/London; EA = East Anglia;
EM = East Midlands; WA = Wales; CE = Continental Europe)

Only similar studies of close-kin marriage in other towns in the colony can provide the comparative framework for firmer conclusions about this aspect of colonial marriage patterns. The town of Newbury, for example, where the Southwesterners lived before coming to Andover and where other Southwesterners remained, would be a good research site to see whether there was a characteristic low incidence of close-kin marriage among them. Neighboring Rowley also needs particular attention to its genealogies. Many there came from Yorkshire, and I would expect them as northerners to have a higher close-kin marriage percentage. In addition, a better understanding of regional marriage patterns in Britain generally in the seventeenth century is needed. But some speculation may be permitted here in the absence of such studies.

I would say that Covenanter town exogamy is related to the reconstruction of the new social hierarchy in the colony, that is, to the fact that the Covenanters were becoming the elites of Andover, indeed of Essex County towns, and the north of Boston generally. They were becoming the new gentry, even though some had been yeomen in the old world. Though without titles, they were behaving as elites do in looking outward to Covenanter families in other towns for their children's marriages. These new social categories would later become the criteria for later generations reclaiming foundational old identities at a later point of transformation. For example, later in the eighteenth century, the honorific Esquire or Esq. began to appear after the names of certain men in the records, men who had descended from this earlier yeoman layer.

This process is exemplified in the marriages made by the eldest son and eldest daughter of John Osgood, the Southwesterner, Hampshireman, and lay leader of the Andover Covenanters, whose career I have already touched upon earlier. Their marriages were of key social location in the second generation at Andover, with implications for the whole community. Osgood married both his eldest children to a son and daughter of Covenanter Robert Clements, his counterpart and leading citizen at Haverhill, the town across the river. In doing so, Osgood reconnected the Andover covenanters with the other part of Ward's intended company, the covenanting Firstcomers at Haverhill led by Ward's son as minister. Marriage exchange between Andover and Haverhill leading families continued for several generations to cement these company ties formed out of the original Parker company at Newbury.

Frequent marriage alliances between the two towns were not just due to the geographical proximity of Andover to Haverhill. Evidence for that pattern may be found in the fact that no known marriages were made by Andover Covenanters with leading families in neighboring Rowley, which was even nearer than Haverhill and on the same side of the river. The Southwesterners of Andover's covenant were apparently not interested in marrying with the Northerners, the Yorkshire families of Rowley. Strong social identity carryovers from Britain were operating in the regional picture of colonists' marriage choices during the early years (see the many genealogies of related families in Abbott n.d.: Osgood; Clements; Ward).

Why the Southwesterners might have practiced town exogamy is clear, as they married with elites of other towns or other with Southwesterner families they knew and had traveled with in the same boat groups. But why they did not practice kin endogamy is another matter. Why such a low incidence of cousin marriage among those families, compared with families from other regions of Britain? Here we probably see another side of the reconstruction of local culture, reflecting British regional distinctions and variations with regard to the acceptability of marrying cousins and step-relatives. Beliefs and habits about kin marriage, lying as they do so close to feelings about incest, would not, I suspect, have changed as quickly in the new world as other habits, or as the sense of regional affinity.[9]

I know of little work that has been done on the topic of kin marriage in regions of the home country, which makes it difficult to proceed very far with understanding variation in the colonies.[10] The Church of England permitted cousin marriage, yet people from certain parts of England, such as Judge Sewall, nevertheless did not approve of it (see below). As for what is known about colonial society, we have already seen that Massachusetts came to the point of debating whether to make first-cousin

---

[9]Some insight into these attitudes may be gained from Defoe's *Moll Flanders* (1923-[1722]). The plot turns on the theme of unwitting incest between two people who meet and marry in the new world, not realizing they are siblings. Anderson (1982; 1986) has done excellent work in the analysis of cousin marriage in the nineteenth century.

[10]See Hall (1650) and Turner (l682a and 1682b) for the two sides of the debate in England in the seventeenth century about marriage of cousins-german. Copies of these texts are available in the microfilm library at Brandeis University. See also Anderson (1986) and Kuper (2002).

marriage illegal or not, and finally ruled to permit it.[11] But legality did not mean approval or agreement among the leaders whose families had come from regions with different customs. The Winthrop family of East Anglia made a number of first-cousin marriages in the second and third generation. But Southwesterner Judge Sewall, on the other hand, records in his diary his strong objections to marriages of "cousins-germane" (Sewall 1973 [1696]:329. Also see Slade 1892 for Daniel Denison's frequent use in his autobiography of the term cousin-germane). Sewall was a Southwesterner whose origin was not far from the region from which the Hampshire families of Andover had come. When it came to kin marriage, he may have been expressing stronger proscriptive rules than were found in other parts of Britain or indeed England.

Beyond these hints, we can say little as to what different British localisms might have been carried over into the colony with regard to cousin marriage. However, in table 4 we saw a breakdown of what Andover families actually did in terms of frequency and distribution. Looking at the distribution as a whole, there is a striking correlation generally between origin north of London and higher incidence of close kin marriage, and origin south, with little or none. If one placed this list of kin marriage frequencies in table 4 alongside a map of Britain (map 3), its distribution could almost be plotted on the north to south axis of the map. If Andover was a representative town of the colony, *blood* and *country* (including kin ties) had as strong an influence on marriage patterns as they did on agricultural and legal ones.

---

[11]Surprisingly, this point was missed by the dean of Puritan studies Edmund Morgan (1966 [1944]:32), who seems to have assumed that (1) the Bible forbids cousin marriage and (2) the Puritans in Massachusetts had thus forbidden cousin marriage on biblical grounds from the beginning The fact that the Bible does not forbid cousin marriage had raised the dilemma for Puritan New Englanders such as Judge Sewall who had come from regions of Britain with longstanding views against it (See Abbot 1981; 1985; also see Smith's (1975) section on cousin marriage in Hingham. Hurd (1983, 1985) has looked at cousin marriage frequencies in a closed community, the "Nebraska" Amish. For examples of recent renewed interest in cousin marriage in America, see the work of anthropologist Ottenheimer (1996). He has become a sort of advocate for a recently formed web-based interest group of cousins wishing to marry and working to change laws in states that forbid it. See C.U.D.D.L.E in the bibliography; also Sefton 2004. They say that recent research disproves the earlier belief propounded by some nineteenth-century eugenicists that there is genetic danger in cousin marriage and on the basis of which many states changed their laws to forbid it. See Heider 1969 and Abbot 1981 for a closer look at the New Hampshire case, one of those states where the law was so changed in the nineteenth century.

6

"An Axe at Andover"
The Course of the Parish Split

News is brought today of Mr Dane's son Robinson, his killing a lion with an axe at Andover. (Judge Samuel Sewall's Diary, February 3, 1681)

The witchcraft crisis that engulfed Salem Village and Andover in 1692 was once thought to pose a certain fascinating problem for the social historians of the period. Why Andover? This question had been a part of the earlier analyses of Boyer and Nissenbaum (1974) and Hansen (1983). Salem Village was festering with conflict. That there should have been an outbreak there was not surprising. But Andover was a harmonious place, or so it was thought, based on Greven's study. Andover's earlier writers sometimes seem to suggest that their town "caught" the craze like a disease from the outside, when Joseph Ballard sent for two of the Salem girls to come over and see if they could determine whether and how his ailing wife was bewitched. "These girls were received with great solemnity, taken to the meetinghouse, and prayer having been made by the Rev. Mr. Barnard...they were adjured to tell the truth," Bailey writes, paraphrasing the Ballard deposition. She adds parenthetically, "Mr Dane seems to have kept aloof from the proceedings, which was perhaps the reason of suspicion's falling on him and his family" later, when "the frenzy...seized the community" (Bailey 1880:197–199).

However, it was not the case that the witchcraft crisis at Andover broke without warning into a situation of previous social harmony. The previous chapters show that Andover, like Salem, had also been suffering increasing trouble and conflict in the years leading up to 1692. In the case of Andover, as a frontier town, there was additional fear of Indian attack and this fear may have coalesced into fear of each other in the form of witchcraft. Heyrman was one of the first to call attention to the possible role of such fears (1984:104–106), as did Webb (1984). The Indian issue has continued to move directly into the spotlight in studies of the witchcraft crisis: see Lepore (1998), Baker and Kences (2001), and Norton (2002). Indian fears may have entered into the situation at Andover, but to the extent it is possible to trace any patterns from the records, old ethnic and regional differences—blood and country—seem to have played a role also.

Many of the ministers of Massachusetts, however, interpreted the loss of peace throughout their little commonwealth in terms of testing, chastisement for sin, or spiritual warfare. As the people "backslid" and Indian troubles increased, they connected the two and warned that God was removing his hand of protection, letting the spirits of the invisible world have their way with the rebellious people of New England. Some ministers specifically mentioned Indians as the devil's agents. As the colony's senior preacher Cotton Mather put it, "some...among the Indians...are well known...to have been horrid Sorcerers and hellish conjurers and such as Conversed with Daemons." (See Godbeer 1992:192–193 for a discussion of this and similar spiritualized characterizations of the native Americans.)

Signs and wonders had been noted from early days in the colony and the ministers taught that spiritually wise people should take them as warnings. On June 28, 1648, John Winthrop recorded an event in his journal that must have been the talk of Boston (as recounted in Northend 1896:300–301). It was a perfectly calm day and the ship *Welcome* was riding at anchor at Charlestown, making preparations for her upcoming departure for the West Indies. All at once she "fell a rolling and continued so about twelve hours, so although they brought a great weight to the one side, yet she would keel to the other, and so deep as they feared her foundering." The magistrates at Boston "hearing that...one Jones (the husband of a witch lately executed in Connecticut) had desired to have passage in her and had come on board but could not pay," sent an officer for him with a warrant. One of the magistrates told the officer that "the ship would stand still as soon as [Jones] was in prison." The officer made his way out to the ship on the harbor ferry and someone said to him "You can tame men sometimes, can't you tame this ship?" The officer answered that he had something that might tame her, and showed his warrant. Winthrop writes, "And at the same instant she began to stop, and presently staid, and after [Jones] was put in prison moved no more." There were both earthly and heavenly signs to be interpreted. Comets had appeared in the skies over New England in 1664, 1665, 1677, and 1680. The comet that appeared in November 1680 stayed visible for three months, prompting the first of Increase Mather's famous comet sermons, *Heaven's*

Alarm to the World. "Fearful sights," said Mather, "are Tokens of God's Anger, they are presages of great and publick Calamities...they are signs that the Lord is coming forth out of his holy habitation to punish the World for their iniquities" (in Williams 1995).

In small towns like Andover, the townspeople were bound to note carefully whatever affected the minister and his family, given his powerful and public position as their spiritual head. Although Andover's controversy with its minister is not as well documented as Salem's, a problem was festering there as it had between Salem Village and its minister. No sermons survive by Andover's minister, Francis Dane, to show how he in particular was teaching his people to interpret and cope with the fears and hardships of their lives or why he later "stayed aloof" from the Salem girls' first visit to Andover. However, he also objected strongly to the use of the infamous "spectral evidence" in a letter to the Court, January 2, 1692/3 (in Mofford 2004:41. See also his petition reprinted in Bailey 218 ff.). But Dane may not have been doing much preaching at all. For one thing, he was apparently not very healthy. As early as 1665 he had begged leave of the Court to be excused from traveling to Salem to depose in the trial of John Godfrey "by reason of prevailing infirmity" (Hall 1991:124). The townspeople were not happy with their minister's situation, judging by a petition of complaint against him from the town's selectmen to the Court in 1681. He was not only infirm, he apparently wanted the town to keep paying his salary even as they took on a younger pastor, even though he was in "comfortable circumstances" (in the words of the petition, in Bailey 1880:422). It was not long after this petition that Dane's son-in-law was attacked by the lion, as recounted in the passage from Sewall's diary which opens this chapter. News of this "alarm" must also have spread throughout the neighboring towns.

If Dane's reputation among the townspeople was in decline, what might they have thought when, in the midst of the controversy, a mountain lion boldly threatened a member of Dane's own family? It was not unusual for people to see much that was preternatural if not downright ominous in the behavior of animals, domestic and wild. Hall's (1991) transcripts provide examples. At the witchcraft trial of Alice Parker of Salem in 1692, John Westgate of Salem testified that he had scolded Alice at the tavern, and that she had "called me rogue and bid me mind my own business and told me I had better have said nothing." On the way home he was strangely threatened by a "black hogg" which made a "great noise and ran at me as if he would devour me." Westgate did not doubt that the beast was connected with the malevolence of Alice Parker. "I then apprehended [it] was either the Divell or some Evill thing not a Real hog...it was either Goody parker or by her means." But years earlier in 1665, Job Tyler and his family also spoke of strange animal behavior. Deposing in the trial of suspected witch John Godfrey, Tyler said they saw "a thing like a bird" come into the house with Godfrey, where it "did fly about" and then "vanished, as they conceived" through a chink in the wall. Questioning Godfrey about it, Tyler was told by him "it came to suck your wife." John Remington deposed in the same trial that Godfrey had threatened him and his father regarding winter pasturage for their cattle. "I did drive up the cattle," said Remington, "and as I was a coming home...the horse I rid on began to snort and the dog that was with me begun to whine and cry...and then I smelt a sweet smell like cider." Before long Remington "did see a Crow come toward me flying and perched upon a tree...and she looked at me and the horse and dog, and it had a very great and quick Eye and it had a very great Bill." Then, said Remington, he began to "mistrust and think it was no crow..." He reassured himself that it "could not hurt my soul though it hurt my body and horse and as I was thinking thus the horse I was upon fell down" injuring Remington's leg. "Then the crow came and flew around me several times." When the crow finally flew off, Remington adds, "then the dog made on me and rejoiceth much" (Hall 1991:125–126).[1]

So, when a wild beast attacked the minister's son-in-law, people could well have seen it as evidence of the larger spiritual battle that was taking place in Dane's family and ministry. By the time of this encounter with the mountain lion, a long series of troubles had already begun for Dane, his family and in-laws, and others from the Hertfordshire contingent of families of which he was a part. These troubles peaked at the witchcraft crisis of 1692. Dane died soon after, but before the final phase of the parish split that followed, he surely had seen his church and town moving towards division. Indeed, the old minister's death may have cleared the way for the final push of the South towards the independent parish status they had wanted for years.

As for Robinson, the lion killer and Dane's son-in-law, his was also a troubled family. He was the stepson of Edmund Faulkner and had come to town as a boy when his widowed mother married Faulkner. Later both he and his Faulkner half-brother married the daughters of Francis Dane. The Faulkner family had known considerable trauma already, their house and family members having been singled out for revenge in the earlier Indian raid. Both

---

[1]The literature on seventeenth-century New England worldview, theology, witchcraft, and magic is vast. For the Westgate testimony against Parker see Boyer and Nissenbaum (eds.) 1972, vol. 2:632–633. The complete Remington-Godfrey witchcraft texts offer a fascinating insight into the native view of the preternatural and of the role of animals in it (RCACMB 1665 lxll:151–161). Godbeer (1992, *passim*) used the term "alternatural" to describe this realm, rather than supernatural. See his discussion and bibliography on this theme. Caporael (1976) proposed a naturalistic explanation of at least some strange animal behavior in her rye ergot (LSD) theory.

the Dane and Faulkner families, children, stepchildren, and grandchildren, were among those who would be most deeply implicated later in the witchcraft crisis. How did such events affect these families? Unfortunately, no known journals or letters survive. But marriage records do survive, and the impact of the events before and after the 1690s can be glimpsed indirectly through tracing the marriage histories of the families involved, especially the minister's family. In the next chapter I will look at marriage in the Dane and Faulkner families following the witchcraft crisis. First, in this chapter I look at settlers' regional and ethnic backgrounds—their *country* and *blood*—in the continuing process by which Andover people established their social world and how it was reflected in a series of conflicts and realignments, including the witchcraft crisis.

Overview of Events: 1676–1710

Trouble in frontier Andover intensified from the time of King Philip's War in 1676, when Indians began to raid Andover more intensely. At that time they had killed one boy and captured another. Various internal conflicts broke out during the turbulent eighties, and Indians struck the town again in 1689. In the Andover records there are accounts of internal trouble as well: drunkenness, fights, and domestic violence, a combination of which resulted in the town's first case of murder. Townspeople found themselves on opposite sides in a number of petitions to settle divisive issues about liquor licenses, land control, the calling of a new minister to assist the aging Dane, and the relocation of the meetinghouse. Smallpox struck several families in 1689 and 1690. Then the infamous witchcraft crisis broke, consuming the energies of the colonists for the entire year of 1692 and afterwards as well. Andoverites hardly had time to recover from this before the third and fourth Indian attacks came in 1696 and 1697, leaving more men, women, and children dead. These local events were embedded in the larger context of turmoil throughout the colony as the Civil War and its aftermath unfolded in England. Cromwell's Puritan republic rose and fell and ended with his head on a pike outside Westminster. The restored British monarchy moved to reassert royal control over the colonies, revoking Massachusetts' charter and putting all the New England colonies under one governor appointed by the Crown.

As the 1700s began, however, the New England colony including Massachusetts seems to have experienced a fairly peaceful period. The Indians retreated. In Andover, the South Enders were finally granted their petition for separate parish status. As elsewhere in the colony towns, the process had begun whereby the school was to be separated from the church. For the first time, the town of Andover hired a schoolmaster who was not also the minister, ending what had been a chronic source of frustration not only for the town but also for the minister himself.

The South Parish drew up its own new covenant. Unlike Andover's first covenant, it was remarkable in that women signed for themselves rather than being covered under a father's or a husband's covenant. Not only that, more women than men signed the first South Parish covenant. In part this reflects the separation of the franchise from church membership. Women still could not vote, but now they could become members of the church in their own right. I think this reflects a pastoral reaction to the recent witchcraft crisis when so many of those involved had been girls and women. Pastors now perceived that women would remain spiritually vulnerable without their own covenant status, personally acknowledged.

The two parishes of Andover were the outworking of both land pressure and the social relationships between the two main subgroups that had made up the original company. In a sense it had taken a crisis to bring about the formal split. Salem Village also divided into two parishes after its crisis. In the words of Boyer and Nissenbaum (1974:219), "The 'reconciliation' of [Salem] Village was thus achieved, in part, simply by giving institutional expression to the fragmentation which had occurred." In time, even marriage alliances in Andover began to reflect the fact that with the two parishes, two new social hierarchies were now in place. As will be described in chapter 7, the eldest son of the leading family of the North Parish and the eldest daughter of the leading family of the South Parish were married, the first marriage between these two families. This was a marriage of key social location and the beginning of more marriages between the families of the two parishes. It must have been a major social and spiritual event. Although no comments survive, possibly townspeople saw it as a reconciliation marriage as was the earlier Winthrop-Dudley marriage exchange, marking the end of their feud and symbolized by Two Brothers Rock (see Winthrop's *Journal,* April 24, 1638 and chapter 2).

The Act of Restitution (to those damaged by the witchcraft trials and their families) came in 1711. It brought a round of formal apologies and the accusations and guilty verdicts were expunged from the records. Marriage records show that it also brought a round of marriages between families that had been involved in the witchcraft crisis. Marriages were even made between children of accused and accuser families. The opening of the new century appeared to be a new age, even locally an "age of enlightenment," as historians would eventually dub the wider period. Boyer and Nissenbaum (1974:218) describe the new minister who took up the pulpit at Salem Village, Joseph Green, as "low-keyed, gregarious and worldly...not unduly preoccupied with religious or ideological issues." Even Judge Sewall himself seems to set the tone for eighteenth-century Andover and the wider colonial world with this comfortable dismissal of affliction in his journal entry for 1702:

> August 12: Rid with Mrs Woodman and others to Andover which is a good In-land Town and of a Good Prospect. Some warned us not to go to the ordinary, because Mr Peters was dangerously ill of the Bloody Flux; so went to Mrs Woodman's daughters & there din'd on Pork and Beans.

Lines of Division in Andover: 1676–1679

In this section I explore long-standing lines of division in Andover, showing how the witchcraft crisis emerged in the context of a series of events before and after the crisis year of 1692, a process that culminated in the formation of a second parish, the new South Parish. I follow the interaction of people over the course of the split, in both their old and new social categories. I look first at Andover's condition at the close of the Indian hostilities in the late 1670s. The militia is now the growing edge of company organization, a structure in action, taking its place with the earlier companies that were emigration units, ecclesiastical units, and town-planting units. I then look at three major conflicts in Andover where fission opened up during this period along old lines, but with new issues. The first of these was the quarrel that began in 1681 between the minister Francis Dane and the church as represented by the town selectmen. The second is the Chandler licensing controversy, and the third, the situation of the Scottish families and their relation to the events at the opening of the witchcraft crisis. Francis Dane, the spiritual head of the Andover community, was not only involved in the first but also connected by ties of blood and country to these latter two situations.[2]

---

[2]Although the evidence is indirect, it points to the possibility that the Danes may have been of Scottish background. They were perhaps one of the anglicized Scottish to whom I referred earlier. Items: the name is often spelled Deane on early records, a more common Scottish surname spelling; Francis Dane married an Ingalls, possibly another anglicized Scot family that had married with a known Scottish family, the Allens; John Dane testified in the defense of a Scotsman in Ipswich (see ECQCR vol. vii [1679]:360–361); several of the Dane grandchildren married Scots after the witchcraft crisis (see chap. 7). If in fact anti-Scot feeling played any part in the early focus of the witch crisis in Andover, and if the Dane family was perceived as having Scottish "blood," these perceptions could account for some of the involvement of the Danes.

Rise of the *militias*

In the view of one historian (Webb 1984), the outbreak of serious hostilities with the Indians in 1675 marked the real end of the founding visionaries' hopes for their Puritan experiment in the Bay Colony. Secular explanations for events can and have been proposed, but from the viewpoint of the believers, those who really took the hand of God seriously, God had withdrawn his favor, making apparent both his terrible anger at their backsliding and their terrible vulnerability without his protection. Many ministers interpreted New England's woes this way and tried to call the people back both by persuasion and by force of law.

Whatever individual colonists and their leaders believed about why in the spiritual realm such problems had assailed them, they had to do something for sheer physical self-protection. In the following I summarize from Bailey the impact upon Andover of more dangerous times. "It is hardly imaginable the panick fears that is upon our upland plantations and scattered places," wrote Major Denison, militia commander for Essex County, to the Council of Safety in Boston in 1676. "The almighty and merciful God pity and helpe us" (Bailey 1880:170; see also Denison's remembrance in Slade 1892). Soon after this, a detachment of militia, gathered from many towns, marched south into the Rhode Island colony where they defeated the Indians in a wintertime battle in the swamps known as the Battle of Narragansett (see map 1). However, Indian survivors of Narragansett marked those individual colonists who had been in the battle and began to track them down for revenge in raids on their hometowns, including Andover.

Andover, as an exposed frontier town, fortified itself after the Narragansett campaign with "twelve substantial Garrisons well-fitted" that met the approval of the committee from Boston sent out to make an inspection tour of the fortifications of the frontier towns (Bailey 1880:172 ff.). But town fortification was not enough. In April 1676, Indians attacked Andover men working out in their fields, killing Joseph Abbot, who had fought in the Narragansett campaign, and capturing his younger brother Timothy. In the following summer of 1677, the Bay Colony militia went north on a campaign into Maine to fight Indians in what became known as the battle of Black Point. According to Bailey, four young men of Andover died at Black Point: a son of Joseph Parker, a son of Nathan Parker, and a son of Edward Phelps; the fourth man was Christopher Osgood's servant Daniel Black, identified as a Scot. Later, the mothers of the first three youths and Christopher Osgood's young wife would all be among the women involved in some way in the witchcraft crisis. It may be that the shock and fear of Indian warfare was especially difficult for the women of affected families. If it was horrible to them, it may have brought on the "melancholy" often described as connected with women's witchcraft stories. Increase Mather, recounting the attacks of the previous year against Andover residents in his *History of King Philip's War* describes the "great fright" of the people as Indians "killed one and burnt one house," causing them to "fly into the garrison houses" while the "barbarous creatures" took their vengeance out on "poor dumb beasts," Edmond Faulkner's cows and horses (p. 174). Again, Indians had made a point of targeting Faulkner, whom they may have still remembered as the one who had taken the lead in the ill-fated (to them) purchase of the land from Cutshamache.

This new phase of war with the Indians meant that the military and the local militia rose in crucial importance as an order of power whose imperatives could challenge the ecclesiastical and civil orders. Dudley Bradstreet, promoted to captain of Andover's foot company soon after the events described above, began at once to improve the town defenses. He petitioned the Court to increase the fine upon all those who persisted in not working and drilling together "in companies." He also asked the Court to order each town to keep a "scouting company" whose task would be "to range the outskirts" so that "the inhabitants may in their spirits be more settled and go about their work for their English and Hay harvest" (Mass. Archives vol. lxix:152 in Bailey 1880:172, 177). Local militia companies, with their tradition of cooperation and loyalty in facing common danger, must have become the main integrating institutions for men in the colony at that time.

In frontier towns like Andover, where Indian menace was felt as a daily matter, the militia grew in importance and rose to a central position among the town institutions, as it became increasingly the focus of safety and pride. At first there had been one "parade" or training field for Andover. As the town grew it was natural to have a training field for each of the two ends of town. The militia then moved towards having two companies, one from the North, one from the South. So in 1683, the militia leaders of Andover petitioned the Court for permission to raise another company in town "to complete their troop to the number of forty-eight men" (Bailey, 1880:168).

Town records of the 1670s and 1680s also show indirectly how military concerns came to the fore. In the records of the 1680s, the lists of men's names begin to include the abbreviations for their military ranks. As the militia grew in importance, the town's selectmen were not only social and economic leaders but also became the militia leaders. The list of the five selectmen Bailey gives for 1682, for example, shows the extent to which the civil and military orders had come to overlap in Andover: "Captain

Bradstreet, Lieutenant Osgood, Ensign Thomas Chandler, Sergeant John Stevens, and Richard Barker Senior." Only Barker, too old to be a soldier, appears with no military title. However, note that men from the leading North End families continued to control the officer ranks, just as they controlled the town offices. Chandler is the only South Ender listed here, holding the junior rank of ensign. The South End militia would not have a captain from among its own families for several more years.

The militia connections overlapped family ties at the colony level as well. Dudley Bradstreet, Andover's captain, was filling his father's place in town. His father Simon had remarried, left Andover, and moved to Salem, where as a magistrate he could more conveniently take part in the central stream of colonial political life. In 1678 he was elected Deputy Governor, and in 1679, Governor of the Colony. Back in Andover, his son Dudley took over his father's place as the town's gentleman, holding the various roles of captain of the militia, justice of the peace, and either town selectman or Representative to the Court. The records show, however, that Bradstreet was occasionally starting to lose elections to Thomas Chandler as Chandler began to rise in the local political offices.

Ensign Thomas Chandler was the first South End man to be elected selectman. He was also the first in the South End to make his way to the rank of captain. The ensign in a troop is the one assigned to hold up the flag until the last possible minute, and Chandler's appointment (or election) to this rank may provide a clue to his temperament and why he was the one who came to lead the South End militia company. However, blood may have played a role there, for the Chandlers were also kinsmen of Major Denison through their mother's family (see Slade 1892 for Denison's autobiographical remarks and his relationship with the Chandlers). Major Denison, son-in-law of Governor Dudley, brother-in-law to Simon Bradstreet, and the Essex county militia leader, was not a resident of Andover but was closely tied to several Andover families through marriage including the Chandlers.

The wills and inventories of the old Firstcomers and Covenanters, many of whom were dying off during this period, provide another source of insight into the language of military office used as social identifiers. For example, Joseph Parker, the miller, died in 1678. Parker left an estate valued at £546, including the old cornmill that he had started in Andover. The will also reveals that Parker still owned his house in England. Parker's generation had lived in unique transition between two sets of identities, those of the old society and the new.[3] The language of his will shows the use of the social and military categories that mattered in the tense days of the 1670s, naming "my loving brother Nathan my loving friend Lieutenant John Abbot my loving friend Sgt Henry Ingalls and my loving friend Ensign Thomas Chandler" to be his overseers (Bailey 1880:102).[4]

Growth and expansion

In the Restoration years after the civil war in England, the Crown began to reassert itself in colonial life, and the Bay Colony came under its scrutiny. In 1678, word came that an oath of allegiance to the king was required of all males in the colonies over sixteen years of age. The oath-taker list for Andover survives, and I will use it to show the significant population growth that had taken place in town. The Firstcomers had arrived in Andover with about twenty-five males over sixteen among them. Thirty-five years later, one hundred and twenty men were recorded as taking the oath. Of these, thirty-one of them have surnames other than those of the Firstcomers (see lists in Bailey 1880:107).[5]

Population growth at this rate entailed pressure for land for farms, as Greven documented. Either holdings had to be divided into ever smaller units, or sons had to move away. The first surviving tax list (*rates list*) for the support of the minister is for the year 1679 (earlier lists having disappeared, probably when town clerk Faulkner's house was burned). The 1679 list warrants a close look. It lists the ratepayers of Andover in terms of the two "Ends" of town. However, the town had clearly moved towards a North-South End division for administrative purposes for some time before 1679. In 1669 other records show there had been four sets of *fence viewers* appointed, a set specified for each End, and one set each for the "new fields" and for the "fields over the Shawsheen." In 1674, two

---

[3]I have not drawn on the evidence in wills in this research except briefly as here with Parker. Greven has put together a clear picture of changing inheritance from the Andover wills. Goodman (1974) in his study of kinship and friendship networks in Newbury makes use of sections like this one as friendship evidence. For a study making use of colonial inventories, see Yentsch 1981.

[4]It is notable that Parker's "loving friends" were a mix of kin and non-kin, North Enders and South Enders, Covenanters and non-Covenanters, Firstcomers and Latecomers. His choice of overseers serves as good warning to the researcher that knowing people's social categories may not make it possible to predict the effect of their relationships.

[5]This list, and others like it, taken in conjunction with genealogies provides an excellent way to judge relative agnatic strength of families in a town. Waters, a historian with an anthropological bent, has made the none-too-surprising observation from his study of colonial Guildford, Connecticut, that families with more surviving sons had the adaptive advantage (Waters 1982).

constables had been appointed for the first time, one for the North and one for the South End. With the 1679 tax list there is at last information about who was now living in each end of town, and what their relative wealth was (see Tax Lists in appendix D). Although records do not survive that reveal the exact composition of the neighborhoods within the Ends, in general, certain clusters of families were associated with each End (Bailey 1880:137–138). The following sections look more closely at these different neighborhoods. Maps 8 and 9 show as much as is presently known about neighborhood composition.[6]

The North End and West Boxford

The names of thirty-nine men appeared on the 1679 tax list for the North End. The three top taxpayers were related: John Osgood II and his two brothers-in-law, Poor and Ingalls. Almost half of the thirty-nine were descendants of the Covenanter families or were their in-laws. Many had been part of the old Parker company of Southwesterners. They had come from Hampshire and Wiltshire in England and been together at Newbury before making the move to Andover. Some, such as Ingalls, were men who had married into Covenanter families and were living uxorilocally (that is, near their wife's family). These people and certain others who were not Covenanters, but were Firstcomers, for the most part now held all the lands of the old central part of town (see map 9). Some had added to their original grants, buying up the lots of those who had left town or moved to the South End.

Judging from the tax list, the North Enders were wealthier than the South Enders in 1679. The highest taxpayers lived in the North, their average tax was higher, and most of those who paid low taxes lived in the South (appendix D). Yet some of the people who paid very low taxes also lived in the North, some in the region that became known as West Boxford. Several families later involved in the witchcraft crisis lived there. Thus the North End not only included the old central part of town and the area up to the bank of the river, it also included an odd little neck of land northeast of Lake Cochichawick, the site of one of the fords over the Merrimack. (See maps 5 and 8. On map 5, what is now Bradford was the disputed area.) It was this piece of land that had caused the dispute between Andover and Rowley men (see the section on Bay Colony Expansion, chapter 3, p. 50). This area was something of a no-man's-land, one of

---

[6]In line with their project on the witchcraft episode, the Andover Historical Societies have undertaken a project to map even more closely the residences of Andover in the 1690s. See maps 10 and 11, also online at the major witchcraft website at <http://www.etext.lib.virginia.edu/salem/witchcraft/maps/andovermap50.jpg>.

the "scattered places" with a population that Major Denison had referred to as difficult to defend from Indian attack and thus especially subject to "panick fears."

Although these families lived in what had been part of Rowley township, their neighborhood was far from the Rowley meetinghouse. The growing population was still too small to have their own parish house and minister. Seemingly, some were neglecting going to meeting in any of the nearby towns; some of them said in a petition to the Court that they preferred to go to Topsfield meeting in any case. However, those living in the area north of the lake, nearest Andover, were also too far from Topsfield. The Court ruled that they would be considered part of the Andover congregation, and thus they would be taxed for the salary of the Andover minister whether they went there or not, so they had better go there (see Perley 1880:64–65).

Many of the families in this marginal area were also Scots or in some way in the Old Briton or Borderer category. Their backgrounds and interrelationships should be noted, as they figure in the witchcraft crisis.[7] Some of these Old Britons appeared in all roles in the crisis: accused, afflicted, and accusers. This situation suggests that something more than one neighborhood or group opposing another was going on in the crisis. Based on their cultural roots in the far north or west of Britain, members of this marginal community may have lived by beliefs and practices about magic, religion, and witchcraft that were different from the dominant group of English Southwesterners.[8] What Godbeer called "the disjunction between theological and [folk] magical conceptions of witchcraft" may well have had these ethnic dimensions as well (Godbeer 1992:181).

---

[7]Boxford bordered on the large landholdings of Richard Barker. Barker was a leading man of Andover, but one of his younger sons, who later described himself in his trial testimony as poor and troubled, had married a woman of Reading and moved to the edge of his father's property on the outskirts of Boxford. John Russ, one of the Scots who had been among the Firstcomers as a bondservant, probably lived on the border of this region (on the basis of testimony in the Godfrey trial), although all the other Scottish families of Andover lived in the South End. Job Tyler (of Shropshire or Welsh border origin) seems to have lived in this area at some point. Tyler's sons remained after their father had left town for Mendon following his bitter litigation with the Chandlers (Metcalf 1880). The Tylers intermarried with the Bridges, who were descended from Edmund Bridges (regional background not certain), a blacksmith of Ipswich who had gotten himself into various kinds of trouble before leaving that area. The Spragues and the Posts, step-kin of the Tylers and Bridges, were also in this neighborhood. (see Abbott n.d on these families; also AHS: Reconstruction of Early Andover Residences)

[8]Cedric Cowing, in a personal communication, proposed this background for Salem witchcraft.

The South End

A point that has sometimes confused researchers needs to be reemphasized here. What was called the South End on the early Andover tax lists is not the same as the geographical South Parish as it was later bounded in 1710.[9] In early days, the South End was the name given to the southern section of the original town center. The dividing line was a certain street about a mile and a half south of the meetinghouse, making a suitable divide between the upper and lower parts of town. This street was called either "Mill Street" as the old road to the river and its mill, or perhaps "Milk Street," so named because the common milking barns were there. William Chandler's house and tavern, the focus of much later controversy, was right in this vicinity (Forbes Rockwell 1988, personal communication (see map 8)). Not enough reconstruction work on land records has been done (and may not be possible) to show where everyone might have been living in 1680, but we do know that people living south of Milk or Mill Street were on the South End constable's list. We do not know how many were living farther away near the Shawsheen by then, where the new parish center eventually formed, and who and how many were living even farther away. The lists do clarify, however, which families were in association in the emerging South End and who were the leading families economically.

Forty-seven men were named on the 1679 South End tax list. Of the forty-seven, only *seven* were from the old Covenanter families, and six of these were either Holts or Fryes. These were the only two of the original Covenanter families whose members left the North End.[10] In the South End as in the North, a cluster of men related by kinship to what might be called a "dominant male" are found at the top end of the taxpayer list. Just as several of the highest taxpayers of the North End were related to John Osgood, several of the top taxpayers of the South End were related. Thomas Chandler, his brother-in-law George Abbot, his son-in-law Phelps (whose pre-emigration regional background is not presently known), and his younger brother William were the top four. Kinsmen and in-laws, their families sharing *blood* and *country*, these were also the families who

---

[9]Greven did not make a distinction between the South End and the South Parish and how one grew out of the other. The reconstructions of Forbes Rockwell of North Andover land holdings, seen in conjunction with the tax lists, make this very clear. I am indebted to Rockwell for pointing this out and for access to his maps.

[10]The persistence of such early associations through time in rural New England may be greater than has been suspected. Holts and Fryes were among the young couples who left Andover to found the town of Wilton in New Hampshire in the 1740s (Livermore and Putnam 1888). These families intermarried many times and remained in that town, and as recently as 1970 distant Holt and Frye cousins married. See also Holt n.d.

had been in Ipswich, not Newbury, prior to the move to Andover. They had their common roots in Hertfordshire *country,* shared a common connection to the *company* that gathered around minister John Norton, and now they were together on common territory in the new *plantation.*

The other strong South End group was clustered around Christopher Osgood. Again, researchers have confused or counted this Osgood family together with the John Osgood family of the North End. As far as any of the family genealogists know, they were not related. Christopher married, in the end, four times (and had fifteen children), and thus he had a wide range of kin connections.[11] He also had at least one servant, Daniel Black or Blake, thought to be one of the Scots from the little enclave of Scots in West Boxford (Abbott n.d: Christopher Osgood).

A third group in the South End was made up of the Firstcomers who had Scots blood, the Allens and Fosters, and the Latecomer Scot, Russell (see table 1, p. 72). They were and continued to be Borderers. These families and their in-laws such as Hugh Stone, Laurence Lacey, and later Thomas Carrier, are all familiar names in the witchcraft crisis records. Indeed, the South End's "Old Briton" neighborhood became an early focus of the witchcraft episode, as did the West Boxford neighborhood of Old Britons in the North End. Several members of these families were among the accused, the afflicted, and the accusers.

Arenas of Conflict: 1680–1692

I have argued that in many respects the factions that surfaced in Andover in the course of conflicts leading up to the witchcraft crisis appear to have followed old lines of *country* and *blood,* British regional and ethnic background loyalties (and antagonisms). In this section I look at several arenas of conflict in which people in the factions concerned do line up with those country and blood ties (whether or not they consciously did so, we cannot know). There was conflict and controversy over the new meetinghouse and in three other situations that dominated the decade of the 1680s in Andover: the conflict between the minister Francis Dane and the church; the Chandler tavern license controversy; and the conflicted relations among and within the Old Briton families, up to and including the witchcraft crisis. As for the meetinghouse controversy, as the central building

---

[11]The career of Christopher Osgood deserves an essay of its own. His relationship to John Osgood of the North End was never ascertained; they do not seem to have been related, and they definitely headed socially distinct families. A major figure in the South End, he was in local and regional politics and a captain in the militia. One of his wives and one of his daughters were accused witches.

of the community, it had been rebuilt at least once. But since it had not been moved from its original location, it was no longer at the center of the population spread. The meetinghouse location became a concrete focus for the controversy because many people disliked having to travel a long way to it, and it was a real enough complaint (especially as Indian threats increased). But the old allegiances and antagonisms entered into the new quarrels, and this overlay I will try to trace. I especially follow Francis Dane and his family, for Dane was not only spiritual head of the community, but he was involved in all of those situations through ties of blood, country, and marriage.

Controversy over the meetinghouse

With the growth of the population the problem arose for the need of land and for a larger meetinghouse. The process frequently stirred up trouble as the records of many New England towns attest. How many times the meetinghouse was rebuilt in Andover is not clear, but problems always centered around, first, where it was to be built if it was to be relocated, and then, once built, what the seating arrangement should be. A committee had to be appointed to "dignify the pews" and "seat the meetinghouse," that is, decide what the pew rents would be and who would sit where. Seating according to social rank had existed in the English church, so this idea was not new. A complex reckoning of rank, wealth, and age determined the seating, and the decisions laid bare the bones and nerves of a town's view of itself and its own social structure. But service on the committee which had to decide these things was an unpopular duty and often caused hard feelings.

The decade of the eighties opened with Andover building a new meetinghouse. The surviving records refer not to the building of it but to the vexed process that went with initiating the use of it. In 1680, a seating committee was made up of the minister Francis Dane, Dudley Bradstreet (North End), and George Abbot (South End). The latter two men were no doubt selected to represent the two sections. According to Bailey (1880:412), Bradstreet went on record "protesting against being compelled to serve in seating the meetinghouse" but to no avail; even he apparently could not get out of it.

No record survives, unfortunately, of the criteria Andover used to assign seats, or of any specific seating arrangement until the nineteenth century (Abbot 1988). However, a text from records of the nearby town of Beverly reveals how meetinghouse seating became a distillation of the new criteria for establishing rank or *degree* in the developing colonial social hierarchy. According to local Beverly historian Thayer, the Beverly committee ruled

> ...that every male be allowed one degree for every complete year of age he exceeds twenty-one; that he be allowed for a captain's commission twelve degrees, for a lieutenant's eight, and for an ensign's four degrees; that he be allowed three degrees for every shilling in the last parish tax...Married women to be seated agreeably to the rank of their husbands, and widows in the same degree as their husbands were they yet living; that the foremost magistrate seat shall be the highest in rank...that the side seat below shall be for elderly men, the foremost first or highest, and the others in order, that the seats behind the fore-front seat shall be for middle-aged men. according to their degree... (Thayer 1942:35–36)

This description sounds almost like a parody. The entire text is reprinted in appendix B for the insight it affords into social hierarchy in late seventeenth-century Massachusetts (but see a note of caution from Godbeer [personal communication] at appendix B). Little wonder in any case that men like Dudley Bradstreet did not want to serve on the committee whose job it was to work out such arrangements.

Controversy with the minister

If the problems of seating the meetinghouse were distracting, how much more so the problems with the minister himself as glimpsed in the records. By 1680, Francis Dane had been minister at Andover for over thirty years. Both his first and second wives had died. His six children were all married, his eldest son following the pattern of Andover-Haverhill elites in marrying the eldest daughter of the prominent Hazletine family from across the river in Haverhill. All of Dane's children were living in the North End except the younger of his two sons, who had married and moved to the South End. But something, possibly some infirmity of the minister's, led to town dissatisfaction with him and a petition to the Court for mediation.

The petition of 1681 presented to the Court against Dane implied that although they recognized his infirmities, he had not been doing much preaching in recent years and the town had suffered because of it. They wanted him to agree to have an assistant minister. Signed by all the six selectmen, the five North End leaders and Dane's own stepson Thomas Chandler of the South, the petition made a

> ...humble request to this honoured Court...that they would be pleased to take our sad and solemn condition into their serious consideration and to put us into such a capacity that we may be able to

maintain a preaching minister amongst us, the want of which makes us in a sorrowful and very uncomfortable condition. (Mass Archives vol. 11:15)

Indeed, the records do show "sad and solemn" troubles in Andover as elsewhere in the New England churches and towns after the Restoration. The sense of loss of control and attempts to regain it by law and punishment are pervasive in the records. In 1662, Thomas Johnson and Christopher Osgood had fought ostensibly over a hoe, a dispute that seems to have resulted in a long enmity and rivalry between these two.[12] The problem surfaced again in the record of the sides taken in the controversy over William Chandler's tavern (see next section). Of further concern throughout the colony was the rise in Sabbath breaking. In 1677 the General Court had passed an act authorizing a cage to be set up on Boston Common for the confinement of Sabbath breakers.

At Andover, there were at first trivial "prophanations." For instance in 1672, a six-pence fine had been levied on the owner for each offense of "doggs in the meeting house on the Sabbath-Day" (Bailey 1880:411). The constables and tythingmen began to confront cases of open conflict and rebellion, especially among the young South Enders. In 1678, an argument over animal trespass between young William Chandler, Jr. and Walter Wright, the miller, ended in a knife fight (ECQCR vol. xxix:93, in Bailey p. 35). In 1679, the town had to appoint two extra officers "to have inspection over the boys in the galleries on Sabbath" (p. 413). This doubtless unpleasant job was often assigned to men who were fairly recent arrivals in town. This status probably did nothing to enhance their authority over unruly young sons and grandsons of the Firstcomers such as William Chandler, Jr.

---

[12]To review, Osgood had arrived in Andover with his mother and stepfather at the age of ten (see chapter 5). His older sister had already moved to the town as wife of John Lovejoy, recently released servant of John Stevens (Lovejoy 1930). The stepfather soon died, and the widow and her children stayed on in Andover. They seemed to have no relationship with the leading family of Osgoods, but Christopher gradually worked his way up into a position of leadership in the South End faction. To do this, he had to assert himself against the Roxbury group led by the Chandlers and against Thomas Johnson, with whom he had had a fight long ago. I give details from the transcript of this fight for the insight it gives into a man (Johnson) for whom the Puritan God and church seemed quite dead.

A court record entitled "A Complaint of Christopher Osgood" gives details of Osgood's presentment against Johnson. It was 1662; Osgood was then nineteen, and Johnson was about thirty. Osgood said that during their fight Johnson nearly killed him. Osgood's mother entered the scene and told Johnson that the Scripture pronounced a curse on such as he for "wronging the widow and the fatherless and that God would plead their cause." According to the deposition, Johnson "replied in a scofing and in a sneering way and sayd, 'Aye: doe: doe: trust to him, trust to him, he will help you no question'" (ECQCR 1662, quoted in Bailey 1880:608, spelling and punctuation unchanged).

Little appears on record before 1680 about how the minister Francis Dane had related to his congregation during his many years in office. One item in the court records of 1665 may be of importance for evaluating the minister's reputation. In 1665 Dane had spoken in defense of troubled and troublesome John Godfrey who had been accused of bewitching or cursing by Job Tyler, although he did not attend the trial (see discussion of this trial earlier in this chapter (p. 126); also Demos [1976:44–45], who describes Godfrey's case but does not mention Dane's role). In 1692 Dane wrote a letter on behalf of the accused Martha Carrier (who was an Allen and Dane's niece by marriage). These actions may have worked against him.

Dane's troubles with the town surfaced in the records again in 1681 in another form. Some townspeople were engaging another minister to help the aging senior pastor. Why they had waited so long is not known. Back in 1648, the writers of the Cambridge Platform had urged all towns to establish associate ministries, with both a preacher and a teacher. What information there is about the Andover situation comes from the petition of the selectmen to the Court at Boston asking for their help in solving the town's problems with Dane. Dane had objected to the cut in pay the selectmen asked him to take because he was not preaching so frequently. But, they said, since he was in "comfortable circumstances" and knew that the town was not rich, he could afford, they thought, to take on more of his own support now that they were about to hire a younger assistant (Massachusetts Archives 1681, vol. 11:16 in Bailey 1880:422).

The magistrates investigated and ordered the town to continue to pay Dane something in view of his long service among them. They advised Dane himself to "encourage" Thomas Barnard, his new colleague, and "forgetting all previous disgusts" with his people, "endeavor to his utmost to conduct the public worship of God with the love and respect to his people as befits a Minister of the Gospell." The following year, 1683, an entry appears, the significance of which is hard to assess. The town voted to give Mr. Dane £5 of his £30 salary in rare silver money instead of "pay" that is, grain (ATR 1683, in Bailey 1880:422ff.). These problems seem to have then subsided.

Thomas Barnard, the associate minister who came to assist Dane in Andover in 1682, was probably a cousin of one of the original ten Covenanters, Robert Barnard (Abbott n.d.: Barnard). Robert had been the first Covenanter to leave town soon after moving there (following a quarrel with Simon Bradstreet, according to Abbott). Thomas Barnard's particular link with Andover at the time of his calling there was through the Stevens family. His sister had married John Stevens' eldest son.[13] This was a marriage with an important social location, for the Stevens family occupied a unique position in the social hierarchy of the North End. Although he had sailed with Osgood, Parker, and Frye, and joined them in the new community at Newbury, John Stevens was not a Southwesterner from Wiltshire-Hampshire as were they and many of the other former Newbury residents. He was from southern Oxfordshire. Once in Andover, he lived among the Covenanters at the core of North End, but he, like Bradstreet, did not join in the covenant with them (Abbott n.d.: Stevens).

John Stevens was brother-in-law to Joseph Parker. They had married each other's sisters. He was a man of means, for he had brought along at least two bondservants to Massachusetts, John Lovejoy and his sister, and received a substantial allotment of land in the first division. But when it came to the inner circle of Covenanters, Stevens for some reason was not among them. From the beginning, Stevens and another man, Barker (probably from Suffolk in Eastern England), did not fit the Covenanter mold and formed something of a separate alliance in the North End. Their genealogies show a number of marriages between their two families and with South End families, but few with the Covenanters.

John Stevens II became heir to a substantial estate upon his father's death in 1662, and both he and Barker II were selectmen for the first time in the year that Barnard was called. Thus it may have been that when the town was ready to call a second minister, Stevens put forth the name of his relative Thomas Barnard. The wide connections of the Stevens and Barker families, and the fact that they were not part of either the Southwesterner or the Hertfordshire group, may have made Barnard an acceptable choice to the dominant groups in both Ends. Unfortunately, one cannot check on these speculations.

Controversy over Chandler's tavern

Another conflict centered around a tavern license controversy. The Bay Colony continued the practice of English society regarding control of strong drink. Licenses were required to sell liquor and keep public houses and they were supposed to be granted to men who were considered respectable and responsible citizens in the towns. Each town was given a quota of licenses to grant to such citizens. These policies would, it was hoped, keep the effect of "strong spirits" under some control. But liquor was ever a wild card in any system of social control and by the 1680s

---

[13]Barnard may also have been an in-law of the wife of Dudley Bradstreet, son of Simon. His wife was a Price from Salem, and Bradstreet's wife was a widow Price, probably also of Salem (Hinman 1985). I have not checked this connection.

cases having to do with the regulation or consumption of liquor were frequently before the courts.

At first, the concern of authorities had been directed towards the problem of Indians and liquor. They were "overcome with swinish drunkenness" by it, according to the General Court, and strict penalties were enacted early on to prevent its sale to them. But there were instances of drunkenness among the colonists. John Godfrey, who seemed to shift residence as he took odd jobs around Andover, Newbury, Haverhill, and elsewhere, was an extreme example whose case made it into the records. Godfrey's trial for witchcraft in 1665 was one of the first in the colony. Records concerning him show earlier arrests for drunkenness and a case where, while drunk, he had willed all his goods to a man in Boston and was now petitioning for the will to be declared null (Bailey 1880:66; ECQCR vol. v:78, 88, 248).

However, the upper ranks of colonists had problems with liquor as well. According to the court record reprinted in Lovejoy (2002), in 1658 "Mr Sergt John Stevens" was charged with intoxication and summoned to court, where his erstwhile servant Lovejoy testified that he "observed him to reele coming to me." Lovejoy then asked his master how he did and he said the liquor "did fume in his head" whereupon Lovejoy tried to help him to his house. But Stevens was "so overcome that he was not able to go nor stand" and was "like a child newly learning to goe." Lovejoy further deposed that "Sergt. Stevens was much troubled that his wife should not know of it, and that he was never so catched in his life." He said that the liquor he had drunk "may well be called KILL DEVIL for he thought it would kill devil and man too." This was not the end of it for Stevens. Later that year by petition of Andover men to the Court, John Osgood was appointed their sergeant in place of Stevens.[14]

At Andover's town meeting in 1678 the selectmen tried to control the apparently growing problem of disorderly conduct by instituting a curfew. They ordered that no person could entertain others in his house after nine o'clock at night. The tythingmen were to report the breaches of these orders and to fine offenders. They ordered the sexton to toll the bell every night at nine (Abbot 1829:49; in Bailey 1880: 411–412).

In the 1680s, the problem of public drunkenness, and even more disturbing, public drunkenness among the better as well the "meaner sort" of citizenry was noted by contemporary observers. True, the monarchy had been restored in England, and some in Massachusetts were delighted that the Puritan age was over. Judge Sewall reported that news of the

---

[14]I am grateful to Barrie Lovejoy for having included the longer court record in his family history (Abbott n.d.: Lovejoy; citation MCR 1650–1693, vol. 1:122, in Lovejoy 2002:21). Bailey, as was appropriate in her situation, gives the text of the petition (1880:167), but does not tell the story behind it or name those involved.

imminent arrival of the royal governor, Sir Edmund Andros, was polarizing the town of Boston. Some of the Anglicans and other Royalist sympathizers were rejoicing.

> September 3, 1686: Mr Shrimpton, Capt Lidgett, and others come in a Coach from Rocksbury about 9 aclock or past, singing as they come, being inflamed with drink; At Justice Morgans they stop and drink Healths, Curse, Swear, talk profanely and baudily to the great disturbance of the Town and the grief of good people. Such highhanded wickedness has hardly been heard of before in Boston. (Sewall 1973:121)

In Andover, a dispute began about this time over control of the sale of liquor in the town. The Court had allowed two ordinary licenses and one retailer's license. As far as can be ascertained, North Enders had held all these licenses from the beginning: Edmund Faulkner and John Osgood, the ordinary licenses and Deacon Frye, the retailer's. But in the South End, William Chandler's home was becoming known as a public house, even before he claimed to have received official permission. By virtue of its location, his house had been for some time a place where travelers stopped or met to do business. It was at Chandler's, for example, that Andrew Allen met in 1681 with men from Chelmsford to conduct their children's marriage negotiations (ECCP lii:116, in Bailey 1880:77).[15] Located at the crossroads of the South End of town, it was more convenient for travelers using the Ipswich-Billerica road than were the Faulkner and Osgood taverns in the North End (map 7).

Chandler's place became a place of refreshment for travelers because of its location, but it was also convenient for neighborhood people, who thought it too far for the South End residents to go to the taverns owned by Faulkner and Osgood in the North. But the South End and the North were socially different as well. The South End was a place where the Scots, and Latecomers non-Covenanter families, were forming another social world through shared space and intermarriage.

Of particular interest is the Scottish neighborhood that was part of the South End. Rockwell's reconstructions show that all the Scots except the Russes lived in the South End and that they lived near each other. Abbott's genealogies show that they intermarried with each other and with Scottish families in other towns. The genealogies also show that there was far more intermarriage between the Scots and the old Hertfordshire families of Dane, Abbot, and Chandler, than between the Scots and the Southwesterners. The

---

[15]Chandler and Allen had both married into the same Chelmsford family. This meeting was another instance of the way in which the Scots and the old Hertfordshire families of the South End were developing ties, which intentionally or not, did strengthen their numbers in relation to the North End.

Frye family, the only Southwesterner Covenanter family that moved from the North to South End, never married with the Scots. In fact, at the parish split, all the Fryes moved back to the North End. On the other hand, many Scots married into the Holt family.[16] Both Holt and Christopher Osgood developed "social broker" families, by which the families of Scots and servants could enter through marriage and thus move from the margins nearer to the center of the town's social stream.

Perhaps the South Enders felt the differing loyalties of country and blood between themselves and the North Enders and a lack of welcome in the public houses in the North section of town (see Hunt and Satterlee 1986 for a study of the social dynamics of "regulars" and strangers in a twentieth century two-pub English village). In any case, according to Bailey's account, sometime in 1689 John Osgood moved to stop William Chandler from keeping a public house in the South. Osgood complained to the Court that Chandler was operating without a license. In the exchange that followed, Chandler claimed the Court had in fact granted him a license. His opponents countered that he had no such permission, and that furthermore he should not be given it because he was irresponsible about the goings-on at his house, allowing the young and the poor to waste time and money they could ill-afford at Chandler's "barrels of sider and strong drinke." Andoverites began a series of depositions and petitions to the General Court in 1689 that provides clues to the factions and positions with regard to this division. But if the curfew of 1679 was the opening protest against Chandler, why was there no more intensified action against him until 1689, ten years later?

That situation may have come to a head in reaction to the murder of Hannah Stone by her husband Hugh in April of 1689. This tragic event was the first murder in Andover. It took place in the Scottish community, involved liquor, and thus, no doubt, Chandler's nearby neighborhood public house. Andover had known several severe fights in the past, especially the fight between Christopher Osgood and Thomas Johnson (see fn. 12, this chapter, p. 140), but this was the town's first fatality. According to Cotton Mather's report, Hugh Stone was drunk and cut his wife's throat during a quarrel over what they should do about the sale of a piece of land. Stone, a Scot, had married Hannah Foster, and they were part of the enclave of Scottish and Scots-related people within the South End. Chandler's house bordered the Scots neighborhood (maps 7 and 8). Stone must have obtained his liquor at Chandler's. The condemned man's last words on the gallows, according to Cotton Mather, included a warning to those assembled to beware of drink.

---

[16]See Abbott n.d.: Frye; Holt, and Holt Association of America, n.d. See also Frye Family Home Page online at < http://www.mv.com/ipusers/the masons >. Accessed 3/12/2004.

> When thou has thy head full of drink, remembrance of God is out of thy heart...I gave way to that sin more than any other...It was Contention in my family. I had been used to something of religion and I once was careful about the worship of God...but upon Contention between me and my wife I left off the ways of God and you see what I am come to. (Cotton Mather's account, quoted in Bailey 1880:80–81)

The Stone murder in 1689 possibly caused the village factions to intensify so that North End citizens decided it was time to act against Chandler. Bailey (1880:65–72) gives many details of the controversy that ensued and I draw from her account here. Supported by South Enders Christopher Osgood and the Frye brothers, North Enders petitioned the Court in 1690 that it might "speedily" help in the "matter of our grievance which is grown so much an epidemicall evil that overspreads and is likely to corrupt the greater part of our towne...viz to put a stopp to William Chandler's license of selling of drink." The petitioners claimed that even "servants & children are allowed by him in his house at all times of day and night unseasonable...till they know not their way to their own habitations." Again, with important exceptions, the factional lines represented by the petitioners still followed the old "country" loyalties but now with new kinship ties added to the mix.

Chandler countered Osgood's complaint, saying that he had received permission from the Boston licensing committee in 1686, and that he had been backed up by a group of South Enders who had sent a petition in his favor to the Court in 1687. Their petition said that without Chandler's place, there would be "no publick house of entertainment" out their way, and that they had often heard strangers complain that "they must goe a mile and a elfe [half] out of there way or goe without refreshing or else intrude upon privit houses which that neighborhood have found very burdensome." These petitioners included William Chandler's brother, Thomas, his neighbor, John Lovejoy, and the Johnson brothers, William and Thomas. The Johnsons were a rather outspoken Latecomer family probably of Kentish background, who had married into Andover families. Lovejoy was William Johnson's father-in-law. Thomas Johnson's concern in supporting Chandler may have been that of a kindred spirit. While serving as South End constable, Johnson had fallen into disgrace by allowing "a barrel of cider" to be drunk "in his house at unseasonable hours by young people," and he had also been charged with selling "strong waters" to Indians (Abbott n.d.: Johnson, April 1671; Ipswich Court Records vol. vi:370).

Johnson's support of Chandler may have been a factor in the entrance of Christopher Osgood into the quarrel on the anti-Chandler side, since there was a history of bad relations between Osgood and Johnson (see

Controversy with the Minister, p. 139). Christopher Osgood was now the leader of the other main subgroup of families in the South End and as well, the town clerk. In 1690 he drew up a counter-petition against Chandler's tavern to send to the Court. Osgood's name leads the list of twelve signers, and the petition includes a spectrum of his kin and others, both North and South End names.[17] The petition is blunt in its condemnation of Chandler.

> ...the earnest desire for money hath proved an evil root to him....Be sure if he is not restrained from the selling of drink our town will be for the greatest part of our young generation so corrupted thereby that we can expect little else but a course of drunkenness of them: and what comfort will that be to parents to see such a posterity coming on the stage after them? (ECQCR vol. 1:74)

But the anti-Chandler petition, signed on March 28, 1690, was somehow delayed and "came not to the view of the Court until after another was approved of." A previous one, signed by the town selectmen on March 21, instead commended Chandler for the good order he kept and said that since he was "an infirm man and not capable of hard labor" they judged him "meet enough and his house convenient for travelers."

Of the five selectmen who signed the approving petition—Dudley Bradstreet, Thomas Chandler, Henry Holt, Joseph Ballard, and John Abbot—four were related by blood or marriage to the Chandlers, the exception being Dudley Bradstreet. The relationships among them are worth noting and are spelled out in the footnote.[18] That year, 1690, was an unusual one in that no Osgood, of either the North or South End families was elected selectman. Even though we cannot know for sure what the content of the

---

[17]Christopher Osgood was joined in this petition by his younger brother Thomas, and Samuel Rowell (probably a step- or half brother); by Latecomers Samuel Blanchard and Ephraim Foster; Joseph Lovejoy (showing the division of the Lovejoy family on the issue); and by Joseph Robinson, Dane's son-in-law, the lion killer. Other key supporters were the Fryes, long-time holders of the retail liquor license: Deacon John Frye senior and the four Frye sons. The Fryes were unusual in that although they had begun as a North End Covenanter family, some of the brothers now lived in the South, some in the North. The tax list shows that after the separation of the South Parish, all the Frye families returned to the North Parish. Details of this case are included in Bailey (1880:66ff.) and may be found in ECQCR vols. xlvii:56, xlviii:74.

[18]The selectmen were Dudley Bradstreet, Henry Holt, Joseph Ballard, John Abbot, and Thomas Chandler. Thomas was the elder brother of William, head of the family and leading man of the South. Thomas and William were John Abbot's uncles, for his mother was their sister, Hannah Chandler. Holt and Ballard were brothers-in-law, Holt having married Ballard's sister. Holt was also brother-in-law to Thomas Johnson, Chandler's ally. Meanwhile, Ballard was married to Elizabeth Phelps, and the Phelps family in turn was closely tied affinally to the Chandlers. It was Elizabeth Phelps who would soon sicken and die precipitating the witchcraft crisis in Andover as Salem girls accused the old Scottish widow Ann Foster of bewitching her (Abbott n.d.: Holt, Allen, Phelps, Ballard).

relationships were, evidence seems to show that the old Chandler cluster had achieved town power. As for Bradstreet, who was unallied to either group by other ties, we cannot know why he supported Chandler. He may have genuinely thought Chandler a good innkeeper, or he may well have been on the side of Chandler as against Christopher Osgood. Or, since Thomas Chandler, William's brother, was Bradstreet's right-hand man in the town militia, Bradstreet may have wanted to show his support of this family. But Bradstreet was also connected by marriage to Jonathan Tyng, the very man in Boston who was in a position to favor Chandler's side in the Court, and who did do so. Tyng was the Council of Safety member who had signed Chandler's permission earlier in 1686. Marriage ties alone are no proof of favor; Bradstreet could have loathed his kinsman Tyng. Whatever the reasons and nature of the relationships, the North Enders lost and Chandler got his license.

Sometime in 1689 or early 1690 during the controversy over Chandler, the minister Francis Dane made a move that may not have helped his reputation. At the age of seventy-four, he married for the third time; this time his wife was Hannah Abbot, now a wealthy widow. She was the former Hannah Chandler, sister of William Chandler and thus Dane's own stepsister. Perhaps Dane should have heeded Cotton Mather's words about what happened to Dane's neighbor minister in Rowley, the redoubtable Ezekiel Rogers, when he married for the third time. "The closing days of Mr. Rogers were far from tranquil," says Essex County historian C. S. Jewett (1878:4). He draws on details of Mather's account. "That very night[of his marriage] a fire burnt his dwelling to the ground, with all the goods he had under his roof," he says, and one can almost imagine Mather's pursed lips as he writes. Rogers and his new wife survived the fire, but "his right arm was soon afterwards rendered useless by a fall from a horse," and finally "after a lingering illness" he died. As for Francis Dane, barely a year passed before he and his family were under accusation for witchcraft and one of his daughters on her way to prison.

Although Dane as minister had had no choice but to remain in the parsonage by the church in the North End, his old Hertfordshire companions, loosely gathered to emigrate fifty years ago, built on their old regional connections and became allies and in-laws, with their own new "country" in the South End of Andover. After some years of struggling with the initially dominant Southwesterners, the Hertfordshire group was now achieving something like a balance of power with them as evidenced first in their control of the ministry, then of the militia, finally in their growing control of town offices. In the process they had incorporated several of the Scottish families, whereas there were no marriages between Scots and

Southwesterners. The Chandler license controversy showed these old and new social identities of country and blood continuing to work out in town affairs as much as forty-five years after the founding of the town.

Blood, Country, and Witchcraft: 1690–1692

The controversy over the new meetinghouse, the struggle with the minister Dane, the liquor license quarrel, Hugh Stone's drunken murder of his wife—whatever the reaction of the townspeople to these events and issues, soon a far greater set of blows struck their town. In May of 1690, it was reported that Indians were on the move again. Captain Thomas Chandler was appointed commander of a company of militia drawn from several towns for the defense of the frontier along the south bank of the Merrimack. In August, Indians attacked Haverhill. Another son of Joseph Parker was killed. The end of 1690 brought a new crisis. Smallpox broke out, and again there was an association between affliction and the Scots families as the channel of the pox if not its source.

People believed smallpox to have come into the town with the Carrier family. When Martha (Allen) Carrier was accused and executed for witchcraft two years later, among the accusations was that she could bewitch people to death through the medium of smallpox without catching it herself. Again the theme of suspicion, of the malevolent cunning of Scottish and Old Briton families, emerges. A kinship connection existed between Martha and the minister Dane, although we do not know what the people thought about it. Martha was an Allen, daughter of Firstcomer Scot Andrew Allen. Her mother was an Ingalls, kin to the minister's first wife and presumably a Scot as well. Dane and his children were therefore uncle and cousins to the Allen and Carrier children.

Martha Allen had married the Welshman Thomas Carrier (alias Morgan in some records), about whom dramatic and troubling rumors circulated. Carrier was said to have been among the bodyguards of Charles the First, bodyguards who later became the king's actual executioners. He was said to have fled at the Restoration with other regicides to the colonies, where he moved from place to place in hiding from agents of the Crown (Abbott n.d.: Allen). No firm evidence for any of this exists, the genealogist points out, but true or not, such rumors about any man in the colony would cause misgivings in the post-Cromwellian mood of the Restoration.[19]

Carrier and his wife Martha had been living on the fringes of neighboring Billerica, where there was also a small Scots enclave (see Abbott n.d.:

---

[19]See Robbins (1869) for more on the regicides' escape to New England.

Foster). Martha's sister Mary also lived there, married to the mysterious Roger Toothacre who was later also arrested for witchcraft. The Carriers were unwelcome in Billerica, and so they went back to Andover where her mother, now the elderly widow Allen, was still living in the old homestead. The Carriers soon learned that they were not very welcome in Andover either, although they were not actually "warned out" (officially asked to leave town). It was believed that they were carrying smallpox, and the selectmen warned them and their families to be careful about their actions. The notice in the town records shows who was considered responsible for checking on them: two Allen brothers and Samuel Holt, Martha's brother-in-law, and one who as a Holt was both broker and connection to responsible citizenry.

> To Samuel Holt, Andrew Allen, and John Allen and To Walter Wright, Constable; "Whereas it has pleased God to visit those of the widow Allen's family which she hath taken into her house with that contagious disease the small-pox...(ATR, in Bailey 1880:202–203)

The Carriers were not to go to meeting or to anyone else's house. Nevertheless, the Allen family was decimated by the pox and six of them died in the four months from September to December 1690. But Martha Carrier herself and her own children remained unscathed. When she was arrested for witchcraft two years later, the first to be arrested in Andover, her sharp tongue, her reputation for malicious talk, and the fact that she and her own children had remained untouched by the pox made it easy for some to believe the accusations against her.

By now it should be very clear that, as I said in the introductory chapter, the crisis year of the witchcraft did not burst out of the blue into the peaceful village life of Andover. The statement by the selectmen at the opening town meeting of the year, just before the crisis was actually under way, makes it clear that they also knew all was not well in their town either, especially with their young people.

> And whereas there is grievous complaints of great prophaneness of the Sabbath, both in the time of exercise and noon time, to the great dishonor of God, scandal of religion & the grief of many serious christians, by young persons, we order & require the tything men & constables to take care to prevent such great & shameful miscarriages, which are so much observed and complained of. (ATR, in Bailey 1880:413)

The tythingmen and constables soon had their hands full of even more scandal, grief, and "great & shameful miscarriages." Joseph Ballard was one of the constables for the South End. In May of 1692, Ballard was the one who served the warrant on Martha Carrier, and took her to Salem prison. In July, Ballard decided that the cause of his own wife's long wasting illness might be witchcraft. Accordingly, he called for the two girls of Salem Village who were then in high repute as identifiers of witches to come to Andover. They identified Ann Foster, an elderly widow also living in the Scottish neighborhood near Ballard. She was one whose experience, behavior, and speech, as well as her Scottish blood, had put her in a marginal state already. She was the mother of Hannah Stone, (the woman who had been murdered by her husband three years earlier). Ann Foster like many of the women involved in the witch crisis had experienced deep trauma followed by deep melancholy in the sudden or difficult death of a child. Her pitiable condition apparently aroused little pity in the magistrates. Foster was found guilty and jailed at Salem, but died in jail before she could be executed. Her daughter and granddaughter, Mary Lacey and Mary Lacey Junior, were also among the accused witches.

Over forty people were accused in Andover by the time it was over. Accusations began against the marginal, such as Scots women Martha Allen Carrier and Ann Foster, and ended with accusations against the wives of leading men like John Osgood and John Frye. Hansen (1983) has pointed out that the evidence from Andover is too fragmentary as to who accused whom to allow very firm conclusions, but much more remains to be done with what is available. The Foster, Lacey, Allen, and Carrier families, and those from other known Scots or Scot-related families make up more than twenty-five percent of those who were accused in Andover and Boxford. If those others are counted in, whom I designated as among the "Old Britons" or Borderers, the Celtic fringe of non-English people, they together with the known Scots would account for well over half of the accused. But a number of them would be found among the *accusers* as well. Many of the accusers came out of the other Old Briton enclave, the Tylers, Spragues, and Bridges, living in the marginal area of Boxford in the North end of town. Finally, if the minister Dane was a Scot, or was believed to be of Scottish background, the eight accused members of his family would be also included in this list.

My point here has not been to detail the cases chronologically, or to map the course of the crisis year in Andover, or to do a systematic comparison with Salem. Many studies have now begun to do just that. Rather, I wished to point out certain unexplored aspects of the early stages of the crisis in Andover having to do with the social identities that people had in their relations with each other. Categories such as those they called *country* and *blood* were terms for classifying each other that were emically most relevant to them.[20] Whatever else was the case spiritually, the conflict also correlated in part with the struggle throughout the early New England community with its many dimensions of ethnicity and regionality, brought with them from the old world.

The Town Divides: 1692–1710

Fifteen years after the witchcraft crisis, the parish split was complete. In the next chapter, on the aftermath, I will note the details of some of the marriages made by those who had been children at the time of the crisis. In this section I look at some of the immediate details. Andover was now to be officially divided in two parts, no longer called ends, but parishes, also precincts. The underlying social composition of each parish was made up of the second- and third-generation descendants and remnants of those old companies that had been recruited by Nathaniel Ward for the move in the first place. Within each parish, an order of family rank had emerged for the central social orders: the civil, the ecclesiastical, and the military. The two parts of Andover were now in a new position to work out themes of cooperation and competition. This they began to do during the next phase of Andover's history, until the onset of the Revolutionary War which in turn brought about new alignments until the next point when the parishes became towns in 1855. That story remains to be told. In this next section I look at the final phase of the parish split.[21]

The death of Francis Dane

Francis Dane did not long survive the traumatic events of 1692, no surprise in that he was not well anyway, he had been implicated, and three of his close family members accused. He died in 1697 after fifty years in office. The role of Dane as a personality in Andover seems to have been complex and pivotal, but there is unfortunately little surviving information about him or from him. Affiliated with the Scots, and with the Hertford segment of the South Enders by regional background, kinship,

---

[20]Demos (1982:71) doubts the role of ethnicity in his study of the witchcraft cases prior to 1692. However, Cedric Cowing, a colonial historian, has said that in his analysis the British regional background issue in Salem was far more crucial in the witchcraft crisis there than has previously been proposed (personal communication, 1989; see also Cowing 1995).

[21]For chronological sequence here I draw upon the materials reprinted in Bailey (1880:427ff.) on the marriage records of the families and on Mooar's history of the South Parish (Mooar 1859).

and marriage ties, he nevertheless had to live out his days in the parsonage in the North End. But with his roots and connections in Hertforshire, he was never the North's man as the Southwesterner Woodbridge had been. Dane's third marriage, in his old age, was to a woman with whom he shared not only old Hertfordshire roots in Bishops Stortford, but more immediate family connections. This was Hannah Chandler, the widow of George Abbot. She was also Dane's stepsister, although they were of such an age that it is hard to know what people might have thought of their marriage. Dane continued living in the North End parsonage after this marriage. In the next generation of his family, one of his two sons stayed on in the North End, while the other moved to the South where the other Hertfordshire families and all the Chandlers and Abbots were.

When the minister died, the last human symbol of Andover as a unified company or body of believers was gone. After this the South began its petitioning in earnest to break away. I do not doubt there was more than coincidence between Dane's death and the press of the South End for separation. Even as an old man and despite his problems with the town, Dane had been structurally still its head, symbol of the old 1640s ideal of unity. Like the Lady Arbella for the passengers on the Winthrop Fleet (see Winthrop's entry for April 23, 1630, p. 43 in chapter 2), Dane had filled a position that provided a focus for unity for disparate elements. Once he was gone, those disparate segments were cut loose at the top, as it were, to fission again. Recall the words of George Phillips in 1636:

> ...a company without a head cannot well sway and guide itself but is subject to many errors, distractions, confusions and what not...dangerous to the cause of religion, dismal to the Common state...and a disturbance to the Church estate.... (MHS 1931, vol. iii:241–242)

Dane was among the last remaining people from the very earliest days of Andover. All the other Firstcomers were gone except Simon Bradstreet, long gone from Andover, and he too died in 1697, a month after Dane. Although Bradstreet had not lived in Andover since the 1670s, he and Dane, as town gentry and minister, had once represented the peak period of the unified social order under the old Winthropian vision.

The new meetinghouse: the controversy renewed

With the passing of Dane, the town could now proceed to divide. It was not, however, easily done in Andover, nor was it easy for the other towns wrestling with their internal factions at this time. The provincial government seemed to have no working policy for facilitating town division. In

Andover the catalyst was once again the need for a new meetinghouse. Bailey (1880:426–429) records the series of decisions and delays with selections from the town and Court records, from which I summarize the following account. I also include Bailey's archival references.

Thomas Barnard had come in as Dane's young assistant and was now the head pastor. The town first voted to improve his housing by adding a "lean-to" probably to shelter firewood. In 1705, the town met and voted to build "a new meeting-house as sufficient and convenient for the whole town as may be." No work was begun, however. The last recorded new meetinghouse had been in 1680; there had been talk of rebuilding and relocating it then, but to no avail. All of the town selectmen were North Enders, who in those days still controlled the town and had the greatest say in matters. But by 1707, when the discussion about a new meetinghouse came up again, the political and economic power had shifted significantly as the tax records show (see appendix D). Again the town voted to build a meetinghouse "for the inhabitants of Andover of the following dimensions, viz: of sixty-foot long and forty-foot wide and twenty-foot stud and with a flat roofe." The South End had achieved a voting majority, and there were now selectmen from the South. Having a strong representation and, they thought, good reason, they requested that the new location be more convenient for the residents of the South End. That request meant building nearer the Shawsheen River, for by then, the South End had expanded to the Shawsheen and beyond and was as populous as the original Cochichawick center.

The new location they proposed was near the Holt property, at a place known as "Holt's Tree." Dissension began at once, but then a distraction arose. The parsonage itself burned in 1707. The town had to give its attention and resources to providing a new home for the Barnard family. Meanwhile they were to be "settled" in "some convenient house" while the new house was built. The meetinghouse relocation question then came up again. John Aslebe, selectman from the North and in control of much of the land at the old town center around the meetinghouse (see map 9), seems to have been the one who thwarted attempts at compromise. Moving the location nearer to the South End would mean that the newly built parsonage and the proposed meetinghouse would not be near each other. Again, a stalemate.

North Enders Samuel Osgood and James Bridges (the latter probably representing the West Boxford faction) sent a petition to the Court proposing that one new meetinghouse be built for the town as a whole for the next ten years at the present location, and after that two meetinghouses be built. At this point Aslebe relented and agreed to consider a new location more suitable to the South Enders.[22] The wording of the record reveals the leaders and the intensity of the search for a solution at a key meeting: "At this meeting Lt. Aslebe, one of the chiefs of *the dissenting party* [my italics] and a petitioner in their behalfs did then at this meeting soon after this vote had passed declare himself with the reaching forth of his hand and say, My brethren, I will freely meet you at this place" (Mass. Archives 11:253). The place referred to by Aslebe was the proposed compromise location near Holt's Tree. However, despite this meeting no agreement was reached on the Holt's Tree proposal.

Note that it was Christopher Osgood, the town clerk from the South End who recorded the above incident. In his view the North was "the dissenting party," which is a classic example of the use of language of social identity. No doubt the North saw the South as the dissenters. Control of the entire board of selectmen had passed that year for the first time in Andover's history into the hands of the South End. Sheer numbers had prevailed, and the South had grown enough to outvote the North. The tax records for the year 1707 show that there were now seventy-seven polls listed for the North End, and ninety-five for the South (see appendix D). The South, now in the position of strength, could well view the North as dissenters. The South End's emergent leader, Christopher Osgood, epitomized the shift in social control. He had come to Andover from Ipswich as a seven-year-old, the stepson of one of the marginal settlers who had married his widowed mother. As far as genealogists can tell he was no kin to the John Osgood Firstcomer and North End family that dominated town affairs for so long. Yet Christopher (perhaps even in reaction to the confusion over his name) grew up to become a leader in the other end of town and in the county as well, elected as selectman, town clerk, and Representative to Court. Not only that, he became captain of Andover's militia.

The other three selectmen, all South Enders, were Francis Dane Jr., John Chandler, and George Abbot. These men were now the second generation of those three families in New England. They were all descendants of the loosely-allied company of immigrants from Bishops Stortford in Hertfordshire, followers of their countryman, the Rev. John Norton, to

---

[22]Whatever his reasons for softening at this point, why should Aslebe have been so firm in his resistance earlier? Aslebe came to Andover as a son-in-law of John Osgood. Not a Newburyite, not a Covenanter, not a Hampshire or Wiltshire man, Aslebe had gained his place in the North End through marriage (Abbott n.d.: Aslebe, or Aslett). Yet he must have been disappointed as he realized he would be the last of his name in Andover, for he turned out to have no sons. Aslebe appears to have turned his energy and wealth to buying up much of the property around the old town center (see the Rockwell Maps for 1700 and 1710 in the Andover Historical Society). Without being able to specify precisely how, I suggest that these facts may point to a tenacity on Aslebe's part to keep himself near the center of the social position he had attained, by keeping physical control of the meetinghouse location.

the Bay Colony sixty years earlier. Now they were closely intermarried, and their homes were built on neighboring properties. The Hertfordshire contingent and their in-laws made up the core of the growing South End. Finally, they had overturned the North End's political domination and been elected to all the civic offices of the town.

Additional genealogical analysis shows that in the South End as in the North, the old ties of country, blood, and company still persisted over against the new geographical proximities. Within the South End there were two dominant groups, the Hertfordshire families and the primarily Old Briton and Scot families clustered around Christopher Osgood and married to his many daughters. They worked together politically, but their children did not intermarry for several more generations. Beyond noting background differences, it is impossible to say for certain why that was. But for one thing, Osgood had few male heirs. Although he had four wives and thirteen children, only three were boys, all of whom left town when they married. He alone dominated his family group. Perhaps the very lack of male strength in his "clan" made it both necessary and possible for him and the Hertfordshire families, who were strong in male heirs, to coexist and cooperate against the North End (see Waters [1982] for a comparison of the careers of families in Guilford, Connecticut, on the basis of relative male strength).[23]

In 1709, the problem of the church at Andover was still not settled. With Christopher Osgood again as Representative to Court, a committee from the Court came to Andover and convened a meeting to hear out both sides. The committee members found that there was still no possibility of compromise and agreed that the town must be divided into two parishes, also called precincts in some documents (the term for them as a civil division). They ordered each parish to have its own minister and meetinghouse. Barnard, the present minister, was to have his choice of which parish he wanted. Construction was begun on a replacement meetinghouse for the North.

Meanwhile the people of the newly created South Parish also began to build their new meetinghouse. It was to be "by the rock on the West side of Rogers Brook" several miles away from the former proposed site at Holt's Tree, and nearer the Shawsheen River (map 10). It was thus nearer the South's population center. In May 1709 the South Parish was at last incorporated and the building was first used in 1710.

---

[23]During this period the South almost achieved parity with the North. But the South never could attain Old Covenanter status. Surpassing the North in that dimension remained forever impossible. By the end of the century, however, the South would develop a status of its own through its famous educational institutions, Phillips Andover Academy and the Andover Seminary.

The new arrangement inevitably meant that some families were on the borderline between the parish borders and would have to choose which side they wanted. Worse, some were expected to be a part of the new South Precinct but really did not want to be. In February of 1709 the minister Barnard wrote to the Governor, showing his sympathies with the North. He said that some people were being compelled to pay rates to the South who would prefer to pay to his church. It was in this letter also that Barnard made his complaint on behalf of the entire North Parish, a famous quote in Andover lore: "The north part of town that was the first settlement are dissatisfied that they are now made the lesser part." Although this is the only portion that Bailey cites, the letter in its entirety shows that Barnard was very concerned that a situation of "perpetual discontent" was brewing in the town if the people were "compelled to do that which is inconvenient to them," especially those who lived on one side or the other of the parish boundaries. Barnard begged the Governor to intervene and revealed that he was not only caught in the middle, but had not been paid any salary for some time (Mass. Archives vol. li:183 in Bailey 1880:429. See appendix C for the complete text of Barnard's letter).

Accordingly, in October 1709, those who said they did not want to be part of the new parish sent a petition to the Court. These men owned lands that ran up and down the length of the new boundary. Kinship and other ties may have played a part here, for in particular, it was John Stevens and John Lovejoy who headed this petition. The first Lovejoy had come as bondservant to the first Stevens. The families had intermarried as Lovejoy was allowed to marry one of the younger Stevens daughters. Some were still living near each other since the days of the master-servant relationship of their forebears; now they were allies on the petition. They and the other petitioners gave two main reasons for their wish to stay with the North Parish. First, it would be too far to go to the proposed new South Parish meetinghouse; second, it would be "too hard to leave the minister," that is, Mr. Barnard. Barnard was also related by his marriage to the Stevens. In general, those on the border wanted to remain part of the North Parish where their old roots lay. This petition was granted and the signers did not have to pay their taxes to the South Parish. That same month, the North Parish, assured of thirteen members back in their fold, voted to build a new meetinghouse (NPCR 1709).

Meanwhile, Barnard had still not yet given his decision as to which parish he would choose. To the townspeople there must have been little question as to what his choice would be. But by November he still had not officially announced it, and the South Parish petitioned the Court to direct him to choose. Evidence of the seriousness of the situation is seen in the number of meetings and petitionings taking place well into December, into the wintertime when people tried to make do with as few trips and public meetings as possible. The Court told Barnard that he must decide by December 11.

On December 10, however, the day *before* Barnard's decision was due, the South Parish met and voted unanimously that "Mr Samuel Phillips shall be our Pastor" (quoted in Abbot 1829:84). One has no way of interpreting the last-minute timing of the announcement. Was it a pro- or anti-Barnard action? Did the South announce its choice ahead of the deadline to save Barnard from having to choose publicly, or is it possible that in the end he was veering towards choosing the South, which really did not want him? And what was the new minister Phillips' perceived connection with the South, if any? In the next chapter, the social composition of the new parishes and the early career of Phillips will be discussed.

It seems clear that the South, in their choice of Phillips, was looking to make a fresh start. Here was a new parish, a new meetinghouse, a new covenant, a new minister, and a new threshold situation. Phillips was descended from an established if atypical line of New England ministers. He was a great-grandson of George Phillips, who had come with Winthrop and been the first minister at Watertown (see Winthrop 1908 vol.i:71 for the early debate between Boston ministers and Phillips). Who his particular supporters in the South Parish might have been is not clear. The records do not say. But Phillips had grown up in the neighboring town of Rowley, son of the minister who had succeeded the redoubtable Ezekiel Rogers. He would have been well known to the Andover church. Furthermore, his father was known to have taken a strong stand in Rowley during the witchcraft crisis year *against* the unquestioned acceptance of accusations from "afflicted" children (see Weisman 1984:162). This background may have appealed to South End parishioners looking for a man who would be representative of the new order in the post-crisis ministry.

Phillips had no kin ties or previous associations with any South Parish families as far as I can determine. But soon after his move to the South Parish, his younger sister was married to the son of a leading parishioner. Whether a "motion of marriage" between the two families was already in the air, or whether the acquaintance was made after Phillips' move is not clear. In any case, there appears once again, as with the three previous ministers at Andover, the pattern of ecclesiastical overlap with socio-economic elite as the minister establishes a relationship by marriage with a dominant parish family.

On December 12, 1710, the South Parish declared a day of fasting and prayer for the settling of the minister, and sometime in 1711 he arrived. On October 11, 1711, he was ordained at a regional convocation.

> [T]he new Covenant was publically read and consented to and they were therefore declared to be a church; and Mr Samuel Phillips was at their desire ordained their Pastor by the Rev Mr Thomas Barnard of Andover, Mr Edward Payson of Rowley, Mr Joseph Green of Salem Village, and Mr Thomas Symmes of Bradford. (Abbot 1829:84)

Significantly, a "new Covenant" was read. This will be taken up in the next chapter. Significantly also, but not surprisingly, the disgruntled Reverend Barnard from the North Parish is the first mentioned among the clergy conducting Phillips' ordination along with the ministers from the neighboring towns.[24] But perhaps even more significant in this case was the presence of Joseph Green, who had been the new minister at Salem Village for several years at this point. Salem Village and Andover had been the two towns that had borne the brunt of the witchcraft crisis. Green had been able to reconcile the deep divisions in Salem (see Boyer and Nissenbaum's "Epilogue," 1974:217-221). Perhaps on that October day in 1711 he took the new South Parish minister aside for some pastoral advice as Phillips, only twenty-one years old and fresh out of Harvard College, began the work of ministering to a similarly wounded congregation.

---

[24]Puritan ordination reflected their logic (see Miller 1961 [1939]:116ff. on the Puritans and the logic of Ramus) that ordination was a rite of relations, which must go with a man's call and commencement of work at a particular church. Ordination was to be performed in that context. As the pattern of the ceremonial year developed in the early Bay Colony, ordinations became the main ceremonial events that brought together people above the town level. They promoted regional spirit and connections, and as such must have been great occasions for travel, visiting, feasting, and all the rest of the social occasions that would have surrounded such an event. A rough check of the timing of several ordinations over the years shows that they took place in spring or autumn, to take advantage of weather and work loads. An autumn ordination such as this would have combined with the firstfruits, the harvest, for a doubly festive time. Visitors came from surrounding towns. Each visiting pastor was assigned a role in the ritual: one gave the sermon, one gave the charge, one gave the prayer, one the "right hand of fellowship," and all participated in the laying on of hands. Puritan ritual life is discussed by Walsh (1979) and Gildrie (1982).

7

"As Bees When the Hive Is Too Full"
The Aftermath of the Parish Split

> When a church shall grow too numerous, it is a way and a fit season to propagate one church out of another, by sending forth such of their members as are willing to remove, and to procure some officers to them...as bees when the hive is too full issue out by swarms and are gathered into other hives... (The Cambridge Platform of 1648)[1]

In 1711, the newly incorporated South Parish of Andover finally held its first service, in its own meetinghouse, with its own minister, Samuel Phillips, fresh out of Harvard, great-grandson of George Phillips who had sailed with Winthrop and been first minister at Watertown. But as the story in the preceding chapters has shown, the new parish hardly seemed like the outcome of the natural hiving-off process metaphorically evoked by the ministers who drew up the Cambridge Platform in the hopeful early days of the Bay Colony (see chapter 3). Rather, the process leading to the two parishes had taken ten years of acrimonious petitioning and counter-petitioning between the dominant old Covenanter families and the rising new order that wanted to establish a new South Parish. The split had divided the original group along fission lines both old and new. Some went back to British regional and ethnic social identities, the old ties of country and blood that had been present even before the migrating groups gathered into their companies for the move. Then there were the new allegiances, and enmities, that had formed over time as the settlers worked out issues of land, settlement, cooperation, conflict, and crisis. For the rising population of those had been born in the colony, the old

---

[1]Reprinted in Vaughan 1972.

loyalties to the blood, country, and company of their parents and grandparents began to fade as a factor in their own lives and actions.

Splits similar to the one at Andover had occurred in several of the early Massachusetts settlements by the end of the seventeenth century. Each had its particular story but all were the local outcomes of long chains of larger colony and transatlantic events. The fall of Cromwell's republic followed by the policies of the Restoration brought to an end the Puritan hegemony. The Bay Colony became part of a reorganized single New England Province, ordered by the Crown to combine, however reluctantly, with the neighboring colonies. The original vision of the Puritan founders was that town and church were to be one; civil government was to be at every level "the setting and support of the church" as Eggleston put it (1896:212). But the royal decree of 1691 put a legal end to all that. When the terrible events of 1692 began to unfold, they seemed to some people the tragic culmination of a wrong-headed social experiment. Others continued to interpret events in various ways, as God's chastening work, or as diabolical acts making use of Indian as well as other human and nonhuman agents. In any case, the conflicted fissioning of towns like Andover did not seem to follow the natural manner of wild bees issuing forth as envisioned by the authors of the Cambridge Platform.

There is still much for the next generation of scholars to learn about the social dynamics of this fissioning process in Andover. Although Philip Greven uncovered its broad trends by treating the population as a more or less homogeneous unit, he had to leave out the cut and thrust of town factions and fissions to do it. A major theme of this book has been to take a different view of Andover's early history by focusing instead on the history of those factions and fissions, on the shifting language of social identity used by colonists, and on the way transplanted segments of British families struggled to establish an early colonial settlement like Andover during its first seventy or so years. In this chapter I want to sharpen and summarize certain points that emerged in taking this approach and point to directions for further research. I will focus particularly on the new South Parish in the aftermath of the parish split. Again, as in chapter 5, I use marriage records, which provide some of the most accessible and intriguing insights into the families of the new parish and their alliances.

Marriage and Social Crisis: Greven Revisited

At this point I want to return to the question of why Philip Greven's study and mine resulted in such different pictures of early Andover. In chapter 5, I contrasted my approach and findings to Greven's with regard to the analysis of marriage, particularly town endogamy and exogamy, that is, whether people marry in or out of their town. In that chapter I showed that using Andoverites' own social categories as units of analysis illuminates Greven's general demographic findings regarding exogamy. With those emic social categories in mind, looking at the families behind the figures for town exogamy, it turned out that it was children of the Covenanters who married out much more frequently than did those of non-Covenanters. In fact Andover Covenanter children often married with children of other Covenanter first families in nearby towns. The category of Covenanter or Firstcomer family had become (and in some cases remains) a social status identity among the Bay Colony towns. It was no surprise, in fact inevitable, that some category of social identity must emerge to replicate the structure of social ranking brought from England. The Covenanters, first as an ecclesiastical and then as a social elite, filled the slot as rising colony gentry. In the emerging new social structure, only a few marriage choices would be available in a region of neighboring towns for families of this status. Fewer choices still were available within their own towns.

Furthermore, certain subcategories within the Firstcomer group in Andover followed particular marriage patterns. People from the same country in Britain tended at first to stay together in Andover as in other colony towns. As the children of the founding generation began to marry, they tended to marry at first with those from the same regional background. They also tended to marry with those of the same ethnicity, or blood, and within that category certain families married blood kin. Andover Covenanters with roots in the north of Britain were more likely to marry kinsmen than were Covenanters from the southwest. Kin or not, Covenanter descendants from these two regions were unlikely to marry with someone from the other region until the first and even second generation had passed. This pattern matched that of the old country. Close-kin marriage was practiced far less in the southwest than in the north of England. The mother country itself was unsettled in its marriage law in the seventeenth century and the matter of cousin marriage and what the Bay Colony's law should be was debated by the colonists as well.

The analysis in chapter 5 was in a sense a static analysis, the focus being on marriage patterns of families in terms of social identities such as Covenanters and non-Covenanters, Southwesterners and Northerners, Scots and Old Britons. But a dynamic perspective on family marriage histories opens up the impact of cumulative historical events on various families.² This impact of events on certain families was not in focus for Greven. But it would not be, given his choice of the generation as a unit of analysis,³ his choice of the demographic method with its pressure for homogeneity of categories, and his decision to consider marriage as primarily biological "getting a mate" rather than a social act.

Greven noted (1970:122) that "it was simpler to demonstrate...than explain" the puzzling changes in marriage patterns in Andover that started at about 1700. I will summarize certain of his findings and offer an explanation. Greven charted the residential origin of over eight hundred people, showing them in groups by date of marriage for three time periods from 1650 to 1749 (his table 26, p. 211). He found that during the years 1700 to 1719 both men and women married other Andoverites in much higher proportion than in the period either before or after. Looking just at the proportion of women who married outsiders, the figure is markedly lower for those years. Only nine women (6%) married outside Andover between 1700 and 1719. But before that, from 1650 to 1699, thirty (18.5%) married outside. And after that, from 1720 to 1747, one hundred twenty-six (28.6%) married outside, the figure showing a town population spurt as well.

Greven does not give a clear explanation for choosing three unequal time frames. Nevertheless, why did so few women marry out during the 1700 to 1719 period? Greven takes up the question:

> Perhaps the higher proportion of men who married outside the town than women who did so during the period between 1700 and 1719 accounts for the increased delays in the marriages for many women during this period, but it is almost impossible to be sure. All that is certain is the fact of the increased average age. Beyond that, the dearth of evidence forces the researcher to speculate (p. 123).

Later he suggests that the increased proportion of women marrying outsiders after 1720 "quite probably reflects the outward mobility of substantial percentages of third- and fourth-generation men and the

---

²I am indebted to Kenneth L. Pike for many teachings, one being his emphasis on learning to move easily between what he called static, dynamic, and relational (or in an analogy with physics: particle, wave, and field) perspectives on phenomena (Pike 1972 [1959]).

³The generation was not yet in this early period a significant emic native social category judging from the texts of the time. With neither a clear relation to a domain in the native's mind, nor a clear analytical definition given to the term by Greven, the generation has no focus as a unit of analysis. But it became a very significant native social category in later New England society. I have discussed the shift from genealogical reckoning displayed by "house" in earlier formats of New England family genealogists, to display by "generation" found in later ones (Abbot 1971:7–10).

concomitant influx of men from outside Andover into the community" (pp. 210–211).

Two problems arise from Greven's approach. One already mentioned in chapter 5 comes from his decision to set aside his excellent dissertation research on the regional backgrounds and social distinctions in Andover society. So, in his book, he did not use those distinctions to see what they might have meant to the people themselves in terms of marriage choice. He treated marriage as if it could be explained in primarily biological and demographic terms, and not as social choice. Greven's other serious problem arose from his resolute dismissal from consideration of how the social trauma of Andover's witchcraft crisis might have affected its townspeople's subsequent behavior, marriage or otherwise. This decision of Greven's seems to be a consequence of the particular viewpoint that informed historical demography in the 1960s and 1970s. As he explained in his introduction, his generation of historians was both initiating a search for the deep slow social trends which can only be found by considering large groups demographically, and also reacting against historicism, or history treated as a *story*. Now the discipline has come full circle, and the story is back in history again.

I will briefly comment again, with examples, on the view of the nature of marriage that becomes detached from the social realities of the people themselves. Here is an instance of how that viewpoint influenced Greven's analysis of endogamous marriage in his 1700–1719 time period. He is wondering why so many more Andover people married other Andoverites during that time. By Greven's count there were, he says, "about the same number of male and female young adults" making up the third generation in Andover. Therefore, "the general ratio of men to women in the community, measured by births and by surviving children among these particular Andover families, was sufficiently close to have provided a husband for most of the women choosing to marry" (Greven 1970:122). But—and this is the crucial consideration—marriage is not simply a matter of "a husband" being available for a woman "choosing to marry." Nor should changes in rates of town endogamy be interpreted as chiefly a function of the changing ratio of males to females of the right age in town at the same time. A marriage (whatever else is involved) is a complex social choice. Most families (with exceptions, of course) were concerned to make a *match*, not just find a mate, for their children. Sheer availability no doubt influenced mate selection upon occasion in the colony, and surely many non-negotiated and carelessly made marriages took place. But on the whole it is clear that colonial families were much involved in finding spouses for their children according to criteria that were relevant to them and their identities in the new society. At first, those decisions probably reflected custom in their British home regions. Then the new social order of the colony began to establish its own customs.

This situation can be illustrated by separating out and looking at the incidences of cousin marriages. After 1695 in Andover, there was a sharp rise in the number of marriages of first cousins, or in the colonists' term, *cousins-german*. Among the marriages in the twenty-five-year period from 1695 to 1720, twenty-eight people married their first cousins, compared to only eight during the fifty years previous. First point, it was in 1695 that the New England clergy settled the issue of whether cousin marriage would be permissible: the answer was yes, on biblical precedent. But again, this ruling does not explain everything nor is the mere count of cousin marriages very revealing. The percentage of kin marriages, their distribution by families, and the social and regional backgrounds of the families reveal more significance. Twenty of the twenty-eight cousin marriages were in the South Parish, only eight in the North. Sixteen of the twenty took place among the descendants of two cousin marriages of the earlier period. Certain families, particularly the Holts and Farnums, who lived on neighboring lands, carried on a tradition of cousin marriages begun years before by the previous generations. Possibly for them, cousin marriages became important for strengthening family alliances, in turn connected with establishing and holding on to territory. Why did the South Enders tend to marry cousins so much more frequently than the North Enders during this time? What else does it correlate with, in the absence of any explanation left to us by them? For one thing, the South End and later South Parish families were those linked to Hertfordshire, to the Scots, and to other Old Britons, where British regional tradition was accepting of cousin marriage. In contrast, most of the families remaining in the North Parish had been of southwestern origin in a particular region of England, where Catholic influence had long restricted cousin marriage.

It seems a bit strange for an anthropologist to chide a historian for not paying enough attention to history, but it is after all the historical particulars that shed light on the figures for the marriages of Andoverites in the 1700–1719 period, the figures that Greven found puzzling. Greven noted a strong tendency for young women and men from Andover to marry each other in the first two decades of the 1700s, followed by a period of higher incidence of out-marriage after 1720. This situation looks to me like one of the after-effects of the witchcraft crisis that the townspeople had just endured. That is, there seems to be a close connection between the events of 1692, which had deeply affected everyone, but certain families especially, and the marriages made by the children of these very families as they reached adulthood and married in the early 1700s. A research project along these lines on all the families involved awaits some other student of the aftermath of the witchcraft crisis, but I will illustrate my point here with one family in particular, that of the minister Francis Dane (Abbott n.d.: Dane).

According to the story as summarized in chapter 6, the Dane family was one of those deeply affected by the witchcraft crisis, its women most directly. Though never directly accused, the minister himself had been implicated early in the crisis by the old Scottish widow Ann Foster, who said she saw a "man with gray hair" at the meeting of the Salem coven. This "sighting" was apparently quickly linked by frightened (and disgruntled anyway?) townspeople to Dane (see Boyer and Nissenbaum 1972 vol. 2:341–344). Dane had already shown his doubts about the admissibility of spectral evidence (see also Owen's 1982 discussion of this issue in the trials). Dane himself was never directly accused, but two of his daughters, two young granddaughters, and a daughter-in-law were accused. His daughter Abigail would have been hanged had she not been pregnant and thus exempt by law from execution. So the question arises, what happened to the Dane family in the period following the crisis? Dane himself died a few years later. He had twenty grandchildren, all of whom married between the years 1694 and 1726. These marriages are of great interest as many of them occurred during the years of the sharply increased frequency in town endogamy, especially among women, the situation that puzzled Greven.

The Dane family's marriage histories parallel the general figures for town endogamy and exogamy that Greven discovered during this period. Of the minister's twenty grandchildren as a group, significantly more (fourteen, or 70 percent) married in town rather than out. But what is of particular interest are the following facts. Of the six in-marrying grandsons of Dane, four married accused women or daughters of accused women. Of the eight in-marrying granddaughters, *all* married men from families involved in the witchcraft crisis. Five of them married men whose immediate family relative (mother, grandmother, or sister) had been accused; two of these marriages were also with cousins. The other three Dane granddaughters married sons of those who had been accusers. In fact, Hannah Dane married the son of the woman who had accused her aunt Abigail. Three Dane grandsons and three granddaughters did marry out of Andover, but even there it is important to look more closely at the choices. Of the three grandsons, no information is at hand. But of the granddaughters, one of them married the son (or grandson) of Rebecca Nurse, one of the Salem women who had been accused and hanged in 1692.

In sum, then, nine of the fourteen Dane grandchildren who married in Andover married children of other Andover families who had been closely involved in the crisis. Of three Dane out-marriages, one was with a Salem family that had been involved. These examples seem more than coincidental. Families of lower social status than the Danes who were involved in the witchcraft, such as the Wardwells and the Hawkes, also showed a strong tendency to marry with each other in the next generation (see Abbott n.d.: Wardwell). One cannot tell from the bare records what drives marriage choice. Were Andover families of all social ranks that had been involved in the witchcraft crisis now anathema to the neighboring townspeople as marriage choices? Or, did the children of those families who had been involved prefer to marry with others who had in some way shared the terrible affliction? Although such questions can never be satisfactorily answered, the point to draw from these considerations is that marriage choice is more than a matter of finding an available mate in the right age range.

Much work has been done on the witchcraft crisis in Salem, and more research is now available on Andover for comparison. For the long-term impact in Andover's story, more systematic studies are needed of marriage histories of other affected families and towns and of particular lines within families according to their experience in the witchcraft crisis. More also remains to be done on the less gripping but nonetheless crucial years following, as families recovered from the crisis and people of subsequent generations had to take their stands on what it meant to be descended from the various principal actors in this fundamental American epic. Descendants of some families continued for years to commemorate (if not venerate) the ancestors' roles in the crisis, as does the whole town of Salem to this day.[4] But in Andover no such commemorations took place nor has a witchcraft cottage industry like Salem's developed. In fact, for many years few students of the witch panic of 1692 realized that more were accused at Andover than at Salem.

Samuel Phillips and the New South Parish

Events of 1692 hastened the push to complete the parish split, I would say, but there is nothing specific in the records about that. In any case,

---

[4]See the account by Charlotte Helen Abbott in the *Andover Townsman* of the annual Hawkes/Wardwell family reunions, being held at least 200 years after the events of 1692, and open to anyone who could trace descent through either male or female lines to the accused ancestors, referred to now as "the Martyrs" (Abbott 1904).

following the split, the two parts of Andover were no longer called its *ends* in the records but instead either its *parishes* or *precincts,* depending on whether the record-keeper had the ecclesiastical or civil order in mind. It is important to note again that what had been formerly called the South End was now geographically part of the North Parish. However, many of the original South End families had sold their properties to Latecomers, or to children or grandchildren of Firstcomers, and moved over to their outlying lands in what was now the South Parish. The new division would cut differently through the two aspects of Andover's former structure, Andover as church and Andover as town. While there were now two parishes, each with its own meetinghouse, there was still one town government. For each resident family and for the local institutions the new dual structure of Andover had different consequences, and it meant a particular reordering problem for relationships and action.

Once the court had given its permission for the town to divide into parishes, Thomas Barnard had to make his decision. In the end he decided to stay on as minister in the North Parish, not that there had been much doubt about it. Sarah Loring Bailey, Andover's nineteenth-century resident historian whose compilation I have drawn upon many times here, gives few details of the parish split. As mentioned earlier, she quotes only one sentence from Barnard's 1710 letter of complaint to the Court: "The north part of town that was the first settlement are dissatisfied that they are now made the lesser part." (See Bailey 1880:429. The letter is reprinted in full in appendix C.)

Bailey does not go on in her town history to follow many events in the South Parish. She was, after all, a North Andover native. Her father had been the minister of the North Parish (which by her day had become Unitarian), and she had lived as a child in the very parsonage where Thomas Barnard had lived. As Bailey describes it, the North Parish "lost" eighty freeholders and thirty-five church members to the new Parish (ibid.). Her choice of verb suggests that even a century and a half later, old-timers in the North continued to view the expanding South Parish not as a "new hive" of their own bees, but as a continuing reminder of competition and loss. Joint history in Andover was at an end. For South Parish details one must now go to the South Parish's local historians (Abbot 1829; Mooar 1859). By Bailey's time, the two parishes had already become separate townships, but even then the South Parish was able to take the name Andover for itself while the old town had to make do with the seemingly "lesser part" name of North Andover.

Although there were two parishes now, each with its own minister, Andover was still one town with one set of selectmen in charge of the civil leadership. The struggle of the Andover parishes to disentangle church and town, if not religion and politics, was a microcosm of that continuing issue in New England, if not American, public life. From the perspective of Andover as a town, the official division of 1710 into precincts marked a territorial and economic split that had already taken place *de facto* many years earlier. From the perspective of Andover as a church, the division into parishes was either a loss, as it seemed in retrospect to Bailey, or an important new beginning, as it was for members of the new covenanting congregation in the South. But even South Parish residents reacted differently. Some became covenant members of the new parish, others never did. Some people's lands fell in the new South Precinct so that they now had to attend and pay taxes for the new South Parish church, which caused resentment and petitioning as Barnard had said in his letter. Some who lived along the border petitioned successfully to be allowed to remain North Parish church members, even if they were reckoned as living in the South Precinct.

While there had been nothing so stark as a South End against North End pattern to the witchcraft crisis in Andover, it was nevertheless the case that almost every one of the thirty-four signers of the new South Parish Covenant was a member of a former South End family that had been involved in the witchcraft crisis. Their involvement had been in one or more of the possible ways: they had been accused themselves or in the immediate family of an accused person; afflicted or in the family of an afflicted person; an accuser or in the family of an accuser. The new minister Phillips had people from all these categories among his parishioners. Joseph Green, the new minister at Salem Village, had encountered the same problems in his congregation (on Green's approach to the witch crisis aftermath problems at Salem, see Boyer and Nissenbaum 1974:217ff.). As Phillips took up his new role, he was taking part in a time of hope for new beginnings all over the Province. On October 17, 1709, only six days after Phillips' ordination ceremony, the Court at Boston finally passed the general Reversal of Attainder. By means of this bill all the judgments against the accused of 1692 were to be reversed and expunged from the records and token damages paid to them or their families.

Little is known of how or by whom Phillips was chosen for the South Parish, but it may well have been for his position on certain pastoral issues that had come to seem important in light of the recent crisis. What is known of the positions he fostered suggests that he was keen to avoid a similar crisis in the future (PhRB, *passim*). For example, perhaps influenced by incoming currents of Presbyterianism, he emphasized the importance of children's baptism. Abiel and Ephraim Abbot in their history of Andover (1847:87ff.) claim that during Phillips' ministry "the practice of recognizing baptismal covenant was earnestly urged, and there were very few that were not baptized...all who received baptism were under the watch and discipline of the church." Phillips "reminded the church of their duty with respect to the children of the church, and showed that it was their duty to watch over them, and that by the neglect thereof, the church had contracted a great deal of guilt." Unspecified is the nature of this "neglect" and "guilt" as Phillips saw it. But the adults' failure of responsibility for the large numbers of children caught up in the witch crisis may have been on his mind.

Phillips also took up another problem with his parishioners, one that had been a concern in town since the days of the Chandler tavern dispute. This had to do with the ill effects of liquor, which was no longer a problem only among the youth and town riffraff. He attacked such growing customs as "the free use of strong liquors at funerals" and actually seems to have effected a change in the practice at least in his own parish ceremonies (Bailey 1880:509). One of the leading citizens of the South Parish was Christopher Osgood, now rising to prominence in the new part of town. He had been a key figure in organizing the petition against William Chandler's tavern (see the tavern controversy in chapter 6). Since Osgood and others had been among those greatly disturbed by the liquor problem in the town, they must have welcomed and supported the new minister's pressure on it.

Phillips' preaching and actions on the security of Christian baptism, the responsibility of the church for children, and on the abuse of alcohol reflected a renewal of the ideals of covenant life. But the South Parish church covenant provides evidence that he brought in another, major change, a clear sign of changing concepts of social identity. This was with regard to the clergy's new concern regarding spiritual protection of women. The text of the first South Parish Covenant is reprinted in Abbot (1829:84–86), and the signers are listed there. What is at once noteworthy is that women as well as men signed their names or put their mark to this covenant, unusual for the petitions and documents of the time. It is also in strong contrast to Andover's first covenant, which was signed by men only. Even more striking is the fact that among the signers of the South Parish covenant, considerably more women (twenty-one) signed than men (thirteen). Many of these women were widows. However, most striking of all, several married women signed the covenant but their husbands did not sign until later, if at all (see Mooar 1859 for the list of South Parish members and their dates of joining). Godbeer noted the same phenomena elsewhere in the newer churches (2002:357, fn.74). Why were so many women signing the covenant? Why might women have signed on their own behalf?

Under both earlier covenant theology and English legal precedent, a woman was covered by her father's or husband's signing of pertinent documents. Perhaps Phillips and others had concluded that recent events showed that the church must now encourage women to sign the church covenant for themselves. New young pastors, ordained in the period following the witchcraft crisis, were doubtless concerned to forestall a similar outbreak. From a pastoral perspective, the witchcraft crisis had revealed the extent to which women were perceived as both dangerous and in special danger, vulnerable to attack and to deception in spiritual warfare. In their testimonies during the witchcraft trials women had frequently told about such things as how the devil got them to renounce their baptisms, how he gave them a "baptism" of his own, and got them to sign "the devil's book." This theme was clear from 1692 trial transcripts such as Mary Marston's, one of many confessions involving this theme.[5] Mary confessed that while she was alone in the house, a "black man" came in and offered her a paper book to sign, "which she did sign with a pen dipped in ink." The confessions of other Andover girls and women suggest why Phillips believed he had to stress not only the importance of baptism for children, but in the case of women, why they should sign the new covenant themselves and no longer be signed for by fathers or husbands. In revealing excerpts from the trial transcripts, girls and women tell of receiving the devil's baptism and signing in books and on birch bark, the latter perhaps evocative of the feared Indian world. Elizabeth Johnson said she was "baptized in Goody [Martha] Carrier's well [and] saw bread and wine at the devil's sacraments." Sarah Carrier (age 7) testified, "My mother made me set my hand to a book." Mary Osgood was "baptized by the devil." Joanna Tyler: "The black man asked her to set her hand to his book; he would let her have fine clothes." Sara Bridges "signed the devil's birch rind [bark]" and Mary Toothacre as well "put her mark on a piece of birch rind" (Bailey 1880:206 ff.; Boyer and Nissenbaum 1972 passim).

Phillips apparently acted to counter whatever false ideas and fears had been raised throughout the episode by stressing the importance, and safety, of the Covenant. But he also expanded the category of Covenanters in his parish by having women now sign for themselves and, in some cases, independently of their husbands. thus the separate spiritual lives and consequent vulnerability of women was recognized and the

---

[5]See Norton (1986) for a discussion of the increased membership of women in congregational churches toward the end of the seventeenth century. However, she does not discuss the implications of the fact that after the Restoration laws of the 1660s, men in the colony no longer had to be church members in order to be enfranchised, and so they may not have bothered to join.

influence, negative and positive, that women had in the spiritual community was acknowledged. By stressing both baptism, especially the Reformation covenant-community view of baptism, and covenant, that each person must sign on his or her own behalf, Phillips may have intended to impress upon people that their baptismal security could not be taken away from them by the devil. Phillips' handling of the South Parish as a new church forming in the aftermath of the witchcraft episode provides insight into how the younger generation of colony ministers approached pastoral care for families who had been struck by the crisis.[6]

"The Peace of the Town"

The desire to uncover the direction of deep structural change over time, free from the surface play of historical particulars, is certainly an understandable and worthy goal. Greven explained it well in the introduction to his *Four Generations* and in an early article on the family in Andover (1966). However, for Andover, this approach resulted in an unintended consequence: a misleading picture of the town's early history, especially for those readers who skim over Greven's demographics and statistical tables or who have not followed the ongoing debates among historians and witchcraft specialists. Indeed, it is the historical particulars of Andover that are essential for understanding its people's actions and reactions.

During the weeks I spent reading and checking references at the Andover Historical Society, I often chatted with one of the volunteers about the history of old Andover. I remarked that I was going to use a particular marriage of the early 1700s to mark the endpoint of my study, but that this marriage could also serve as a proper starting point for a sequel about the two parishes should I or anyone else wish to explore the next phase of Andover's social history. Effortlessly identifying with the people of her town three hundred years earlier, she said, "You know what? I think we had to split up in order for the people to start caring about each other again." Perhaps she had put her finger on it. Thomas Barnard in his letter of appeal to the governor of 1710 had urged, "Sir, I think the regulation of the division is necessary to the peace of the town."

---

[6]Little is yet known of Phillips' own theology, although there are some untranscribed sermons available in the North Andover Historical Society. Phillips seems to have returned to a more sacramental concept of ritual life and its spiritual transactions, which makes much pastoral sense in terms of the struggles that the people had been having. Perhaps there is a line of family ideological affinity with his great-grandfather George Phillips, the minister at Watertown, who, back in the 1630s, had maintained against the Boston ministers that the churches of Rome were "true churches" (Winthrop 1908 vol. i).

After the long divisive process that has been recounted in these chapters and just before the official separation into two parishes, a marriage took place in Andover between the leading families of the two parishes-to-be. It was one among many marriages recorded in 1708, but it was a prime example of a marriage in a key social location. The eldest son of the leading North Parish family married the eldest daughter of the leading South Parish family. Specifically, George Abbot of the South Parish married his eldest daughter Hannah to John Osgood III, eldest grandson of the first John Osgood of the North Parish. Both fathers were among the five town selectmen that year (Bailey 1880:142). On the tax lists of 1707 they were among the highest taxpayers of their respective parishes. By 1709, they were paying the highest taxes in their parishes (see appendix D).

In a broad demographic approach, this particular marriage would be just one more in the count of marriages that year and classified in the "town endogamy" category. The two persons involved were indeed both from Andover. But given the history of Andover, this marriage was far more important as a symbol of alliance and peace-making. It united the social factions that had been connected with Andover down through the years, from the settlers' English roots to the town's ends, precincts, and parishes. As an alliance between the two main historical groupings, the marriage was perhaps a symbolic and promising occasion for the townspeople. Unfortunately, no record survives with contemporary comment on this marriage, but, given the town history, this first-time marriage between members of the two leading families assumes significance when seen in terms of the joining of rivals that it represented. John Waters (1968) in his study of the changing marriage alliances of regionally based factions in colonial Hingham, Massachusetts, came to similar conclusions about his data. Waters found that not until the third generation did the East Anglian and the West Country factions that had founded Hingham begin to intermarry. In the initial period people chose from within their British regional background groups when they married. In Waters' view, intermarriage became possible because horizontal class interests had finally emerged strong enough to override the foundation of old vertical regional loyalties initially brought by Hingham's founding companies.

It is true that by the third generation at Andover the descendants of the two factions, the Southwesterners and the Hertsfordshire group, had become socially and economically equal enough to begin the exchange of children in marriage between families at the top levels. But class interests notwithstanding, perhaps people of Andover also saw this first marriage between the two parishes in their own terms as well, as a type of reconciliation marriage to unite and make peace between rival *companies,* much as the Winthrop-Dudley marriage memorialized years earlier at Two Brothers Rock had been for the first generation of colonists (see chapter 2). In the next generation, marriage as both medium and symbol of social reconciliation in Andover took a further important step in the 1738 marriage of Samuel Phillips and Elizabeth Barnard. They were the son and granddaughter of the two ministers of the North and South Parishes (Abbott n.d.: Barnard; Bond 1860:872–877 for Phillips genealogy). Here was another marriage of even more significant social location in view of all that had passed in Andover. It must have been a grand occasion. Perhaps, after all, the people of Andover had become like those bees when the hive is too full in the outcome of their parish split, "issuing out" in a "fit season," as the writers of the Cambridge Platform put it.

As Sarah Loring Bailey concluded her long journey back through Andover's early history, she wrote in her final paragraph, "Few towns offer so wide a field for historical research for understanding the founding years of the country." Having now made a similar journey I concur, but I wonder what she thought of as "the country." Indeed, Bailey was writing to honor the American Centennial. However, the researches and changing viewpoints of many historians since Bailey's time have shown that there is no prototypical New England much less an American "country." Nor can it be said that there was even such a thing as a typical town in Essex County. True, there were common elements, but the early towns were each stamped with the particular mix of blood and country which the members of the companies that formed to found them brought along from the Old World. A place like Andover could never again be proposed as a type for all the colonial towns, or a story that can be told in a single voice.

Nathaniel Ward's plans for his son to lead the company to plant a town at "Cochichawick" were unrealized, but the project went ahead anyway. During the seventy years that followed, the plantation transformed itself into ends, then into precincts and parishes. By 1710, the first three generations of Andover's families, like others in the Bay Colony, had struggled through to social arrangements not envisioned by the founders. They had shed old social identities and put on new ones; yet there remained those connections to the regional social worlds they had left behind in Britain. The next milestone in Andover's official history would be the establishment of the West Parish in 1826. Then in 1855, came the decision to divide at last into two separate townships. The South and West Parishes became Andover, while the old town, the North Parish, became North Andover. May the company of future historians of Andover increase, for there is much more to be discovered about how these next phases of division occurred and how the feuds and alliances of the old companies were played out in them.

Appendix A
Town Seals and Anniversary Banners

A.1. Andover Town Seal

A.2. North Andover Town Seal

A.3. Andover's 250th Anniversary Banner

Artist unknown, 1896
Oil on canvas 57" x 77"
Collection of the Andover Historical Society

The banner was created for the town's 250th Anniversary Celebration in 1896 and displayed on the balcony of the Andover Town House. The Andover town seal of 1903 was based on the banner's design. Chief Cutsumache is shown pointing west, holding a coat and a bag clearly marked 6£ (six pounds). The Banner is shown in color at <http://andoverma.gov/about/250th.php>.

A.4. Andover's 350th Anniversary Banner

For its 350th anniversary celebration banner in 1996, Andover chose the theme "home of *America*", in red, white, and blue. The patriotic song *America* (known to generations of school children as "My country, 'tis of thee") was written in 1831 by Samuel Francis Smith, a student at the Andover Theological Seminary. Perhaps few then realized the words were set to the music of the national anthem of the United Kingdom, *God Save the King*. The Banner may be seen in color and with more information at <http://andoverma.gov/about/350th.php>.

Appendix B

Documents: Seating the Meetinghouse

B.1 The Beverly text: Seating the Meetinghouse (Thayer 1868:34–35)[1]

"...that every male be allowed one degree for every complete year of age he exceeds twenty-one; that he be allowed for a captain's commission twelve degrees, for a lieutenant's eight, and for an ensign's four degrees; that he be allowed three degrees for every shilling in the last parish tax, and one degree for every shilling for personal estate and faculty; every six degrees for estate and faculty of a parent alive, to make one degree among his sons, or, where there are none, among the daughters that are seated; every generation heretofore living in this town to make one degree for every male descendant that is seated; parentage to be regarded no farther otherwise than to turn the scale between competition for the same seat; that taxes for polls of sons and servants shall give no advancement for masters or fathers, because such sons and servants have seats; that no degree be allowed on account of anyone's predecessors having paid towards building the meeting-house, because it had fallen down before now, but for repairs since made; that some suitable abatement in degrees be made, where it is well known that the person is greatly in debt; that the tenant of

---

[1]Richard Godbeer (personal communication, 2004) has raised the question of whether this text may have been, unbeknownst to Thayer, a parody. Therefore I have included in appendix B.2 another text on seating the meetinghouse from a history of the town of Tewksbury, although from a somewhat later date. Tewksbury borders Andover. It was once a part of Billerica and became a separate township in 1734.

a free hold for term of years shall be allowed as many degrees as half the real estate entitles him to and the landlord the other half; that the proprietor of lands in any other parish shall be (if under his own improvement) allowed as much as he would be if they lay in this parish, but if rented out, only half as much...

"Married women to be seated agreeably to the rank of their husbands, and widows in the same degree as their husbands were yet living; that the foremost magistrate seat (so called) shall be the highest in rank, and the other three in successive order; that the next in rank shall be in the foremost of the front seats below, then the foreseat in the front-gallery, then the foreseat in the side-gallery; that the side seat below shall be for elderly men, the foremost first or highest, and the others in order; that the seats behind the fore-front seat shall be for middle-aged men, according to their degree; that the second or third seats in the front and side galleries shall be for younger men, to rank the second first, and the third next."

B.2 The Tewksbury text: Seating the Meetinghouse (Pride 1888:7)

In December 1737 the townspeople decided "to seat their meetinghouse, and to have respect both to money and age in seating the meetinghouse, as to age, all above sixty years...to seat the meetinghouse, going back to the first assessment that was made in Tewksbury...to dispose of the room that is left for the pews to the highest payers, giving the highest payer the first choice, and if he refuse to make his choice, the next highest payer, and so on till the above said pew room be taken up; that such persons as shall make choice of the above said pews are obliged to ceil [plaster] the meetinghouse sides against their pews up as high as the bottom of the lower windows."

Later the town obliged the pew owners to glaze the windows opposite their respective pews, and keep their portion of the meetinghouse in proper repair.

Appendix C

The Reverend Thomas Barnard's Letter to Governor Dudley (1710)

Letter from the Reverend Thomas Barnard, North Andover Parish, to Governor Dudley, dated Andover, February 2, 1709/10. This is the full text of the letter referred to by S. L. Bailey (1880:429). I copied it on October 12, 2004, from the microfilm files at the Massachusetts State Archives, University of Massachusetts, Harbor Campus, Boston. Spelling is retained and words in doubt are shown in brackets.

May it please your Excellency:

If I may not be thought troublesome I would crave leave once more to represent to your Excellency the unsettled condition of this town, by reason of the dissatisfaction of many of our people. Some of our people that are within the South Precinct pray'd the Great Court at their last session that they might have the liberty to belong to the North part, that being more convenient for them. But the committee that was ordered to come and hear the pleas of the petitioners seemed to decline it. One of the gentlemen told me he thought the court had appointed some others to do it. I shall be so glad if the petitioners should have had the liberty granted which they desired without the charge of a committee and the paying of their tax to the building of the new meetinghouse and minister's house, which they think are hard terms. I have thought they might be released without great inconvenience to the New precinct, which by the division is made the greater part, both for number of freeholders, quantity of land, and divisions of lands that are not settled. The North part of the town that was the first settlement, are dissatisfied that they are made the lesser part, and yet [if I continue with them as I am inclined to do] they are obligated by the order of court to perform the obligation of the whole town to me. But I suppose they might be willing to do it if they might have those familyes that desire to continue with them. And if that were granted there would be still more than 80 freeholders belonging to the South Precinct, which is the growing part of town. And if they have as many as are willing to joyn with them I think it is as much as they can reasonably desire. Sir, I think the Regulation of the Division is necessary to the peace of the town. For I fear that if people are compelled to that which is inconvenient to them and that which they are so extremely averse to, it will be an occasion of Perpetual Discontent. I should be glad therefore if things might be settled that future troubles may be prevented. I am the more solicitous in this matter, because the people have neglected to provide for me and I know not when they will do it, unless things are better settled among us. The redressing [refreshing?] of those that are aggrieved would very much [contribute?] to our welfare which if your Excellency please to promote it would be a great satisfaction to those that received it as well as to

      Yr Excellency's
       most humble and obedient servant
       Thomas Barnard

Andover Feb 2 1709/10

Appendix D
Andover Tax Records, 1679–1716

These lists were reordered and compiled by the author in 1986 from "Town of Andover Tax Records" on microfilm in the Memorial Library, Andover, Massachusetts.

The surnames are abbreviated but recognizable. See table 1 (p. 72) for full surnames of most men on this list. Relatives of the two Osgood families are distinguished by a (J) for John and a (C) for Christopher. The two Abbot(t) families are distinguished by different spellings on the lists, although not consistently so on the primary documents: Abbt (from Roxbury), and Abtt (from Rowley). Families of the two Parker brothers are distinguished by a (J) for Joseph's and a (N) for Nathan's.

Titles and military ranks have been included wherever noted on tax lists. Abbreviations: Mr, Dea (Deacon), Esq (Esquire), Cpt (Captain), Lt (Lieutenant), Ens (Ensign), Sgt (Sergeant), Cpl (Corporal), Crt (Cornet), Dr (Drummer, QM (Quartermaster), "Sr" and "Jr" for Senior and Junior, and "Wdw" for Widow are also included as they appear.

(D) in appendix D3 stands for the entry "Doomed," which appears by the names of eight North End taxpayers in the 1716 list, five of them Barkers. According to the Oxford English Dictionary, "doomage" was an American colonial localism meaning assessment in default when the taxpayer failed to submit a proper invoice of his rateable estate to the assessors.

D.1 North End Tax Records

Rank order of taxpayers in Andover
at intervals from 1679 to 1690

(Total polls; name; tax in shillings-pence; rank number in brackets)

Year Tax type	1679 (minister)			1684 (minister)			1690 (province)		
01.	Osgd, JnLt	17-09	[1]	Osgd, JnCpt	10-10	[1]	Osgd, JnCpt	17-01	[1]
02.	Poor, Dn	14-02	[2]	Stvn, JnEns	09-07	[2]	Fry, Sm	13-09	[2]
03.	Igls, HnSgt	13-03	[3]	Brkr, RiSr	06-07	[3]	Stvns, Bn	12-06	[3]
04.	Brkr, RiSr	11-02	[4]	Mstn, JnSr	06-00	[4]	Rbnsn, Js	11-03	[4]
05.	Mstn, JnSr	10-11	[5]	Abtt, GeJr**	05-08	[5]	Brkr, JnLt	11-03	[4]
06.	Abtt, GeJrDr	08-03	[6]	Brkr, JoJrSgt	05-07	[6]	Stvns, Eph	10-03	[5]
07.	Frmm, RJr	07-06	[7]	Jnsn, Ti	05-06	[7]	Jnsn, StEns	09-4.5	[6]
08.	Wdw Stvn	07-05	[8]	Stvn, Bn	05-06	[7]	Aslbe, Jn	08-11	[7]
09.	Brkr, Jn	07-02	[9]	Flknr, Fr	05-04	[8]	Osgd, Ti(J)**	08-09	[8]
10.	Stvn, JnSgt	07-00	[10]	Igls, HnSgt	05-03	[9]	Osgd, JnJr	08-04	[9]
11.	Brdst, DuCpt	06-10	[11]	Stvn, Js	04-10	[10]	Fstr, Abr	08-1.5	[10]
12.	Sesns, Al	06-03	[12]	Brdst, DuCpt	04-10	[10]	Frmm, JnSr	08-1.5	[10]
13.	Aslb, Jn	06-00	[13]	Poor, Dn	04-09	[11]	Lacy, La	07-11	[11]
14.	Lacy, La	06-00	[13]	Aslb, Jn	04-07	[12]	Abtt, ThSr	07-11	[11]
15.	Prkr, Js	05-08	[14]	Frmm, JnSr	04-04	[13]	Prkr, St	07-06	[12]
16.	Fry, Jm	05-08	[14]	Mrtin, Sm	04-03	[14]	Stvn, NaCrt	07-06	[12]
17.	Prkr, Na	05-06	[15]	Frmm, RaSr	04-03	[14]	McCln, Sa	07-04	[13]
18.	Rbsn, Js	05-03	[16]	Abtt, Th	04-01	[15]	Brdgs, Jn	07-3.5	[14]
19.	Brkr, Wm	05-02	[17]	Brdgs, Jn	04-01	[15]	Prkr, Jn (J)	07-3.5	[14]
20.	Jnsn, Ti	05-00	[18]	Lacy, La	04-00	[16]	Elknr, Jn	07-3.5	[14]

D.1 North End Tax Records

21.	Abtt, Th	05-00	[18]	Osgd, JnJr	03-11	[17]	Grves, Mk	06-10	[15]
22.	Brnd, St	05-00	[18]	Sesns, Al	03-10	[18]	Brkr, RiJr	06-10	[15]
23.	Stvn, Js	04-09	[19]	Mrbl, Sm	03-09	[19]	Mrbl, Sm	06-10	[15]
24.	Frnm, ThSgt	04-09	[19]	Dane, Na	03-09	[19]	Frnm, Ra	06-5.5	[16]
25.	Mrtn, Sm	04-09	[19]	Prkr, Na	03-09	[19]	Prstn, Jn	06-03	[17]
26.	Stvn, Eph	04-08	[20]	Brkr, Wm	03-09	[19]	Holt, Ja	06-03	[17]
27.	Flknr, Fr	04-08	[20]	Stvn, Na	03-08	[20]	Poor, Dn	06-03	[17]
28.	Frnm, Jn	04-07	[21]	Rbsn, Js	03-08	[20]	Htchsn, Sm	06-03	[17]
29.	Prkr, St(J)**	04-06	[22]	Prkr, Js	03-07	[21]	Brdst, DuCpt	05-10	[18]
30.	Dane, Na	04-06	[22]	Ingls, Sm	03-04	[22]	Ingls, Ja	05-10	[18]
31.	Brkr, Eb	04-00	[23]	Grngr, Jn	03-03	[23]	Dane, Na	05-09	[19]
32.	Mstn, JnJr	04-00	[23]	Prkr, St	03-03	[23]	Abtt, GeJr	05-7.5	[20]
33.	Stvn, Na	04-00	[23]	Stvn, Eph	03-03	[23]	Mstn, Jcb	05-7.5	[20]
34.	Prkr, Jn(N)	04-00	[23]	Mstn, JnJr	03-00	[24]	Grngr, Jn	05-7.5	[20]
35.	Ingls, HnJr	03-08	[24]	Fstr, Eph	02-11	[25]	Brkr, Wm	05-05-	[21]
36.	Flknr, Jn	03-06	[25]	Poor, DnJr	02-10	[26]	Prkr, Js	05-05	[21]
37.	Fstr, Eph	03-02	[26]	Brkr, RiJr	02-10	[26]	Mstn, JnJr	05-00	[22]
38.	Brkr. RiJr	03-02	[26]	Frnm, ?Sgt	02-10	[26]	Frnm, JnJr	04-07	[23]
39.	Russ, JnJr	01-16	[27]	Tylr, Jn	02-09	[27]	Ingls, HnJr	04-07	[23]
40.				Brkr, Eb	02-07	[28]	D[?], Jn	04-06	[24]
41.				Flknr, Jn	02-07	[28]	Wdw Stvns	04-4.5	[25]
42.				Grvs, Abr	02-06	[29]	Abtt, JnJr	04-4.5	[25]
43.				Poor, Jn	02-05	[30]	Stvns. NaJr	04-04	[26]
44.				Frnm, JnJr	02-04	[31]	Flknr, Fr	04-02	[27]
45.				Brkr, St(?)	02-02	[32]	Ingls, HnSgt	04-02	[27]
46.				Ingls, HnJr	01-11	[33]	Chdlr, WmSr	04-02	[27]
47.				Frnm, RaJr	01-11	[33]	Lvjy, Js	3-11.5	[28]
48.				Ingls, Jn	01-11	[33]	Tylr, Jn	3-11.5	[28]
49.				Abtt, Geo(?)	01-11	[33]	Brkr, St	3-11.5	[28]
50.				Crmwl, Jn	01-08	[34]	Abtt, ThJr	03-09	[29]

#	Name	Amount	Ref		Name	Amount	Ref
51.	Saltr, Ri	01-08	[34]		Mstn, Jn	03-09	[29]
52.	Russ, JnSr	00-09	[35]		Ingls, Fr	03-09	[29]
53.	Wdw Prkr	00-08	[36]		Brkr, Bn	03-09	[29]
54.	Flknr, Edm	00-06	[37]		Frmgtn, Ed	03-09	[29]
55.					Andrw, Js	03-06	[30]
56.					Chubb, Ps	03-06	[30]
57.					Austn, Sm	03-06	[30]
58.					Austn, Th	03-06	[30]
59.					L (?), Hn	03-06	[30]
60.					Brkr, RiSr	03-4.5	[31]
61.					Mstn, JnSr	03-04	[32]
62.					Holt, Ni	02-06	[33]
63.					Wdw Poor	01-10-	[34]
Totals		£11-19-05				£10-03-08	

£19-14-04.5

D.1 North End Tax Records

Rank order of taxpayers in Andover
at intervals from 1693 to 1707
(Total polls; name; tax in shillings-pence; rank number in brackets)

Year Tax type	1693 (minister)			1699 (minister)			1707 (town)		
01.	Osgd, Sm(J)	09-07	[1]	Osgd, JnLt	09-00	[1]	Osgd, JnLt	06-05	[1]
02.	Brkr, JnLt	08-04	[2]	Frye, SmSgt	09-00	[1]	Frye, SmSgt	05-02	[2]
03.	Frye, Sm	06-06	[3]	Wdw Chdlr	09-00	[1]	Holt, Ni	04-11	[3]
04.	Aslb, JnSgt	06-04	[4]	Aslb, JnEns	08-04	[2]	Osgd, SmSgt	04-09	[4]
05.	Brdst, DuCpt	06-01	[5]	Brkr, JnLt	07-07	[3]	Stvns, BnCpt	04-08	[5]
06.	Osgd, Jn	06-00	[6]	Osgd, SmSgt	07-03	[4]	Aslb, JnLt	04-07	[6]
07.	Ingls, HnSgt	05-10	[7]	Mrbl, Sm	07-02	[5]	Frmm, JnSr	04-07	[6]
08.	Osgd, Ti(J)	05-09	[8]	Brkr, Bn	07-00	[6]	Wdw Stvns	04-07	[6]
09.	Stvns, Bn	05-08	[9]	Brdst, DuCpt	06-09	[7]	Brkr, WmSr	04-06	[7]
10.	Stvns, Js	05-07	[10]	Stvns, EphSgt	06-09	[7]	Poor, Dn	04-05	[8]
11.	Mrtn, (?)Ens	05-06	[11]	Rbnsn, JsCpl	06-07	[8]	Gray, Hn	04-02	[9]
12.	Mrbl, Sm	04-11	[12]	Wdw Stvns	06-06	[9]	Osgd, Ti (J)	04-02	[9]
13.	Pbnsn, Js	04-09	[13]	Mstn, JnSr	06-06	[9]	Fstr, Eph	04-01	[10[
14.	Fstr, Ab	04-09	[13]	Lacy, La	06-03	[10]	Brkr, JnCpt	03-10	[11]
15.	Mstn, JnSr	04-0	[14]	Poor, Dn	06-00	[11]	Stvns, Js	03-10	[11]
16.	Dane, Ntl	04-07	[14]	Stvns, JsDea	05-10	[12]	Lacy, La	03-09	[12]
17.	Poor. Dn	04-04	[15]	Stvns, BnCpt	05-09	[13]	Rbnsn, JsCpt	03-09	[12]
18.	Abtt, ThSr	04-04	[15]	Fstr, Eph	05-08	[14]	Brkr, RiSr	03-07	[13]
19.	Stvns, Eph	04-02	[16]	Brkr. Wm	05-37	[15]	Crltn, Jn	03-07	[13]
20.	Prkr, St(J)	04-01	[16]	Osgd, Ti	05-36	[16]	Dane, Ntl	03-06	[14]
21.	Gray, Rbt	04-02	[16]	Crltn, Jn	05'06	[16]	Fstr, Ab	03-06	[14]
22.	Crltn, Jn	04-02	[16]	Lvjy, Jn	05-04	[17]	Tylr, Mo	03-06	[14]

23.	Tylr, MoSr	04-00	[17]	Tylr, MoQM	05-04	[17]	Ingls, Sm	03-06	[14]
24.	Grvs, Mk	04-00	[17]	Prkr, St	05-02	[18]	Grngr, Js	03-05	[15]
25.	Frnm, JnEns	04-00	[17]	Ingls, Sm	05-00	[19]	Flknr, Fr	03-04	[16]
26.	Brkr, Ri	03-11	[18]	Mstn, JnJr	05-00	[19]	Htchsn, Sm	03-04	[16]
27.	Chdlr, Wm	03-09	[19]	Htchsn, Sm	04-11	[20]	Brdgs, Ja	03-03	[17]
28.	Frnm, Sm	03-08	[20]	Jnsn, Jn	04-08	[21]	Prkr, Js	03-02	[19]
29.	Mstn, Jn	03-06	[21]	Prkr, Jn(N)	04-08	[21]	Frnm, JnJr	03-01	[20]
30.	Lacy, La	03-06	[21]	Dane, Ntl	04-07	[22]	Brkr, Bn	03-00	[20]
31.	Stvns, Na	03-06	[21]	Holt, Ni	04-05	[23]	Ingls, Ja	03-00	[20]
32.	Flknr, Jn	03-06	[21]	Fstr, Ab	04-05	[23]	Frnm, Eph	02-11	[21]
33.	Brkr, Bn	03-05	[22]	Dlknr, Jn	04-05	[23]	Brkr, StLt	02-10	[22]
34.	Frye, Bn	03-05	[22]	Frnm, Eph	04-04	[24]	Stvns, Eph	02-10	[22]
35.	Prstn, Jn	03-04	[23]	Frnm, JnJr	04-03	[25]	Abtt, Th	02-06	[23]
36.	Prkr, Jn	03-04	[23]	Grngr, Jn	04-00	[26]	Jnsn, Jn	02-06	[23]
37.	Prkr, Js	03-04	[23]	Mstn, Jcb	04-00	[26]	Jnsn, Ti	02-06	[23]
38.	Ingls, Sm	03-03	[24]	Frnm, Sm	04-00	[26]	Wdw Mrtn	02-06	[23]
39.	Htchsn, Sm	03-03	[24]	Brdgs, Ja	04-00	[26]	Wdw Ingls	02-05	[24]
40.	Brkr, Wm	03-03	[24]	Abtt, Geo	04-00	[26]	Mstn, Eph	02-04	[25]
41.	Bridges, Jn	03-02	[25]	Prstn, Jn	03-11	[27]	Frnm, Th	02-03	[26]
42.	Mstn, Jcb	03-00	[26]	Stvns, NaSr	03-10	[28]	Mstn, JnJr	02-03	[26]
43.	Ames? Rbt	03-00	[26]	Ingls, HnSgt	03-09	[29]	Emry, Js	02-02	[27]
44.	Tylr, Jn	03-00	[26]	Brkr, Ri	03-09	[29]	Stvns, NaCrt	02-02	[27]
45.	Swan, Rbt	03-00	[26]	Stvns, NaCrt	03-08	[30]	Prkr, Js	02-01	[28]
46.	Fstr, Eph	03-00	[26]	Emry, Js	03-08	[30]	Chdlr, Js	02-00	[29]
47.	Abtt, GeoJr	02-08	[27]	Abtt, Th	03-08	[30]	Flknr, Jn	02-00	[29]
48.	Grngr, Jn	02-08	[27]	Flknr, Fr	03-07	[31]	Stvns, NaSr	02-00	[29]
49.	Austn, Sm	02-06	[27]	Ingls, Ja	03-07	[31]	Lvjy, Jn	02-00	[30]
50.	Frnm, Jn	02-06	[28]	Brkr, Js	03-06	[32]	Holt, Ti	01-11	[30]
51.	Wdw Stvns	02-06	[28]	Austn, Sm	03-06	[32]	Rbnsn, Dne	01-11	[30]
52.	Chdwk, JnSgt	02-06	[28]	Frnm, Jn	03-05	[33]	Austn, Sm	01-10	[31]

D.1 North End Tax Records

#	Name	Date	Ref		Name	Date	Ref		Name	Date	Ref
53.	Stvns, NtlJu	02-05	[29]		Rbnsn, Dne	03-02	[34]		Abtt, Geo	01-10	[31]
54.	Ingls, HnJr	02-04	[30]		Brkr, JnJr	02-10	[35]		Mrbl, Sm	01-10	[31]
55.	Brkr, St	02-03	[31]		Frnm, JnJr	02-10	[35]		Ingls, Jn	01-10	[31]
56.	Post(?), Jn	02-03	[31]		Wdw Mrtn	02-08	[36]		Frye, Jn	01-09	[32]
57.	Lvjy, Jn	02-02	[32]		Ingls, Jn	02-08	[36]		Mstn, Jcb	01-09	[32]
58.	Stvns, Jsh	02-01	[33]		Frnm, Th	02-06	[37]		Sessns, Alx	01-09	[32]
59.	Wdw Holt, Ha	02-00	[34]		Frngtn, Ed	02-06	[37]		Stvns, Eb	01-08	[33]
60.	Jnsn, Fr	02-00	[34]		Gray, Hn	02-06	[37]		Stiles, Eb	01-08	[33]
61.	Ames, Jn	02-00	[34]		Jnsn, Jna	02-04	[38]		Brkr, JnJr	01-06	[34]
62.	Holt, Ni	02-00	[34]		Nchls, Ni	02-00	[39]		Brkr, JnJr	01-06	[34]
63.	Flknr, Fr	02-00	[34]		Abtt, Js	01-09	[40]		Frnm, Sm	01-06	[34]
64.	Bdwll, Hn	02-00	[34]		Ingls, Jsah	01-09	[40]		Frngton, Ed	01-06	[34]
65.	Abtt, JnJr(T)	02-00	[34]		Abtt, Ntl(T)	01-08	[41]		Gray, RbtJr	01-06	[34]
66.	Emry, Js	01-11	[35]		Wdw Ingls	00-08	[42]		Jnsn, Fr	01-06	[34]
67.	Brdgs, Ja	01-11	[36]		Wdw Poor	00-04	[43]		Mrbl, SmSr	01-06	[34]
68.	Wdw JnsnRe	01-08	[37]						Stvns, Sm	01-06	[34]
69.	Frnm, Jn	01-08	[37]						Smith, Sm	01-06	[34]
70.	Frngtn, Ed	01-08	[37]						Stvns, Abl	01-05	[35]
71.	Frnm, Th	01-08	[37]						Gray, Edw	01-04	[36]
72.	Davis, Eph	01-08	[37]						Crltn, Th	01-03	[37]
73.	Ingls, Jn	01-07	[38]						Ingls, Jsah	01-03	[37]
74.	Nchls, Ni	01-06	[39]						Prstn, Jn	01-02	[38]
75.	Stone, Sim	01-06	[39]						Mstn, JnSr	01-01	[39]
76.	Crltn, Jn	01-06	[39]						Tylr, Jn	01-01	[39]
77.	Mstn, Jn	01-03	[40]						Abtt, Ntl(T)	01-00	[40]
78.	Crmwl, Jn	01-03	[40]						Abtt, Jn(T)	01-00	[40]
79.	Swan, Sm	01-00	[41]						Brnd, St	00-10	[41]
80.	Swan, Jsh	01-00	[41]						Grvs, Sm	00-10	[41]
81.	Brdly, Hn	01-00	[41]						Nchls, Ni	00-10	[41]
82.	Andrws, Js	01-00	[41]						Ingls, SmJr	00-10	[41]

83.	Wdw Poor	00-10	[42]			
84.				Wdw Frye	00-05	[42]
				Wdw Alln	00-03	[43]
Totals		£13-09-11			£10-12-04	
					£15-08-04	

D.2 South End Tax Records

Rank order of taxpayers in Andover
at intervals from 1679 to 1690

(Total polls; name; tax in shillings-pence; rank number in brackets)

Year Tax type	1679 (minister)			1684 (minister)			1690 (province)	
01.	Chdlr, Th	11-01	[1]	Chdlr, ThCpt	08-11	[1]	Jnsn, Th	16-09	[1]
02.	Abbt, G.Sr	10-05	[2]	Wdw Abbt	08-10	[2]	Chdlr, ThCpt	15-03	[2]
03.	CPhlps, Ed	09-00	[3]	Frye, DeaJn	07-10	[3]	Frye, Ja	13-02	[3]
04.	Chdlr, Wm	08-06	[4]	Wrght, Wa	06-08	[4]	Holt, Sm	12-02	[4]
05.	Osgd, Chr	08-03	[5]	Holt, NiJr	05-08	[5]	Wrght, Wa	11-11	[5]
06.	Bllrd, WmSr	07-11	[6]	Rsll, Rbt	05-04	[6]	Hagit, Mo	11-10	[6]
07.	Alln, And	07-06	[7]	Frye, Ja	05-04	[6]	Frye, DeaJn	11-06	[7]
08.	Fstr, Abr	07-02	[8]	Frye, Sm	05-04	[6]	Rsll, Rbt	11-03	[8]
09.	Frye, JnJr	07-02	[8]	Jnsn, St	05-04	[6]	Abbt, GeJr	11-03	[8]
10.	Holt, NiSr	07-00	[9]	Jnsn, Th	05-01	[7]	Abbt, JnSr	08-09	[9]
11.	Hagit, Mo	06-08	[10]	Fstr, Abr	04-11	[8]	Bussl, Jn	08-09	[9]
12.	Wlsn, Js	06-06	[11]	Osgd, Chr	04-10	[9]	Dane, FrJr	08-09	[9]
13.	Osgd, St(J)	06-05	[12]	Osgd, St(J)	04-10	[9]	Osgd, Chr	08-09	[9]
14.	Jnsn, Th	06-04	[13]	Wlsn, Js	04-09	[10]	Lvjy, Wm	08-09	[9]
15.	Abbt, Jn	06-00	[14]	Abbt, Jn	04-06	[11]	Chdlr, W.Sr	08-08	[10]
16.	Bllrd, Js	05-09	[15]	Abbt, G.Sr	04-05	[12]	Blchd, Sm	08-04	[11]
17.	Frye, Sm	05-08	[16]	Osgd, Th(C)	04-05	[12]	Jnsn, Wm	07-09	[12]
18.	Stone, Hu	05-06	[17]	Chdlr, Jn	04-04	[13]	Mrbl, Js	07-03	[13]
19.	Lvjy, Wm	05-05	[18]	Russ, JnJr	04-04	[13]	Brnd, St	07-03	[13]
20.	Frye, Bn	05-03	[19]	Jnsn, Wm	04-02	[14]	Chdlr, WJr	06-08	[14]

21.	Chdlr, Jn	05-02	[20]		Stone, Hu	04-01	[15]		Stvns, Jn	06-08	[14]
22.	Fstr, AnJr	05-02	[20]		Frye, Bn	04-00	[16]		Tylr, Hpl	06-06	[15]
23.	Mrbl, Js	05-00	[21]		Holt, Sm	04-00	[16]		Alln, Jn	06-05	[16]
24.	Phlps, Sm	04-11	[22]		Hagit, Mo	03-11	[17]		Bllrd, Jn	06-03	[17]
25.	Mrbl, Sm	04-09	[23]		Bllrd, WmJr	03-10	[18]		Phlps, Ed	06-03	[17]
26.	Bllrd, WmJr	04-09	[23]		Bllrd, Jn	03-09	[19]		Lvjy, Jn	06-03	[17]
27.	Blunt, Wm	04-09	[23]		Holt, Hn	03-08	[20]		Carier, Th	06-03	[17]
28.	Rsll, Rbt	04-08	[24]		Fstr, AnSr	03-08	[20]		Abbt, Bn	05-10	[18]
29.	Holt, Hn	04-08	[24]		Mrbl, Js	03-08	[20]		Colmn, (?)	05-06	[19]
30.	Jnsn, Wm	04-06	[25]		Phlps, EdSr	03-08	[20]		Wlsn, Js	05-05	[20]
31.	Bgsby, Dn	04-06	[25]		Lvjy, Wm	03-07	[21]		Blchd, Jna	05-05	[20]
32.	Wright, Wa	04-05	[26]		Holt, Ja	03-05	[22]		Stone, Jn	05-05	[20]
33.	Lvjy, JnSr	04-02	[27]		Phlps, Sm	03-04	[23]		Holt, Hn	05-03	[21]
34.	Nchls, Ni	04-02	[27]		Bllrd, WmJr	03-04	[23]		Fstr. AnJr	05-03	[21]
35.	Holt, NiJr	04-00	[28]		Bllrd, WmJr	03-03	[24]		Brkr, Eb	05-03	[21]
36.	Holt, Ja	03-11	[29]		Prkr, (?)	03-02	[25]		Abtt, Neh	05-03	[21]
37.	Jnsn, St	03-11	[29]		Bllrd, WmSr	03-01	[26]		Jnsn, Jn	05-00	[22]
38.	Ayres, Za	03-10	[30]		Blunt, Wm	03-00	[27]		Prstn, Sm	05-00	[22]
39.	Osgd, Th(C)	03-08	[31]		Phlps, EdJr	02-11	[28]		(?)	05-00	[22]
40.	Prstn, Sm	03-08	[31]		Bgsby, Dn	02-10	[29]		Busll, Jn	04-08	[23]
41.	Whin, Ed	03-03	[32]		Dane, Fr	02-09	[30]		Abbt. Wm	04-07	[24]
42.	Lvjy, JnJr	03-02	[33]		Gray, Rbt	02-09	[31]		Abbt, ThJr	04-07	[24]
43.	Gray, Rbt	03-02	[33]		Chdlr. WmLt(?)	02-08	[32]		Frmm, Ra	04-07	[24]
44.	Ayres, Jn	03-00	[34]		Tylr, Hpl	02-07	[32]		Lvjy, Chr	04-00	[25]
45.	Wrdwl, Sm	02-09	[35]		Alln, An	02-07	[33]		Abbt, Ti	03-09	[26]
46.	Sltr, Hn	02-06	[36]		Alln, Jn	02-05	[33]		Carier, Th	03-08	[27]
47.	Jnsn, Jn	01-00	[37]		Chdwk, Wm(?)	02-05	[33]		Post, Jn	03-06	[28]
48.					Wrdwl, Sm	02-05	[34]		Wlsn, Js	03-06	[28]
49.					Prstn, Sm	02-03	[35]		Hoopr, Th	03-06	[28]
50.					Chdlr, WmEns	02-02			Wrdwl, Sm	03-04	[29]

D.2 South End Tax Records

51.	Gutsn, Jn	02-01	[36]		Brkr, Wm	03-04	[29]
52.	Lvjy, Chr	02-00	[37]		Bgsby, Dn	03-04	[29]
53.	Rsll, Th	01-11	[38]		(?)	03-04	[29]
54.	Jnsn, Jn	01-11	[38]		Abbt, JnJr	03-02	[30]
55.	(Lord?), Jn	01-11	[38]		Moor, Ab	03-00	[31]
56.	Crltn, Jn	01-08	[39]				
57.	Alln, An	01-05	[40]				
Totals		£13-02-10			£11-03-01		£18-09-09

Rank order of taxpayers in Andover
at intervals from 1693 to 1707
(Total polls; name; tax in shillings-pence; rank number in brackets)

Year	1693			1699 (province)			1707 (minister)		
Tax type (minister)									
01.	Holt, Hn	07-11	[1]	Osgd, Chr	10-06	[1]	Holt, Hn	05-11	[1]
02.	Jnsn, Th	07-06	[2]	ChdlrlrnWrks	10-00	[2]	Wdw Abbt	05-06	[2]
03.	Bllrd, Js	07-06	[2]	Abbt, Jn	10-00	[2]	Blunt, Wm	05-04	[3]
04. *	Frye, Ja(Lt?)	07-04	[3]	Blchd, Sm	10-00	[2]	Petrs, AnMr	05-01	[4]
05.	Russ, Jn	07-00	[4]	Holt, Hn	10-00	[2]	Rsll, Rbt	05-00	[5]
06.	Blunt, Wm	06-02	[5]	Rsll, Rbt	09-07	[3]	Chdlr, JnCpt	04-11	[6]
07.	Petrs, MrAn	06-01	[6]	Chdlr, ThSr	09-03	[4]	Dane, FrSgt	04-09	[7]
08.	Abbt, Geo	06-00	[7]	Bllrd, JsEns	09-03	[4]	Chdlr, WmSgt	04-08	[8]
09.	Blchd, Sm	05-10	[8]	Blunt, Wm	08-04	[5]	Abbt, GeLt	04-06	[9]
10.	Frye, JnDea	05-08	[9]	Abbt, Geo	08-00	[6]	Abbt, JnSgt	04-04	[10]
11.	Wrght, Wa	05-06	[10]	Frye, JaCpt	08-00	[6]	Bllrd, Jna	04-03	[11]
12.	Lvjy, Wm	05-06	[10]	Chdlr, JnLt	07-09	[8]	Frye, JaCpt	04-02	[12]
13.	Osgd, Chr	05-05	[11]	Prstn, An	07-02	[9]	Blchd, Jna	04-01	[13]
14.	Rsll. Rbt	05-05	[11]	Jnsn, Th	07-01	[9]	Lvjy. Wmen	04-01	[13]
15.	Hagit, Mo	05-03	[12]	Mrbl, JsSr	07-00	[10]	Phlps, Sm	04-01	[13]
16.	Mrbl, Js	05-00	[13]	Dane, FrSgt	06-11	[11]	Frye, JncCl	03-11	[14]
17.	Dane, Fr	04-11	[14]	Holt, SmJr	06-08	[12]	Fstr, Wm	03-11	[14]
18.	Jnsn, Wm	04-06	[15]	Abbt, Bn	06-07	[13]	Brnd, St	03-09	[15]
19.	Stvns, Jn	04-05	[16]	Frye, Jn	06-07	[13]	Rsll, Th	03-09	[15]
20.	Brnd, St	04-04	[17]	Wrght, Wa	06-02	[14]	Wrght, Wa	03-09	[15]
21.	Chdlr, Jn	04-03	[18]	Russ, JnEns	06-02	[14]	Osgd, ChCpt	03-07	[16]
22.	Chdlr. Js	04-03	[18]	Lvjy. Wm	06-01	[15]	Prkr. Js	03-07	[16]

D.2 South End Tax Records

#	Name	Date	Ref	Name	Date	Ref	Name	Date	Ref
23.	Phlps, Ed	04-02	[19]	Hagit, Mo	05-08	[16]	Abbt, Wm	03-05	[17]
24.	Holt, Sm	04-01	[20]	Wlsn, Js	05-07	[17]	Bllrd, JsEns	03-05	[17]
25.	Busll, Sm	04-00	[21]	Abbt, Neh	05-03	[18]	Abbt, Neh	03-00	[18]
26.	Bllrd, Jn	03-11	[22]	Lvjy, Na	04-10	[19]	Osgd, HSgt(J)	03-00	[18]
27.	Tylr, Hpl	03-09	[23]	Brnd, St	04-09	[20]	Jnsn, WmSg	03-00	[18]
28.	Abbt, Bn	03-07	[24]	Jnsn, Wm	04-08	[21]	Jnsn, Jn	02-11	[19]
29.	Bgsby, Dn	03-06	[25]	Chdlr, Jn	04-06	[22]	Wlsn, Js	02-11	[19]
30.	Abbt, Neh	03-06	[25]	Bllrd, Jn	04-06	[22]	Brkr, Eb	02-10	[20]
31.	Phlps. Sm	03-06	[25]	Osgd, Hkr(J)	04-05	[23]	Frnm, Ra	02-08	[21]
32.	Stone, Jn	03-05	[26]	Abbt, Ti	04-04	[24]	Grvs, Ab	02-08	[21]
33.	Osgd, Hkr(J)	03-03	[27]	Chdlr, Hn	04-03	[25]	Abbt, Ntl	02-07	[22]
34.	Moor, Ab	03-03	[27]	Abbt, Ntl	04-03	[25]	Chdlr, Js	02-06	[23]
35.	Wlsn, Js	03-02	[28]	Stvns, JnEns	04-02	[26]	Chdlr, HnCpl	02-06	[23]
36.	Chdlr, WmSr	03-02	[28]	Blchd, Jna	04-01	[27]	Stvns, JnCpl	02-06	[23]
37.	Fstr, An	03-02	[28]	Chdlr, Wm	04-01	[27]	Rsll, Bn	02-06	[23]
38.	Lvjy, Eb	03-02	[28]	Fstr, Am	04-01	[27]	Phlps, Ed	02-06	[23]
39.	Bllrd, Wm	03-00	[29]	Jnsn, Jn	03-11	[28]	Russ, (Jn?)	02-05	[24]
40.	Lvjy, Chr	03-00	[29]	Phlps, Ed	03-11	[28]	Bllrd, JsJr	02-05	[24]
41.	Osgd, Th(C)	03-00	[29]	Holt, SmJr	03-10	[29]	Bllrd, WmJr	02-05	[24]
42.	Blchd, Jna	03-00	[29]	Osgd, St(J)	03-10	[29]	Jnsn, Ja	02-04	[25]
43.	Abbt, Ti	02-11	[30]	Jnsn, Ja	03-09	[30]	Prstn, SmSr	02-04	[25]
44.	Osgd, St(J)	02-10	[31]	Moor, Ab	03-09	[30]	Chdlr, JnCpl	02-03	[26]
45.	Rsll, Th	02-10	[31]	Phlps, Sm	03-09	[30]	Abbt, Ti	02-03	[26]
46.	Gttsn, Jn	02-10	[31]	Stvns, Jsh	03-08	[31]	Prstn, SmCpt	02-03	[26]
47.	Jnsn, Jn	02-09	[32]	Gttsn, Jn	03-07	[32]	Gttsn, Jn	02-02	[27]
48.	Holt, SmJr	02-09	[32]	Lvjy, Eb	03-07	[32]	Russ, Th	02-01	[28]
49.	Chdlr, ThJr	02-09	[32]	Rsll, Th	03-07	[32]	Lvjy, Na	02-01	[28]
50.	Brkr, Eb	02-07	[33]	Abbt, Th	03-04	[33]	Jnsn, ThLt	02-00	[29]
51.	Abbt, Th	02-07	[33]	Brkr, Eb	03-04	[33]	Chdlr, Th	02-00	[29]
52.	Chdlr, Wens	02-06	[34]	Lvjy, Chr	03-04	[33]	Holt, HnSr	02-00	[29]

53.	Chdlr, Cpt(?)	02-06	[34]	Brnd, Jn	03-03	[33]
54.	Frnm, Ra	02-05	[35]	Mrbl, JsJr	03-03	[33]
55.	Jnsn, Ja	02-04	[36]	Bllrd, Wm	03-02	[34]
56.	Grvs, Ab	02-00	[37]	Grvs, Ab	03-01	[35]
57.	WdwOsgd St)	02-00	[37]	Chdlr, CptJn?	03-00	[36]
58.	Abbt, Ntl	01-11	[38]	Frnm, Ra	03-00	[36]
59.	Lvjy, Ntl	01-08	[39]	Holt, Olv	02-11	[37]
60.	Austn, Th	01-03	[40]	Austn, Th	02-11	[37]
61.	Carier, Th	01-03	[40]	Osgd, Js(J)	02-10	[38]
62.	Prstn, SmJr	01-03	[40]	Rsll, Rbt	02-10	[38]
63.	Stvns, Eph	01-02	[41]	Bllrd, Js	02-09	[39]
64.	Wrght, Jn	01-02	[41]	Wrght, Jn	02-09	[39]
65.	Wdw Phlps	01-02	[42]	Stvns, Eph	02-07	[40]
66.	Blknp, Sm	01-00	[42]	Bgsby, Dn	02-06	[41]
67.	Chubb, Pas	01-00	[42]	WdwChdlrW?	02-06	[41]
69.	Prstn, SmJr	01-00	[42]	Stone, Sim	02-06	[41]
70.				Wrdwl, SmJr	02-06	[41]
71.				Prstn, SmSr	02-05	[42]
73.				Holt, Ja	02-03	[43]
74.				Holt, Geo	02-03	[43]
75.				Carier, Th	02-00	[44]
76.				Holt, Bchs	02-00	[44]
77.				Fstr, Ab QM	01-01	[45]
78.						
79.						
80.						
81.						
82.						
83.						
84.						

Fstr, Ab	01-11	[30]
Osgd, Js(J)	01-10	[31]
Blunt, Hm	01-10	[31]
Abbt, Th	01-10	[31]
Stvns, Jsh	01-09	[32]
Osgd, StJr	01-09	[32]
Lvjy, Eb	01-09	[32]
Lvjy, WmSr	01-09	[32]
Holt, Jn	01-09	[32]
Holt, Sm	01-09	[32]
Holt, Olv	01-09	[32]
Chdlr, ThSr	01-09	[32]
Blchd, Th	01-09	[32]
Abbt, Js	01-08	[33]
Wrdwl, SmJr	01-07	[34]
Austn, Th	01-07	[34]
Lvjy, Jn	01-06	[35]
Bllrd, WmJr	01-06	[35]
Mrbl, Js	01-06	[35]
Lvjy, Chr	01-06	[35]
Abbt, JnJr	01-05	[36]
Abbt, Eph	01-05	[36]
Brkr, Ri	01-05	[36]
Jnsn, ThJr	01-05	[36]
Stone, Sim	01-05	[36]
Bgsby, Th	01-04	[37]
Hagit, Wm	01-04	[37]
Holt, Geo	01-04	[37]
Wdw Moor	01-04	[37]
Wrght, Jn	01-04	[37]

D.2 South End Tax Records

85.	Wrdwl, Wm	01-04	[37]
86.	Alln, Ja	01-03	[38]
87.	Blchd, SmJr	01-03	[38]
88.	Carier, ThSr	01-02	[39]
89.	Osgd, Chr	01-00	[40]
90.	Osgd, Ezk	01-00	[40]
91.	Prstn, Jcb	01-00	[40]
92.	Holt, Ja	01-00	[40]
93.	Carier, ThJr	00-11	[41]
94.	Hagit, Ti	00-11	[41]
95.	Stvns, Eph	00-11	[41]
96.	Frye, Ja	00-10	[42]
97.	Jnsn, Jsah	00-10	[42]
Totals		£12-12-01 £18-20-01	£12-04-08

D.3 North and South End Tax Records

Rank order of taxpayers in Andover
for the year 1716: The Province Tax

(Total polls; name; tax in pounds-shillings-pence; rank number in brackets)

	North				South	
001.	Stvns, BnCpt	02-03-03	[01]	Abbt, GeoCpt	02-00-06	[01]
002.	Osgd, Ti (J)	02-01-00	[02]	Dane, NaLt	01-10-09	[02]
003.	Frye, JnSr	01-08-05	[03]	Abbt, Neh	01-09-09	[03]
004.	Fry, Ja (D)	01-18-800	[04]	Blchrd, Jna	01-09-09	[03]
005.	Aslbe, Jn	01-15-03	[05]	Bllrd, (?)Ens	01-09-06	[04]
006.	Mrtn, Jn	01-14-00	[06]	Osgd, (?)Cpt	01-08-06	[05]
007.	Grngr, Jn	01-13-00	[07]	Phlps, SmSr	01-07-10	[06]
008.	Mstn, Jo	01-11-09	[08]	Holt, HnSr	01-06-00	[07]
009.	Petrs, Sm	01-09-10	[09]	Abbt, Ti	01-06-00	[07]
010.	Osgd, JnSr	01-09-00	[10]	Blunt, Wm	01-05-09	[08]
011.	Rbnsn, Js	01-08-06	[11]	Fstr, Wm	01-04-09	[09]
012.	Frye, Sm	01-08-06	[11]	LvJy, Eb	01-04-03	[10]
013.	Stvns, Jn	01-08-03	[12]	LvJy, (?)Dea	01-03-06	[11]
014.	Chdlr, HnEns	01-08-01	[13]	Gray, Hn	01-02-00	[12]
015.	Brkr, Bn	01-08-800	[14]	Jnsn, Ja	01-02-00	[12]
016.	Prkr, Jn	01-07-0?	[15]	Chdlr, ThSr	01-01-03	[13]
017.	Wlsn, Jn	01-07-00	[15]	Rsll, Th	01-01-03	[13]
018.	Fstr, EphSr	01-05-09	[16]	Abbt, Jna	01-01-03	[13]
019.	Stvns, Js	01-05-09	[16]	Jnsn, Wm	01-00-06	[14]
020.	Osgd, Sm(J)	01-05-06	[17]	Osgd, St(J)	01-00-03	[15]
021.	Prkr, Js	01-05-01	[18]	Abbt, Ntl	01-00-00	[16]

D.3 North and South End Tax Records   201

#	Name	Code	Ref		Name	Code	Ref
022.	Brkr, WmJr	01-04-06	[19]		Holt, Olv	00-10-09	[17]
023.	Austn, Sm	01-04-06	[19]		Blchd, Sm	00-19-00	[18]
024.	Ingls, Sm	01-03-07	[20]		Frnm, Ra	00-18-03	[19]
025.	Fstr, Ab	01-03-03	[21]		Abbt, St	00-17-09	[20]
026.	Dane, Na	01-03-03	[21]		Holt, Sm	00-17-09	[20]
027.	Lvjy, Na	01-03-03	[21]		Holt, Ni	00-17-09	[20]
028.	Tylr, Mo	01-03-01	[22]		Lvjy, Chr	00-17-06	[21]
029.	Ingls, Ja	01-02-06	[23]		Chdllr, Jn	00-17-04	[22]
030.	Wrght, Jn	01-01-09	[24]		Holt, Hn	00-17-01	[23]
031.	Jnsn, Ti	01-01-09	[24]		Brnd, Jn	00-16-07	[24]
032.	Stvns, Eph	01-01-06	[25]		Holt, Th	00-16-06	[25]
033.	Emry, Js	01-01-06	[25]		Chdlr, Wm	00-16-03	[26]
034.	Ingls, Hn	01-01-07	[26]		Abbt, Jn	00-16-03	[26]
035.	Brkr, Jn	01-01-00	[27]		Chdlr, Zb	00-16-02	[27]
036.	Crltn, JnSr	01-01-00	[27]		Abbt, Bn	00-16-00	[28]
037.	Osgd, JnJr	01-00-09	[28]		Bllrd, Shb	00-16-00	[28]
038.	Jnsn, Jn	01-00-09	[28]		Rsll, Jn	00-15-06	[29]
039.	Brdgs, Ja	01-00-06	[29]		Abbt, Th	00-15-06	[29]
040.	Frnm, Jn	01-00-06	[29]		Jnsn, JnSr	00-15-04	[30]
041.	Frmgtn, Ed	01-00-00	[30]		Blchd, Th	00-15-00	[31]
042.	Frnm, Eph	00-19-10	[31]		Brnd, Rbt	00-14-09	[32]
043.	Abtt, Geo	00-19-01	[32]		Fstr, Ab	00-14-07	[33]
044.	Lacy, La (D)	00-18-10	[33]		Rsll, Ja	00-14-07	[33]
045.	Abtt, Dn	00-18-07	[34]		Lvjy, Wm	00-14-03	[34]
046.	Frnm, Jna	00-18-07	[34]		Chdlr, ThJr	00-14-03	[34]
047.	Mrbl, Na	00-18-00	[35]		Moor, Ti	00-18-09	[35]
048.	Stvns, Na	00-18-00	[35]		Holt, Th	00-13-09	[35]
049.	Brkr, Eb	00-17-10	[36]		Abbt, Js	00-13-06	[36]
050.	Lvjy, Ntl	00-17-00	[37]		Bllrd, Hz	00-13-06	[36]
051.	Mstn, Jcb	00-16-06	[38]		Gray, Rbt	00-13-00	[37]

052.	Flknr, Dn	00-16-03	[39]		Chdlr, Js	00-13-00	[37]
053.	Brkr, Jo (D)	00-16-03	[39]		Grves, Ab	00-12-07	[38]
054.	Stvns, Eb	00-15-10	[40]		Abbt, Eph	00-12-16	[39]
055.	Jnsn, Fr	00-15-06	[41]		Osgd, Js(J)	00-12-16	[40]
056.	Htchsn, Sm	00-15-06	[41]		Poor, Jn	00-12-03	[40]
057.	Abtt, Th	00-15-13	[42]		LvJy, Hn	00-11-09	[41]
058.	Sesns, Sm (D)	00-15-00	[43]		Wrght, Js	00-11-09	[41]
059.	Brkr, Ri (D)	00-14-09	[44]		Chdlr, Jsah	00-11-06	[42]
060.	Chdlr, Jn	00-14-09	[44]		Prstn, Jcb	00-11-04	[43]
061.	Ingls, Jn	00-14-06	[45]		Abbt, Eb	00-11-03	[44]
062.	Mstn, Js	00-14-03	[46]		Holt, Jsah	00-11-00	[45]
063.	Flknr, Fr	00-14-01	[47]		Prstn, SmJr	00-11-00	[45]
064.	Stvns, NaCpl	00-14-01	[47]		Prstn, Jn	00-11-00	[45]
065.	Brkr, Wm	00-13-03	[48]		Holt, Jn	00-11-00	[45]
066.	Frye, JnJr	00-13-00	[49]		Abtt, Sm	00-11-00	[46]
067.	Stvns, Sm	00-12-10	[50]		Hagit, Mo	00-10-09	[47]
068.	(?), Eb	00-12-05	[51]		Hobs(?), Jna	00-10-06	[48]
069.	Smith, Sm	00-12-04	[52]		Banby(?), Dn	00-10-03	[48]
070.	Rbnsn, Dane	00-12-01	[53]		Holt, Mo	00-10-00	[49]
071.	Frnm, Th	00-12-00	[54]		Phlps, SmJr	00-09-909	[50]
072.	Osgd, Jn	00-11-09	[55]		Stone, Sim	00-09-07	[51]
073.	Stvns, Bn	00-11-07	[56]		Wrdwl, Sm	00-09-07	[51]
074.	Crtis, Th	00-11-06	[57]		Osgd, Ex (C)	00-09-06	[52]
075.	Stvns, Abl	00-11-04	[58]		Nchls, Ni	00-09-06	[52]
076.	Frye, Ntl	00-11-03	[59]		Holt, Paul	00-09-06	[52]
077.	Gray, Ed	00-11-00	[60]		Bllrd, Js	00-09-06	[53]
078.	Stvns, Dv	00-11-00	[60]		Phlps, Js	00-09-00	[54]
079.	Stvns, Ja	00-10-10	[61]		Abbt, Dv	00-08-09	[55]
080.	Jnsn, ThJr	00-10-09	[62]		Hagit (?), Wm	00-08-06	[55]
081.	Alln, An	00-10-09	[62]		Grvs, Th	00-08-06	[55]

D.3 North and South End Tax Records

082.	Brkr, Na	00-10-07	[63]
083.	Frye, Eb	00-10-07	[63]
084.	Pckns, Jn	00-10-07	[63]
085.	Kmbl, Dn	00-10-06	[64]
086.	Wdw Prkr, Ab	00-10-06	[64]
087.	Jnsn, Jsah	00-10-06	[64]
088.	Frnm, Jn	00-10-03	[65]
089.	Pckns, Ti	00-10-03	[65]
090.	Brkr, Hnh (D')	00-10-00	[66]
091.-	Frnm, Sm	00-09-09	[67]
092.	Brkr, SmSr	00-09-03	[68]
093.	Ingls, Jsah	00-08-09	[69]
094.	Frye, Na	00-08-09	[69]
095.	Fisk, Wm	00-08-09	[69]
096.	Abbt, Jn	00-08-09	[69]
097.	Brkr, Jn (D)	00-08-06	[70]
098.	Jnsn, ThSr	00-08-06	[70]
099.	Poor, DnJr	00-08-00	[71]
100.	Crltn, JnJR	00-07-09	[72]
101.	Flknr, Paul	00-07-09	[72]
102.	Fstr, Jn	00-07-00	[73]
103.	Frye, EphJr	00-06-10	[74]
104.	Htchsn, Jn	00-06-07	[75]
105.	Brkr, SmJr (D)	00-06-06	[76]
106.	Prkr, Bn	00-06-00	[77]
107.	Ingls, Fr	00-05-06	[78]
108.	Flknr, EdmJr(?)	00-05-06	[78]
109.	Fstr, Dn	00-05-06	[78]
110.	Mtchll, Ja	00-05-00	[79]
	Stvns, Eph	00-08-04	[56]
	Wrdwl, Wm	00-08-01	[57]
	Brnd, St	00-08-800	[58]
	Fstr, Js	00-07-09	[59]
	Bllrd, Uriah	00-07-09	[59]
	Gray, Brav	00-07-09	[59]
	Dane, Fr	00-07-03	[60]
	Dane, Jn	00-07-03	[60]
	Holt, Ja	00-07-03	[60]
	Jnsn, JnJr	00-07-00	[61]
	Abbt, (?)Dea	00-06-06	[62]
	Prstn, SmJr	00-06-06	[62]
	Frnm, Hn	00-06-05	[63]
	Abbt, Ja	00-06-03	[64]
	Holt, Hmph	00-06-03	[64]
	Chdlr, Phlmn	00-05-06	[65]
	Clerk, Js	00-05-04	[66]
	Banby, Ph(?)	00-05-04	[66]
	Bllrd, Hmph	00-05-00	[67]
Totals		£97-12-04	£74-17-05

Glossary

Seventeenth-century British and New-England English social category terms from early texts, relating to Massachusetts Bay Colony and the town of Andover.

adventurers: those undertaking a "venture," usually stockholders in a seafaring enterprise for some sort of profit. Many ventures were for colonization. The organizers of the Massachusetts Bay Company were called *adventurers.*

blood, also *bluid:* essence or characteristics of one's nature, especially what people share as members of a race or ethnic group, as in *his scottie's blood rose up.*

brother: basic kinship term extended to mean the father of one's child's spouse, as in "Two Brothers Rock" in Concord, Mass., so designated by Winthrop and Dudley as a memorial to the marriage of their children.

company: a voluntary association of people undertaking some sort of common action under the direction of a leader, each with his particular skill; there are many usages including a military company, a church/town planting company, a stock-holding company, or a group of people temporarily gathered for a task.

country, also *countrey:* one's home region, especially counties in Britain but not initially a political unit, as in *west-country,* the western counties of Cornwall, Devon, Dorset.

cousin-german, also *cousin-germane:* first cousin; judging from usage, applicable to any first cousins on the paternal or maternal side.

covenant: a sacred agreement; in early Massachusetts a group of Puritan men intending to plant a church-town covenanted together. A *Covenanter,* usually capitalized, was one who had signed such a covenant.

fenceviewer: a town officer usually appointed by the *selectmen* to walk property lines and be sure that householders were keeping up proper fencing.

firstcomers: usually capitalized; this term designated the founding group of lot holders in Andover; also used by other but not all early towns. Firstcomers had first choice in subsequent allocations of land, according to their order of arrival. All Covenanters were Firstcomers, but, as in Andover, not all Firstcomers were necessarily Covenanters.

freeholder, also *freedholder* and *free holder:* a man who was not, or was no longer, a bondservant, thus free to own land and pass it on to his heirs. Freeholders in good Puritan church standing in the Bay Colony were at first the only ones allowed to vote.

householder, also *househoulder:* in Andover, if not in the Bay Colony generally, either a category of lot owner second to the *freeholders,* or a term that may have replaced *freeholder* when the voting rights law changed so that church membership was not required.

latecomers: usually capitalized; in Andover, a term coined to distinguished the settlers who came after the first twenty-three, who then were called the *Firstcomers.* Not used in all towns.

ordinary: licensed place where liquor could be bought and consumed; *tavern* or *public house.*

meetinghouse: central building of early settlements, used for church, garrison, and any public meeting.

plant, (plantation, planter): to establish or *set down* a new settlement or church-town, called a *plantation.* Those who took part were called *planters* and in some towns *proprietors.* In Andover, proprietor came into use later as a way to refer to both Firstcomer and Latecomer property owners.

poll: the human head (archaic); used to modify tax, as in *poll tax,* or to count votes, as in *to poll.*

rate: the tax a resident or householder paid, determined yearly by the town clerk or selectmen and collected by the *tythingman.*

scottie: one of several ways the settlers referred to Scots; stronger terms were *Scotch rogue* and *Scottish dog.*

selectmen: the group of men elected to handle town affairs, usually five in Andover; still done in small New England towns.

set down: see *plant.*

Southton man: a man from the port of Southampton in southern England, or the region around.

trainband: a term for the town militia which each town was required by law to maintain; also appears in some records as *trained band.*

tythingman: town tax or *tythe* collector (see *rate*); from *tythes,* the biblical term, since taxes were initially collected from all for the support of the minister and the upkeep of the meetinghouse.

west-country man: a man from the western counties of England, especially Cornwall and Devon, but also Dorset and Somerset.

Bibliography

Sources

Primary sources

Church records

Early records of the two parishes churches, Andover and North Andover (Andover Old Town), are stored at the two Historical Scieties, the Andover Historical Society (AHS) and the North Andover Historical Society (NAHS). Abbreviations used in this book for church record materials are:

> (ANPCM) Andover North Precinct Church Meetings Records.
> (BP) Barnard Papers. Journals of the ministers, father and son, Thomas Barnard and John Barnard, 1688–1743.
> (NPJCM) North Parish Journal of Church Matters, 1686–1810.
> (SPCR) South Parish Church Records.
> (PhRB) The Rev. Samuel Phillips' Record Book, 1711–1722.

Town records

The originals of many of the earliest town records of Andover were unavailable during the time I was conducting research. The Historical Societies requested researchers to use the Microfilm versions in the Andover

Public Library. I used the following microfilmed records, referred to in this book by the abbreviations in parentheses:

(ATR) Ancient Town Records, 1656–1708.
(TR&B) Record of Town Roads and Town Bounds, 1698–1852.
(TXRB) Old Tax and Record Book, 1670–1716.

County records

Andover and most of the towns mentioned in this book are in Essex County. Records at the county level are kept in two locations at Salem, the county seat: (1) the Registry of Deeds and Probate Court Building, and (2) the Office of the Clerk of the County Court, Essex County Court House. Early Essex County Probate and Quarterly Court Records have been transcribed and published. I refer to them in this book as follows:

(ECPR) Essex County Probate Records. Probate Records of Essex County, Massachusetts, 1635–1681. 3 Volumes.
(ECQCR) Records and Files of the Quarterly Courts of Essex County, Massachusetts. 8 Volumes.

Colony records

Records of the Massachusetts Bay Company and Colony have been printed and published. They are available at the Massachusetts Archives, now stored at the University of Massachusetts, Harbor Campus. They are abbreviated in this book as:

(RMBC) Records of the Governor and Company of the Massachusetts Bay Colony in New England. 5 Volumes.
(RCAMBC) Records of the Court of Assistants of the Massachusetts Bay Colony, 1630–1692. 3 Volumes.

Province records

Massachusetts became part of the expanded Province of the Massachusetts Bay in October 1691. Records from this period are listed as:

(ALPMB) Acts and Laws, Province of Massachusetts Bay. Readex Microprints #695. Early American Imprints 1639–1880. Worcester: American Antiquarian Society.

Secondary sources

Genealogies

It has been said somewhere that the best histories of the twentieth century depend on the labors of the antiquarians and genealogists of the nineteenth. In the twenty-first century, we are still depending on them. We had better carry on our own antiquarian labors now for those coming after us. Charlotte Helen Abbott (1844–1921) was an indefatigable antiquarian, genealogist, and historian of the Andover towns and their families. Abbott's genealogies of early Andover families, typed up in the 1930s from her notes by a WPA (Works Project) worker, provided much basic information for my research, as they did for Greven. Wherever possible I crosschecked Abbott with other privately printed family genealogies, listed in the References below.

The New England Historical and Genealogical Register, the publication of the New England Historical and Genealogical Society, also contains many new and supplementary notes to the researches of earlier genealogists. These sources are referred to as follows:

> (Abbott n.d.: family surname) Charlotte Helen Abbott, Andover Family Genealogies.
> (NEHGR) New England Historical and Genealogical Register.

Town histories

Town histories written by local citizens provide invaluable help to a cautious researcher. Many exuberant amateur historians and family genealogists of the nineteenth century prepared and timed their publications to celebrate the anniversary of the founding of the town or the country. I have leaned heavily on Sarah Loring Bailey's classic citizen history of Andover (now available in full online at the website of the Andover Historical Society). Bailey's was one of many produced throughout New England for the centennial celebrations of 1876. These town histories, unencumbered by the need to develop an academic thesis, are an indispensable source of additional genealogical material, as well as information on historical relationships among towns in the region and refreshing anecdotes about events and people.

Reordered tax records and genealogies

Using microfilms of the original tax records of Andover, I copied and reordered a selection of tax lists at five-year intervals from 1670 to 1716, showing highest to lowest taxpayer (appendices B1–3).

Using Abbott's and other genealogies, I also constructed a three-generation genealogical chart for all Andover families in the research population, using the various family histories and genealogies mentioned above. These charts together cover some 3,000 individuals. Copies of these charts were placed on file in the Andover Historical Society.

In revising and updating the manuscript for this book, I was able to make use of many website resources which have sprung up since the coming of the Internet. I visited numerous family websites maintained by people tracing some connection to Andover, and in some cases have added to or modified the material on that family's history from the way it was in my dissertation. This is the case particularly with the Holt and Barker histories.

Historic Houses (HH) of Andover (1946)

HH Andover refers to the Historic Houses Map, helpful for early South Parish houselot layout. No equivalent of the Rockwell Maps (a time series) exists for the South Parish that I know of, but useful for a beginning understanding of neighborhoods in the early South Parish is the following publication, available at the AHS: *Historic Houses in Andover,* which was compiled with maps and photographs for the Tercentenary Celebration of the founding of Andover in 1946. In the 1990s members of the Historical Societies began a project of mapping the houses related in some way to the witchcraft outbreak: <http://www.nmrls.org/enha/exhibit/nandover/1692_m.shtml>. Portions of that map have been adapted with permission for use in this book; see maps 10 and 11.

References

Abbot, Abiel. 1829. *History of Andover from its settlement to 1829.* Andover, Mass.: Flagg and Gould.

Abbot, Abiel and Ephraim Abbot, compilers. 1847. *A genealogical register of the descendants of George Abbot of Andover, George Abbot of Rowley, Thomas Abbot of Andover, Arthur Abbot of Ipswich, Robert Abbot of Branford, Connecticut, and George Abbot of Norwalk, Connecticut.* Boston: James Munroe & Co.

Abbot, E. Stanley. 1916. The causal relations between structure and function in biology. *American Journal of Psychology* 27:245–250.

Abbot, Elinor. 1971. Change and continuity through eight generations in a New England family. ms.

Abbot, Elinor. 1974. Review of *Four generations: Population, land, and family in Colonial Andover, Massachusetts* by Philip Greven. *American Anthropologist* 76(3):593–594.

Abbot, Elinor. 1981. Heider's "Anthropological models of incest laws in the United States" continued: The New Hampshire case. ms.

Abbot, Elinor. 1985. Close-kin marriage in early Andover. *Andover Historical Society Newsletter* 10:3.

Abbot, Elinor. 1988. Notes on "seating the meetinghouse" in nineteenth-century Andover. ms.

Abbot, Elinor. 1990. Transformations: The reconstruction of social hierarchy in early colonial Andover, Massachusetts. Ph.D. dissertation, Department of Anthropology, Brandeis University.

Abbot, Elinor. 1992. Early Andover social structure. *Andover Historical Society Newsletter* 17:2.

Abbot, Elinor. 1996. Seventeenth century Andover: The people's point of view. *Andover Historical Society Newsletter* 20:4.

Abbott, Charlotte Helen. 1904. The Hawkes Reunion. *The Andover Townsman* (August 5, 1904). Andover, Massachusetts.

Abbott, Charlotte Helen. n.d. *The Charlotte Helen Abbott collection of genealogies of Andover families.* Typescript manuscripts [1936] on file at the Andover Historical Society, Andover, Massachusetts.

Abu-Lughad, L. 1986. *Veiled sentiments: Honor and poetry in a Bedouin society.* Berkeley: University of California Press.

Adams, Charles Francis. 1893. *Massachusetts: Its history and its historians.* Cambridge, Mass.: Riverside Press.

Alcott, Louisa May. 1929a. [1876] *Eight cousins.* Boston: Little, Brown, and Company.

Alcott, Louisa May. 1929b. [1878] *Rose in bloom*. New York: Grosset and Dunlap.

Allen, David Grayson. 1981. In *English ways: The movement of societies and the transferal of English local law and custom to Massachusetts Bay in the seventeenth century*. Chapel Hill: University of North Carolina Press.

ALPMB. Acts and Laws, Province of Massachusetts Bay. Readex Microprints #695. Early American Imprints 1639–1880. Worcester: American Antiquarian Society.

Anderson, Nancy Fix. 1982. The "Marriage with a deceased wife's sister" bill controversy: Incest anxiety and defence of family purity in Victorian England. *Journal of British Studies* 21:67–86.

Anderson, Nancy Fix. 1986. Cousin marriage in Victorian England. *Journal of Family History* 11:295–301.

ANPCM. *Andover North Precinct Church Meetings, 1710–1827*. Records of early Andover. Originals and Microfilm copies at the North Andover Historical Society.

ATR. *Ancient Town Records, 1656–1708. Records of early Andover*. Microfilm copies at the Andover Town Library.

Bailey, Sarah Loring. 1880. *Historical sketches of Andover, Massachusetts*. Boston: Houghton, Mifflin and Co. Facsimile reprint (1974) by the North Andover Historical Association, North Andover, Massachusetts.

Bailyn, Bernard. 1984. New England and a wider world. In David Hall and David Grayson Allen (eds.), *Seventeenth-century New England. Transactions of the Colonial Society of New England* 63. Charlottesville: University of Virginia Press.

Bailyn, Bernard. 1986. *The peopling of British North America*. New York: Alfred E. Knopf.

Bailyn, Bernard, and Philip D. Morgan, eds. 1991. *Strangers within the realm: Cultural margins of the First British Empire*. Chapel Hill: University of North Carolina Press.

Baker, Emerson W., and James Kences. 2001. Maine, Indian land speculation, and the Essex County witchcraft outbreak of 1692. Online: <http://www.hawthorneinsalem.org/Scholars Forum/MMD1705.html>. Accessed 2/11/2004.

Banks, Colonel C. 1928. Scotch prisoners deported to New England by Cromwell, 1651–1652. *Proceedings of the Massachusetts Historical Society*, vol. xli. Boston: Massachusetts Historical Society.

Banks, Colonel C. 1969 [1937]. *Topographical dictionary of 2885 English emigrants to New England, 1620–1650*. Edited by Elijah E. Brownell. Baltimore, Md.: Baltimore Publishing Company.

Barker, Mitch. 2004. On Barker Family website at <http://www.rootsweb.com/~mecnewry/barker_brothers.htm>.
Barnard Papers. n.d. *Journals of the Revs. Thomas Barnard and John Barnard, 1688–1743.* Original manuscripts and microfilm copies at North Andover Historical Society.
Binford, Lewis. 1982. The archaeology of place. *Journal of Anthropological Archaeology* 1:5–31.
Bixby, Willard G. 1914. *A genealogy of the descendants of Joseph Bixby, 1621–1701, of Ipswich and Boxford, Massachusetts.* Privately printed. On file in the North Andover Historical Society.
Black, G. L. 1968. Descendants of Daniel Black. On file in the Boxford (Massachusetts) Village Library. ms.
Bond, Henry. 1860. *Genealogies of the families and descendants of the early settlers of Watertown, Massachusetts, including Waltham and Weston, to which is appended the early history of the town.* Second edition. Boston: NEHGR.
Boyer, Paul, and Stephen Nissenbaum, eds. 1972. *Salem-Village witchcraft: A documentary record of local conflict in colonial New England.* Belmont, Calif.: Wadsworth Publishing Company.
Boyer, Paul, and Stephen Nissenbaum. 1974. *Salem possessed: The social origins of witchcraft.* Cambridge, Mass.: Harvard University Press.
Bradford, William. 1912. *History of Plymouth Plantation, 1606–1646.* 2 vols. New York: Barnes and Noble.
Breen, T. H. 1973. Moving to the New World: The character of early Massachusetts migration. *William and Mary Quarterly* 30:189–122.
Breen, T. H. 1978. Transfer of culture: Chance and design in shaping Massachusetts Bay. *NEHGR* cxxxii:3–17.
Breen, T. H. 1980. *Puritans and adventurers: Change and persistence in early America.* New York: Oxford University Press.
Brigham, Willard I. Tyler. 1912. *The Tyler genealogy: The descendants of Job Tyler of Andover, Massachusetts, 1619–700.* Privately printed. On file at the Andover Historical Society.
Brown, B. Katherine. 1954. A note on the Puritan concept of aristocracy. *Mississippi Valley Historical Review* xii:105–112.
Brown, Jennifer. 1980. Informants in the archives: Doing anthropology through historical documents. *Journal of Anthropology* 2:138–146.
Campbell, Helen. 1891. Anne Bradstreet and her time. Boston: Lothrop. Online: <http://www.blackmask.com/books10109c/nnbst.html>. Accessed 12/20/2004.
Campbell, Mildred. 1959. Social origins of some early Americans. In J. M. Smith (ed.), *Seventeenth-century America: Essays in colonial history,* 63–89. Chapel Hill: University of North Carolina Press.

Caporael, Linnda. 1976. Ergotism: The Satan loosed in Salem? *Science* 192. Online: <http:www.//web utk.edu/~kstclair/221/ergotism.html>. Accessed 2/19/2004.

Cawston, George, and A. H. Keane. 1968 [1896]. *The early chartered companies (AD 1296–1858)*. New York: B. Franklin.

Chandler, George. 1883. *The descendants of William and Annis Chandler*. Worcester: Charles Hamilton.

Chase, George Wingate. 1861. *History of Haverhill, Massachusetts, from 1640–1860*. Haverhill: privately printed.

Clement, Percival Wood. 1927. *Ancestors and descendants of Robert Clement of Leicestershire and Warwickshire, England, first settler of Haverhill, Massachusetts*. Philadelphia: Patterson and White.

Cliffe, J. T. 1984. *The Puritan gentry: The great Puritan families of early Stuart England*. London: Routledge & Kegan Paul.

Coffin Joshua. 1977 [1845]. *A sketch of the history of Newbury, Newburyport, and West Newbury, from 1635 to 1845*. Boston: Samuel G. Drake. Facsimile reprint for the Sons and Daughters of the First Settlers of Newbury. Hampton: Peter E. Randall Company.

Columbia encyclopedia. 2001–2005. New York: Columbia University Press.

Cook, A. M. 1956. *Lincolnshire links with the U.S.A.* Published at the Sub-deanery, Lincoln, England.

Cowing, Cedric. 1995. *The saving remnant: Religion and the settling of New England*. Chicago: University of Chicago Press.

Cressy, David. 1986. Kinship and kin interaction in early modern England. *Past and Present* 11(3):38–69.

Cressy, David. 1987. *Coming over: Migration and communication between England and New England in the seventeenth century*. Cambridge: Cambridge University Press.

C.U.D.D.L.E. [Cousins United to Defeat Discrimination Laws through Education] Online: <http://www.cuddleinternational.org.> Accessed 2/2/2004.

Dane, John. 1894 [1670]. A declaration of remarkabell providenses in the corse of my lyfe. *NEHGR* vol. viii:147–156.

Dawes, Norman. 1949. Titles as symbols of prestige in seventeenth-century New England. *William and Mary Quarterly* 6:69–84.

Deetz, James. 1996 [1977]. *Small things forgotten: An archaeology of early American life*. Revised edition. New York: Anchor.

Defoe, Daniel. 1923 [1722]. *The fortunes and misfortunes of the famous Moll Flanders*. Reprinted from the first edition. London: Constable and Company.

Demos, John. 1970. *A little Commonwealth: Family life in Plymouth.* Oxford: Oxford University Press.
Demos, John. 1976. John Godfrey and his neighbors: Witchcraft and the social web in colonial Massachusetts. *William and Mary Quarterly* xxxiii:242–265.
Demos, John. 1982. *Entertaining Satan: Witchcraft and the culture of early New England.* New York: Oxford University Press.
du Boulay, Juliet. 1984. The blood: Symbolic relations between descent, marriage, incest prohibitions, and spiritual kinship in Greece. *Man* 19:533–546.
Duby, Georges. 1980. *The three orders: Feudal society imagined.* Chicago: University of Chicago Press.
Dumont, Louis. 1984. *Affinity as a value.* Chicago: University of Chicago Press.
Dunn, Richard S. 1962. *Puritans and Yankees: The Winthrop dynasty of New England, 1630–1717.* Princeton: Princeton University Press.
Durrie, Daniel. 1864. *A genealogical history of the Holt family in the United States: More particularly the descendants of Nicholas Holt of Newbury and Andover, Massachusetts, 1634–41 and of William Holt of New Haven, Connecticut.* Albany: J. Munsell. Online: <http://www.holt.org/holtgen.html>. Accessed 4/19/2004.
ECPR. *Essex County Probate Records, 1635–1681.* 3 vols. Printed at Salem, Massachusetts, 1916–1920.
ECQCR. 1679. *Essex County Quarterly Court Records.* Records and files of the Quarterly Courts of Essex County, Massachusetts. 8 vols. George F. Dow (ed.). Printed at Salem, Massachusetts, 1911–1921.
Eggleston, Edward. 1896. *The beginners of a nation: A history of the source and rise of the earliest English settlements in America with special reference to the life and character of the people.* New York: D. Appleton and Company.
Evans-Pritchard, E. E. 1962. Anthropology and History. In E. E. Evans-Pritchard (ed.), *Social Anthropology and Other Essays.* Glencoe: Free Press.
Farber, Bernard. 1970. Heider's "Anthropological models of incest in the United States": A comment. *American Anthropologist* 72:846–847.
Farber, Bernard. 1972. *Guardians of virtue: Salem families in 1800.* New York: Basic Books.
Felt, Joseph B. 1834. *History of Ipswich, Essex, and Hamilton.* Cambridge, Mass.: Charles Folsom.
Field, Edward. 1897. *The colonial tavern.* Providence: Preston and Rounds.

Fischer, David Hackett. 1991 [1989]. *Albion's seed: Four British folkways in America.* New York: Oxford University Press.

Fleming, Patricia H. 1973. The politics of marriage among non-Catholic European royalty. *Current Anthropology* 14:231–249.

Foster, Stephen. 1971. *Their solitary way: Puritan social ethic in the first century of settlement in New England.* New Haven: Yale University Press.

Fox, Robin. 1978. *The Tory Islanders: A people of the Celtic fringe.* Cambridge: Cambridge University Press.

Frye Family. Frye Genealogy. Frye Family Home Page. Online: <http://www.mv.com/ipusers/ the masons>. Accessed 3/12/2004.

Fuess, Claude. 1953. Witches at Andover. *Proceedings of the Massachusetts Historical Society* 70:14.

Fuess, Claude. 1959. *Andover: The symbol of New England.* Historical Publications: North Andover and Andover Historical Societies.

Galenson, D. 1979. "Middling people" or "common sort": The social origins of some early Americans reexamined. *William and Mary Quarterly* 35:499–524, with a rebuttal by Mildred Campbell, 525–535.

Geertz, Clifford. 1976. "From the native's point of view": On the nature of anthropological understanding. In Keith H. Basso and Henry A. Selby (eds.), *Meaning in anthropology.* Santa Fe: School of American Research.

Giddens, Anthony. 1979. *Central problems in social theory: Action, structure and contradiction.* Berkeley: University of California Press.

Giddens, Anthony. 1984. *The constitution of society: Outline of the theory of structuration.* Cambridge: Polity Press.

Gildrie, Richard P. 1971. Salem 1626–1668: History of a covenant community. Ph.D. Dissertation, Department of History, University of Virginia. Ann Arbor: University Microfilms. [Published 1975.]

Gildrie, Richard P. 1982. The ceremonial Puritan. *NEHGR* cxxxvi:3–16.

Godbeer, Richard. 1992. *The devil's dominion: Magic and religion in early New England.* Cambridge: Cambridge University Press.

Godbeer, Richard. 1995. "Love raptures": Marital, romantic, and erotic images of Jesus Christ in Puritan New England. *New England Quarterly* 68:355–384.

Godbeer, Richard. 2002. *Sexual revolution in early America.* Baltimore: Johns Hopkins Press.

Godbeer, Richard. 2004. *Escaping Salem: The other witch hunt of 1692.* Oxford: Oxford University Press.

Goode, William. 2003. Family changes over the long term: A sociological commentary. *Journal of Family History* 29(1):15–30.

Goodman, Robert L. 1974. Newbury Massachusetts, 1635–1685: The social foundations of conflict. Ph.D. Dissertation, Michigan State University.

Greene, Jack R., and J. R. Pole, eds. 1984. *Colonial British America: Essays in the new history of the early modern era.* Baltimore: The Johns Hopkins Press.

Greven, Philip J. Jr. 1964. Four generations: Population, land and family in colonial Andover. Ph.D. Dissertation, Department of History, Harvard University. Ann Arbor: University Microfilms.

Greven, Philip. 1966. Family structure in seventeenth-century Andover, Massachusetts. *William and Mary Quarterly,* 3rd Series 23:234–256.

Greven, Philip. 1977. *The Protestant temperament.* New York: Meridian, New American Library.

Greven, Philip J. Jr. 1970. *Four generations: Population, land, and family in colonial Andover, Massachusetts.* Ithaca: Cornell University Press.

Greven, Philip J. Jr. 1972. A note on the ages of converts in Andover, Massachusetts, 1711–1749. *Essex Institute Historical Collections* 108:119–134.

Hall, David D. 1972. *The faithful shepherd: A history of the New England ministry in the seventeenth century.* Institute of Early American History and Culture, Williamsburg. Chapel Hill: University of North Carolina Press.

Hall, David D. 1991. *Witch-hunting in seventeenth-century New England: A documentary history, 1638–1692.* Edited and with an introduction by David D. Hall. Boston: Northeastern University Press.

Hall, Joseph, Bishop of Norwich. 1650. Whether the marriage of cousins-german be lawful. In *Four decades, with some additionals: Resolutions and decisions of diverse practical cases of conscience.* Fourth decade, 331–342. London.

Hammatt, Abraham. 1980. *Early inhabitants of Ipswich, Massachusetts, 1633–1700. The Hammatt papers, 1880–1889.* Baltimore: Genealogical Publishing Company.

Hansen, Chadwick. 1969. *Witchcraft at Salem.* New York: George Braziller.

Hansen, Chadwick. 1983. Andover witchcraft and the causes of the Salem witchcraft trials. In Howard Kerr and Charles L. Crow (eds.), *The occult in America,* 38–57. Urbana: University of Illinois Press.

Hanson, Edward W. 1985. The non-English New Englanders. *NEHGR* cxxxiv:3–20.

Harris, Marvin. 1968. *The rise of anthropological theory.* New York: Thomas W. Crowell.

Hartley, L. P. 1953. *The go-between.* London: Hamish Hamilton.

Hardwick, Katherine D. 1962. *"As long as charity shall be a virtue": Boston private charities from 1657–1800.* Boston: Boston Atheneum Press.

Hawthorne, Nathaniel. 1981 [1851]. *The house of the seven gables.* New York: Bantam Classics.

Haskins George Lee. 1960. *Law and authority in early Massachusetts: A study in tradition and design.* New York: MacMillan Company.

Hazen, Henry. 1883. *History of Billerica, Massachusetts.* Boston: A. Williams.

Headland, Thomas N., Kenneth L. Pike, and Marvin Harris. 1990. *Emics and etics: The insider/outsider debate.* Newbury Park: Sage Publications

Heider, Karl. 1969. Anthropological models of incest laws in the United States. *American Anthropologist* 71:693–701.

Heider, Karl. 1988. The Rashomon effect: When ethnographers disagree. *American Anthropologist* 90:71–81.

Heyrman, Christine. 1984. *Commerce and culture: The maritime communities of colonial Massachusetts.* New York: Norton.

Higginson, Francis. 1629. *New England's plantation, or a short and true description of the commodities and discommodities of that country.* Redacted and introduced by John Beardsley, editor in chief, The Winthrop Society Quarterly. Online: <http// www.imsa.edu/socsci/jvictory/txt_colonial /newengland_higginson.htm>.

Hinman, Barry. 1985. Anne (Wood) (Price) Bradstreet: An identity revealed. *NEGHR* cxxxix:139–142.

HH Andover. 1946. *Historic houses in Andover.* Compiled with maps and photographs and published for the Tercentenary Celebration. Andover Historical Society.

Holmes, Frank R., compiler. 1964 [1923]. *Directory of the ancestral heads of New England families, 1620–1700.* Reprint. Baltimore: Genealogical Publishing Co.

Holt Association of America. n.d. *The first three generations of Holts in America.* Newburg: N. Y. Moor Printing Company. Privately printed for the subscribers.

Homans, George C. 1970 [1941]. *English villagers of the thirteenth century.* New York: Harper Torchbooks.

Hotten, John Camden, compiler. 1962 [1880]. *The original lists of persons of quality who went from Great Britain to the American plantations, 1600–1700.* Baltimore: Genealogical Publishing Company.

Hunt, Geoffrey, and Saundra Satterlee. 1986. Cohesion and division: Drinking in an English village. *Man* 21:521–537.

Hurd, D. Hamilton. 1888. *History of Essex County, Massachusetts.* Boston: J. W. Lewis & Co.

Hurd, James P. 1983. Kin relatedness and church fissioning among the "Nebraska" Amish of Pennsylvania. *Social Biology* 30:56–60.

Hurd, James P. 1985. Kissing cousins: Frequencies of cousin types in "Nebraska" Amish marriages. *Social Biology* 32:82–84.

Innes, Stephen. 1983. *Labor in a new land: Economy and society in seventeenth-century Springfield.* Princeton: Princeton University Press.

Jameson, J. Franklin, ed. 1910 [1654]. *Johnson's wonder-working providence, 1628–1651.* New York: Charles W. Scribner & Sons.

Jewett, C. F. 1878. Standard History of Essex County, Massachusetts. Boston: C. F. Jewett & Co. Online: <http://homepages.rootsweb.com/~kwc/boynton/rowley_hist.html>. Accessed 2/18/2004

Johnson, Edward. 1654. *Wonder-working providence of Sions Saviour in New England.* Original narratives of early American history. Online: <http//www. rootsweb.com/~usgenweb/special/history /providence/book3.htm>. Accessed 3/18/2003.

Jones, Maldwyn. 1991. The Scotch-Irish in British America. In Bernard Bailyn and Philip Morgan, (eds.), *Strangers within the realm: Cultural margins of the First British Empire,* 284–313. Chapel Hill: University of North Carolina Press.

Karlsen, Carol. 1987. *The devil in the shape of a woman: Witchcraft in colonial New England.* New York: Norton.

Karlsen, Carol. 2003. Devils in the shape of good men. Review of *The devil's square: The Salem witchcraft crises of 1692,* by Mary Beth Norton. Online: <ww.common-place.org/vol-03/no-02/reviews/Karlsen/shtml>.

Kendall, Edward Augustus. 1809. *Travels through the northern parts of the United States in the years 1807 and 1808.* New York: I. Riley.

Kent, Joan. 1981. The English village constable, 1580–1642: The nature and dilemmas of the office. *Journal of British Studies* 20:26–49.

Kimball, David T. 1823. *A sketch of the ecclesiastical history of Ipswich.* Haverhill, Mass.: Gazette and Patriot Office.

Knight, Madam. 1935 [1702]. *The journal of Madam Knight.* Introduction by George Park Winship. New York: Peter Smith.

Kuper, Adam. 2002. Incest, cousin marriage and the origin of the human sciences in nineteenth-century England. *Past and Present* 174. Online: <http//www3.oup.co.uk/past/hdb/volume_174/issue-01/pdf/174258.pdf>. Accessed 3/10/2004.

Lepore, Jill. 1998. *The name of war: King Philip's War and the origins of American identity.* New York: Alfred A. Knopf.

Lett, James. 1990. Emics and etics: Notes on the epistemology of anthropology. In Thomas N. Headland, Kenneth L. Pike, and Marvin

Harris (eds.), *Emics and etics: The insider/outsider debate,* 127–142. Newbury Park: Sage Publications.

Leyton, Elliott. 1975. *The one blood: Kinship and class in an Irish village.* Newfoundland Social and Economic Studies 13. Institute of Social and Economic Research, Memorial University of Newfoundland. Toronto: University of Toronto Press.

Lindholdt, Paul J., ed. 1988. *John Josselyn, colonial traveler. A critical edition of Two Voyages to New England (1672 and 1674).* Hanover: University Press of New England.

Livermore, Abiel Abbot, and Sewall Putnam. 1888. *A history of the town of Wilton, Hillsborough County, New Hampshire.* Lowell: Marden and Rowell.

Lockridge, Kenneth A. 1970. *A New England town: The first one hundred years.* New York: Norton.

Lovejoy, Clarence Earle. 1930. *The Lovejoy genealogy, with biographies and a history, 1460–1930.* Privately printed by the author.

Lovejoy, W. Barrett Jr. 2002. *Lovejoy family history, 800–2001.* Homepage of Jerry Lovejoy. Online: <http//home.comcast.net/~bennabre/lfh.doc>. Accessed 3/16/2004.

Main, Gloria L. 1996. Naming children in early New England. *Journal of Interdisciplinary History* 27:1–27.

Main, Gloria L. 2001. *Peoples of a spacious land: Families and cultures in colonial New England.* Cambridge, Mass.: Harvard University Press.

Malinowski, Bronislaw. 1984 [1922]. *Argonauts of the Western Pacific.* Reissue, Prospect Heights, Ill.: Waveland Press.

Marston, Nathan Washington. 1888. *Marston genealogy.* Privately printed for the subscribers. On file at the Andover Historical Society.

Mather, Cotton. 1695. *The answer of several ministers to that case of conscience whether it is lawful for a man to marry his wife's own sister.* B. Green: Boston. Massachusetts Historical Society Archives.

Mather, Cotton. 1977 [1702]. *Magnalia Christi Americana,* Kenneth B. Murdock (ed.). Cambridge, Mass.: Belknap Press.

Mather, Richard. 1643. *An apologie of the churches in New England for church-covenant.* London.

McChesney, Elinor Blanchard. 1976. *Blanchard: A Huguenot family in America.* Privately printed for the family. Copy on file at the Andover Historical Society.

McDonald, Maryon. 1986. Celtic ethnic kinship and the problem of being English. *Current Anthropology* 227:333–348.

Mendelson, Sara Heller. 1980. Debate: the weightiest business: Marriage in an upper-gentry family in seventeenth-century England. *Past and Present* 85:126–135. [See also Slater 1980.]

Metcalf, John G. 1880. *Annals of the town of Mendon, 1659–1880.* Providence, R.I.: E. L. Freeman and Co.

MHS. 1931. *The Winthrop papers,* vol. 2, Stewart Mitchell, (ed.). Boston: The Massachusetts Historical Society Publications xii:367.

MHS. 1934. *The Winthrop papers.* vol. 3, Allyn Bailey Forbes (ed.). Boston: The Massachusetts Historical Society Publications. xxxvii:544.

MHS. 1944, *The Winthrop papers,* vol. 4, Allyn Bailey Forbes (ed.), Boston: The Massachusetts Historical Society Publications. xxxvii:531.

Millar, David R. 1967. The militia, the army, and independency in colonial Massachusetts. Ph.D. Dissertation, Cornell University. Ann Arbor: University Microfilms, Inc.

Miller, Perry. 1961 [1939]. *The New England mind: The seventeenth century.* Boston: Beacon Press.

Mofford, Juliet Haines. 1985. *"And firm their ancient vow": The history of the North Parish Church of North Andover.* North Andover, Mass.: North Andover Historical Society.

Mofford, Juliet Haines. 2004. *Andover, Massachusetts: Historical selections from four centuries.* History of the Merrimack Valley Series. Andover, Mass.: Merrimac Valley Preservation Press.

Molloy, Maureen. 1986. "No inclination to mix with strangers": Marriage patterns among Highland Scots migrants to Cape Breton and New Zealand, 1800–1916. *Journal of Family History* 11:221–243.

Mooar, George, compiler. 1859. *Historical manual of the South Church in Andover, Massachusetts.* Andover: Warren Draper.

Morgan, Edmund S. 1966 [1944]. *The Puritan family.* New York: Harper Torchbooks.

Moriarty, G. Andrews. 1931. The ancestry of William Chandler of Roxbury, Massachusetts. *NEHGR* cxxxv:142–145.

Murrin, John M. 2003. The infernal conspiracy of Indians and grandmothers. *Reviews in American History* 31(4):485–494.

Nash, Gary. 1970. *Class and society in early America.* Englewood Cliffs, N.J.: Prentice-Hall.

NEHGR. *New England Historical and Genealogical Record.* Publication of the New England Historic Genealogical Society.

Northend, William Dummer. 1896. *The Bay Colony: A civil, religious and social history of the Massachusetts Colony.* Boston: Estes and Lauriat.

Norton, Mary Beth. 1986 The evolution of white women's experience in early America. *American Historical Review* 89:593–619.
Norton, Mary Beth. 2002. *In the Devil's snare: The Salem witchcraft crisis of 1692.* New York: Knopf.
NPJCM. *North Parish Journal of Church Matters. 1686–1810.* Original records and Microfilm copies at the North Andover Historical Society.
O'Malley, Patricia. 1975. Rowley, Massachusetts, 1639–1730: Dissent, division, and delimitation in a Colonial Town. Ph.D. dissertation, Boston College. Ann Arbor: University Microfilms.
Osgood, Ira. 1894. *A genealogy of the descendants of John, Christopher, and William Osgood who came from England and settled in New England early in the seventeenth century,* Eben Putnam (ed.). Salem: Essex Institute.
Ottenheimer, Martin. 1996. *Forbidden relatives: The American myth of cousin marriage.* Urbana: University of Illinois Press.
Owen, Dennis E. 1982. Spectral evidence: The witchcraft cosmology of Salem village in 1692. In Mary Douglas (ed.), *Essays in the sociology of perception.* London: Routledge & Kegan Paul.
Palfrey, John Gorham. 1882. *History of New England during the Stuart dynasty.* 3 vols. Boston: Little, Brown, and Company.
Parkhurst, Winifred C. 1952. *History of the First Congregational Church, Boxford, Massachusetts, 1702–1952* [with map of early Boxford residences keyed to Perley 1893]. Topsfield: Perkins Press.
Paynter, Robert. 1982. *Models of spatial inequality: Settlement patterns in historical archaeology.* New York: Academic Press.
Perkin, Harold. 1972 [1969]. *The origins of modern English society, 1780–1880.* London: Routledge & Kegan Paul.
Perley, Sidney. 1880. *The history of Boxford.* Boxford, Mass.: privately printed by the author.
Perley, Sidney. 1893. *The dwellings of Boxford, Essex County, Massachusetts.* Privately printed by the author.
Perley, Sidney. 1912. *The Indian land titles of Essex County.* Salem: Essex Book and Print Club.
Perzel, Edward. 1967. The first generation of settlement in colonial Ipswich, Massachusetts, 1633–1660. Ph. D. dissertation, Rutgers University. Ann Arbor: University Microfilms.
Peters, Edmond F., compiler. 1903. *Peters of New England: A genealogy and family history.* New York: Knickerbocker Press.
PhRB *The Rev. Samuel Phillips' record book, 1711–1722.* Original in the Andover Historical Society.
Pike, Kenneth L. 1967. Etic and emic standpoints for the description of behavior. In *Language in relation to a unified theory of the structure of*

human behavior, part 1:8–12. [2nd revised edition] Janua Linguarum. Series Maior 24. The Hague: Mouton.

Pike, Kenneth L. 1972. [1959] Language as particle, wave, and field. In Ruth M. Brend (ed.), *Kenneth L. Pike: Selected writings,* 129–143. The Hague: Mouton.

Plakans, Andrejs. 1984. *Kinship in the past: An anthropology of European family life, 1500–1900.* Oxford: Basil Blackwell.

Pride, Edward W. 1888. *Tewksbury, a short history.* Issued under the auspices of the Tewksbury Village Improvement Association. Cambridge: Riverside Press. Online: <http://www.tewksbury.com/pride.html>.

Powell, Sumner Chilton. 1963. *Puritan village: The formation of a New England town [Sudbury, Mass.].* Middleton, Conn.: Wesleyan University Press.

Pratt, Phineas. 1662. Account of the Wessagussett plantation. Redacted version. Online: <http://www.winthropsociety.org/doc_pratt.php>.

Proceedings of 1896. 1896. *Proceedings of the celebration of the two hundred and fiftieth anniversary of the incorporation of the town of Andover.* Andover: The Andover Press.

RCACMB. 1904. *Records of the Court of Assistants of the Colony of Massachusetts Bay, 1630–1692.* 3 vols. Printed under the supervision of John Noble, Clerk of the Supreme Judicial Court, Boston.

RMBC. 1853–1854. *Records of the Massachusetts Bay Colony: Records of the governor and company of the Massachusetts Bay Colony in New England,* 5 vols., Nathaniel B. Shurtleff (ed.). Printed at Boston.

Robbins, Chandler. 1869. The Regicides sheltered in New England. *Lectures on subjects relating to the early history of Massachusetts.* Boston: Massachusetts Historical Society Publications.

Roberts, Gary Boyd. 1987. Immigrants to early New England for whom royal descent has been proved, virtually proved, improved, or disproved since about 1960: A bibliographical survey. *NEHGR* cxli:92–109.

Robinson, Enders. 1991 (paperback edition 1992). Paperback edition of *The devil discovered: Salem witchcraft, 1692.* Hippocrene Books: New York.

Rockwell, Forbes. n.d. Rockwell map series of early Andover houselot ownership. Andover Historical Society Collection.

Rumsey, David. *The David Rumsey map collection.* Online: <http://www.davidrumsey.com> Accessed 4/28/2004.

Rutman, Darrett. 1965. *Winthrop's Boston: A portrait of a Puritan town, 1630–1649.* New York: W. W. Norton and Company.

Sabean, David Warren. 1984. *Power in the blood: Popular culture and village discourse in early modern Germany.* Cambridge: Cambridge University Press.

Schneider, David. 1968. *American kinship: A cultural account.* Englewood Cliffs, N. J.: Prentice Hall.

Sefton, Dru. 2004. First cousins speak out for right to wed. Online: <http://www. newhousenews.com/archive/sefton/012004.html.> Accessed 2/2/2004.

Sewall, Judge Samuel. 1973. *The diary of Samuel Sewall, 1674–1729.* M. Halsey Thomas (ed.). New York: Farrar, Straus and Giroux.

Shurtleff, Nathaniel B. 1853. *Records of the governor and company of Massachusetts Bay in New England.* 5 vols. Boston.

Shy, John W. 1963. A new look at the Colonial militia. *William and Mary Quarterly* 20:175–185.

Sidky, H. 2004. *Perspectives on culture.* Upper Saddle River, N. J.: Pearson Prentice-Hall.

Simmons, Frederick Johnson. 1959. *Emmanuel Downing.* Forest City: Forest City Printing.

Simpson, Alan, and Mary Simpson, eds. 1975. *Benjamin Church's diary of King Philip's War, 1675–76.* Tercentenary edition. Published for the Little Compton Historical Society. Chester, Conn.: Pequot Press.

Slade, Daniel Denison, ed. 1892. Autobiography of Major General Denison. *NEHGR* xlix:127–133.

Slater, Miriam. 1976. The weightiest business: Marriage in an upper-gentry family in seventeenth-century England. *Past and Present* 72:25–54.

Slater, Miriam. 1980. A rejoinder to Mendelsen. *Past and Present* 85:136–140.

Slotkin, Richard. 1973. *Regeneration through violence: The mythology of the American frontier, 1600–1860.* Middletown, Conn.: Wesleyan University Press.

Sly, John F. 1928. Geographical expansion and town system. In Albert B. Hart (ed.), *Commonwealth history of Massachusetts,* ch. 4. New York: The States History Company.

Smith, Carol. 1976. Analyzing regional social systems. In Carol Smith (ed.), *Regional analysis.* New York: Academic Press.

Smith, Daniel Scott. 1975. Population, family, and society in Hingham, Massachusetts, 1635–1880. Ph.D. dissertation, Department of History, University of California, Berkeley. Ann Arbor: University Microfilms.

Smout, T. C. 1981. Scottish marriage, regular and irregular, 1500–1940. In R. B. Outhwaite (ed.), *Marriage and society: Studies in the social history of marriage*. New York: St Martin's Press.

SPCR. 1711. South Parish Church Records. *A book bought by the church in the south part of Andover for their use, with a record book of the south precinct*. Ms. stored at the Andover Historical Society.

Staloff, Dennis. 1998. *The making of an American thinking class: Intellectuals and intelligentsia in Puritan Massachusetts*. Oxford: Oxford University Press.

Stearns, Raymond P. 1937. Correspondence of John Woodbridge and Richard Baxter. *New England Quarterly* x:572–578.

Summers, Montague. 1927. *The geography of witchcraft*. New York: Alfred A. Knopf.

Thayer, Christopher T. 1868. An address delivered on October 2, 1867, in the First Parish Beverly, on the two-hundredth anniversary of its formation, 34–35. Boston: Nichols and Noyes.

Thompson, Roger. 2001. *Divided we stand: Watertown, Massachusetts, 1630–1680*. Amherst: University of Massachusetts Press.

Town of Topsfield. 1899. *The historical collections of the Topsfield Historical Society*. Topsfield, Mass.: Topsfield Historical Society.

Towner, Lawrence. 1962. "A fondness for freedom": Servant protest in Puritan society. *William and Mary Quarterly* 19:201–219.

TR&B. Records of town roads and town bounds, 1698–1852. *Records of early Andover, Massachusetts*. Microfilm copies at the Andover Town Library.

TXRB. Old tax and town of record book, 1670–1716. *Records of early Andover, Massachusetts*. Microfilm copies at the Andover Town Library.

Turner, John. 1682a. *A letter of resolution concerning marriage of cousin-germans*. London: Printed by H. H. for Walter Kettilby.

Turner, John. 1682b. *Two discourses introducing to a disquisition demonstrating the unlawfulness of the marriage of cousins-german: From law, reason, Scripture, and antiquity*. London: Printed by H. H. for Walter Kettilby.

Turner, Victor. 1969. *The ritual process: Structure and anti-structure*. Chicago: Aldine.

Turner, Victor. 1974. *Dramas, fields, and metaphors: Symbolic action in human society*. Ithaca: Cornell University Press.

Underdown, David E. 1973. *Somerset in the Civil War and Interregnum*. Newton Abbot: David and Charles.

Vaughan, Alden T., ed. 1972. *The Puritan tradition in America: A sourcebook*. Columbia: University of South Carolina Press.

Wallace, Anthony F. C. *1978. Rockdale: The growth of an American village in the early Industrial Revolution.* New York: Alfred A. Knopf.

Walne, Peter. 1978. Emigrants from Hertfordshire, 1630–1640: Some corrections and additions. *NEHGR* cxxxii:18–24.

Walsh, J. P. 1979. Holy time and sacred space in Puritan New England. *American Quarterly* 32:79–95.

Ward, Nathaniel. 1641. *Liberties of New England.* <www.winthropsociety.org>.

Waters, John J. 1968. Hingham, Massachusetts 1631–1661: An East Anglian oligarchy in the New World. *Journal of Social History* 1:350–370.

Waters, John J. 1982. Family, inheritance, and migration in colonial New England: The evidence from Guilford, Connecticut. *William and Mary Quarterly* 39:64–86.

Waters, Thomas Franklin. 1905. *Ipswich in the Massachusetts Bay Colony, part 1.* Ipswich: Ipswich Historical Society.

Webb. James. 2004. *Born fighting: How the Scots-Irish shaped America.* New York: Random House, Broadway Books Division.

Webb, Stephen S. 1984. *1676, the end of American independence.* New York: Alfred A. Knopf.

Weisman, Richard. 1984. *Witchcraft, magic, and religion in seventeenth-century Massachusetts.* Amherst: University of Massachusetts Press.

Williams, Andrew P. 1995. Shifting signs: Increase Mather and the comets of 1680 and 1682. *Early Modern Literary Studies* 1(3):4.1–34. Online: <http://www.purl.oclc.org/emls/03-1/willmath.html>. Accessed 4/20/2004

Willson, David Harris. 1967. *A history of England.* New York: Holt, Rinehart, and Winston.

Winslow, Ola Elizabeth. 1952. *Meetinghouse Hill.* New York: MacMillan.

Winthrop, John n.d. Reasons to be considered for justifying the undertakers of the intended plantation in new England, & for encouraging such whose heart God shall move to joine with them in it. circa 1628. In Robert C. Winthrop (ed.), 1864, *life and letters of John Winthrop,* 309–310. Boston: Treknor and Fields. Online: <http://www2.sjsuedu.faculty/Watkins/Newengland02.htm>. Accessed 2/18/2004.

Winthrop, John. 1630. A model of Christian charity. Sermon given aboard the ship Arbella. Online:<http://religiousfreedom.lib.virginia.edu/sacred/charity.html>. Accessed 4/14/2004.

Winthrop, John. 1908. Journal. In James Kendall Hosmer (ed.), *John Winthrop's History of New England, 1630–1649,* 2 vols. New York: Charles Scribner and Sons.

Wise, Mary Ruth, Thomas N. Headland, and Ruth Brend, eds. 2003. *Language and life: Essays in memory of Kenneth L. Pike.* SIL International and the University of Texas at Arlington Publications in Linguistics 139. Dallas: SIL International.
Wormald, J. 1980. Blood-feud, kindred, and government in early modern Scotland. *Past and Present* 87:54–97.
Wrigley, E. A. 1966. *An introduction to historical demography.* London: Weidenfeld and Nicolson.
Yentsch, Anne Elisabeth. 1981. Expressions of cultural diversity and social reality in seventeenth-century New England. Ph.D. dissertation, Brown University. Ann Arbor: University Microfilm.
Zaret, David. 1985. *The heavenly contract: Ideology and organization in pre-revolutionary puritanism.* Chicago: University of Chicago Press.
Zodiac Atlas of Great Britian. 1976 edition. London: Bemrose and Sons Ltd.

Name Index

Listed below are the names of most Massachusetts Bay Colony settlers and early Andover residents mentioned in this book. A note on spellings: Town and court clerks did not always spell people's names the same way twice in the early documents. One of my favorite seventeenth-century characters in the Massachusetts record in this regard (not listed here) is a Frenchman who somehow landed among the Massachusetts Englishmen and found himself transformed by the clerks from "Jacques Ibert" to "Jacky Bear."

To readers who may be searching for their ancestors on this list: any inquiries, corrections, or updates on the family information in this account would be much appreciated and may be directed to the author at the publisher's address.

A

Abbot, George, 62, 63, 94, 118, 136, 138, 153
Abbot, George, Jr., 155, 174
Abbot, John, 133, 147
Abbot, Joseph, 130
Abbott, George, 21, 118
Allen, Andrew, 21, 118, 137, 144, 149, 150
Allen, John, 150
Aslebe, John (also Aslett), 87, 92, 118, 154, 155
Aslett (see Aslebe), John, 21
Aubrey, John, 25

B

Ballard, John, 84
Ballard, Joseph, 84, 123, 147, 150
Ballard, William, 21, 84, 94, 111, 118
Barker, Richard, 21, 92, 97, 111, 112, 115, 116, 118, 132, 135, 142
Barnard, Elizabeth, 175
Barnard, Robert, 21, 92, 141
Barnard, Thomas, 3, 141, 142
    as minister, 97, 154
    choice of parish, 157, 158, 159, 169, 173
    text of letter to the Court, appendix C, 183
Black, Daniel, 130, 137
Blake, Richard, 21, 91, 111
Blanchard, Samuel, 118
Bradford, William, 7

Bradstreet, Anne, 7
Bradstreet, Dudley, 68, 70
   Andover gentry, 92, 97
   meetinghouse seating committee, 85, 138, 139
   promoted to Captain, 131, 132
   supports Chandler tavern petition, 147, 148
Bradstreet, Mercy, 100
Bradstreet, Simon, 30, 37, 40, 43, 58, 60, 61, 65, 67, 70, 79, 80, 82, 92, 99, 103, 142
   and title "Mr", 9, 23, 69
   builder of first sawmill, 83
   death of, 153
   first civic and military leader of Andover, 7
   in the Faulkner list, 21
   marriage history, 108, 110, 118
   move to Salem, 89, 92, 132
Bridges, Edmund, 135
Bridges, James, 154
Bridges, Sara, 172
Browne, Nathaniel, 64

C

Carrier, Martha, 141
   and witchcraft crisis, 149, 150, 172
Carrier, Mary
   and witchcraft crisis, 151
Carrier, Sarah, 172
Carrier, Thomas, 65, 137, 149, 150
Chandler, Hannah Abbot, 148, 153
Chandler, John, 155
Chandler, John Jr., 155
Chandler, Thomas, 21, 63, 94, 132, 133, 136, 139, 146, 147, 148, 149
Chandler, William, 62, 63, 94, 118
   tavern dispute, 87, 136, 140, 144, 145, 146, 148, 171
Clements, Robert, 119
Conant, Roger, 59
Cotton, John, 40, 42
Cradock, Matthew, 35, 45
Cromwell, Oliver, 28, 52, 65, 76
Cutshamache, 2

D

Dane, Abigail, 167
Dane, Francis, 63, 70, 138, 149
   Dane (or Deane) family, 64
   death, 153
   family troubles, 126
   in ill health, 125
   quarrel with church, 129, 137, 139, 141
   reputation, 148
   witchcraft crisis, 151, 152, 167
Dane, Francis Jr., 155
Dane, John, 7, 61, 62, 64, 71, 94, 97, 118, 129
Davison, Damoe 64
Denison, Daniel, 7, 130, 132, 135
Downing, Emmanuel, 40
Dudley, Anne, 30, 100
Dudley, Thomas, 100, 183
   as gentry, 43, 45
   as governor, 65, 68
   background, 30, 40, 61
   letter to Countess of Lincoln, 30, 31, 32, 35, 38, 44
   move to Ipswich, 58
   quarrel with Rogers, 52
   reconciliation with Winthrop, 47, 60, 101, 128

E

Endecott, John, 31, 39, 44, 59

F

Farnum, Ralph, 72, 93, 118
Faulkner, Edmond, 21, 80
   as gentry, 82, 108
   as town clerk, 77, 133
   Faulkner list, 19, 20, 23
   holder of ordinary license, 86, 87, 144
   marriage history, 110, 117, 118, 126
   negotiations with Indians, 69, 131
Foster, Andrew, 21, 65, 106, 111, 118, 137
Foster, Ann, 111, 151, 167
Frye (or Frie), John, 118, 142
   holder of ordinary license, 144
   in militia, 36
   in South End, 136, 146
   in witchcraft crisis, 151

Name Index 233

G

Gilbert, Mr., 26
Godfrey, John, 125, 126, 135, 141
Gorges, Sir Ferdinando, 38
Gould, John, 26
Green, Joseph, 129, 159, 170

H

Henryson, John, 28
Higginson, Francis, 8
Holt, Henry, 147
Holt, Nicholas, 21, 72, 80, 111
   as a settler, 90, 93
   close-kin marriage, 112, 116, 117, 118
   Holt Hill, 93
   in South End, 136, 145
Holt, Nicholas Holt
   as a settler, 95
Holt, Samuel, 150
Hooker, Mr Thomas 36

I

Ingalls, Henry, 71, 84, 93, 118

J

Jaques, Henry, 21
Johnson, 118
Johnson, Edward, 8, 24, 75, 76
Johnson, Elizabeth, 172
Johnson, John, 51
Johnson, Lady Arbella, 42, 45, 109, 153
Johnson, Sir Isaac, 43, 45, 109
Johnson, Sir Issac, 42
Johnson, Thomas, 140, 145, 146
Johnson, William, 146
Josselyn, John, 1, 2, 7, 8, 13, 25, 76

L

Lacey (Lacy), Laurence, 137
Lacy (or Lacey), Mary, 151
Levett, Capt., 44
Lincoln, Countess of, 30
Lincoln, Earl of, 30, 35, 40, 42, 45, 100
Lovejoy, John, 21, 94, 118, 140, 142
   as a tavern petitioner, 146
   in a court case, 143

Lovejoy, John Jr., 157

M

Marston, John, 92, 118
Marston, Mary, 172
Mather, Cotton, 25, 145, 148
Mather, Increase, 124, 131
Miller, Thomas, 28
Morton, Charles, 25

N

Norton, John, 58, 61, 62, 63, 94, 137, 156
Nurse, Rebecca, 167

O

Osgood, Christopher, 94, 107, 118, 130, 145, 148
   dispute with Johnson, 140
   history, 94, 95
   in military, 132
   in South End, 137, 146, 147, 155, 156, 171
Osgood, John, 21, 59, 87, 94, 107, 118, 136, 137, 142, 155, 174
   Andover (England) background, 22, 61
   first covenanter, 92, 97, 119
   holder of ordinary license, 86, 144, 145
   in military, 143
   in witchcraft crisis, 151
   prior residence in Newbury, 80
Osgood, John III, 174
Osgood, John Jr., 93
Osgood, Mary, 172
Osgood, Samuel, 154

P

Parker, Alice, 125
Parker, Joseph, 15, 21, 23, 29, 55, 57, 60, 84, 118, 130, 132, 142, 149
Parker, Nathan, 21, 60, 91, 118, 130, 133
Parker, Thomas, 59, 60
Payson, Edward, 159
Peeters, Andrew, 118
Phelps, Edward, 94, 118, 130, 136
Phillips, George, 33, 35, 158, 161, 173

Phillips, Samuel, 11
  as minister of South Parish, 158, 159, 161, 170, 171
  encourages women to sign covenant, 172, 173
Phillips, Samuel, Jr., 175
Poor, Daniel, 21, 92, 118
Poore, Thomas, 21
Pyncheon, William, 28

R

Remington, John, 126
Robinson, Joseph, 126
Roger, Indian, 69
Rogers, Ezekiel, 62, 148, 158
  as "Mr" Rogers, 15
  background, 53
  establishing Rowley, 33
  expanding Rowley, 52, 66
Rowell, Thomas, 94
Russ (or Russe), John, 21, 94, 118, 135
Russell, Robert, 118, 137

S

Saltonstall, Sir Richard, 35, 42, 59, 65
Sewall, Samuel, 7, 143
  against cousin marriage, 121
  as judge, 26
  Hampshire County origin, 32
  visit to Andover, 129
Skelton, Mr., 44, 45
Stevens, John, 21, 67, 82, 91, 111, 118, 140, 141
  as a non-Covenanter, 92, 97, 115
  in court, 143
  in the military, 132
  petitioner for North Parish, 157
Stone, Hannah, 145, 146, 151
Stone, Hugh, 137, 145, 149

Sutton, Richard, 92
Symmes, Thomas, 159

T

Toothacre, Mary, 149, 172
Toothacre, Roger 150
Tyler, Job
  as unofficial settler in Andover, 75
  in Boxford, 52, 65, 135, 141
  in witchcraft trial, 125, 126
Tyng, Jonathan, 148

V

Vane, Governor Henry, 66

W

Wade, Jonathan, 99
Wade, Nathaniel, 100
Ward, John, 2, 65, 67, 87
Ward, Nathaniel, 2, 7, 49, 50, 58, 62, 102, 103, 152, 175
  background, 41, 47, 53, 57, 59, 60, 65, 87
Westgate, John, 125
Winthrop, Governor John, 2, 7, 15, 25, 30, 31, 32, 35, 36, 43, 49, 50, 66, 124, 128, 158, 161
  as a leader, 45
  background, 32, 38, 39, 40, 42, 44, 65, 76
  marriage alliance, 47, 101, 103
Winthrop, John Jr., 35, 40, 50, 58
Woodbridge, Benjamin, 21, 60, 68
Woodbridge, John, 21, 55, 60, 66, 79, 84, 97, 114, 118, 153
  as a leader, 30, 63, 65, 68, 69, 70, 87
Wright, Walter, 140

Subject Index

A

Abbot, Abiel, 169
Abbot, Elinor, 4
Abbott, Charlotte Helen, 73
Abu-Lughad, L., 10
Act of Restitution of 1611, 128
adventurers, 39
Allen, David Grayson, *In English Ways*, 12, 78
Andover
    division into parishes, 152, 156
    emergence of the two Ends, 97
    North and South Ends, 133
    official name, 76
    parish split, 123
    planting of, 65, 67, 69
    population growth, 133
Andover families, backgrounds, 72
Andover settlers
    summary table, 70, 71, 73
Andover Theological Seminary, 2, 3
Andover, England, 2, 22
Andros, Sir Edmund, 143
animal behavior
    as sign, 125
animals
    and disputes, 140

B

Bailyn, Bernard, 65
Bailyn, Bernard and Philip D. Morgan, 13
battle of Black Point, 130
Battle of Narragansett, 130
Bay Colony social order, 43
biblical metaphors
    colonists use of, 38
Billerica, Mass., 88, 149
Binford, Lewis, 81
blood (as emic category), 18, 24, 26, 28, 30, 31
blood and *country*, 24
Borderers, 13
Boxford, Mass., 52
Boyer, Paul and Stephen Nissenbaum, 28, 123, 128, 167, 170, 172
    on witchcraft at Andover, 6
Breen, Stephen, 12
brother (as emic category), 10, 18

C

Cambridge Platform of 1648, 34, 141, 161
Campbell, Helen, 7
Caporael, Linnda, 126
Carrier family, 149, 150
Chase, George Wingate, 88
Chelmsford, Mass., 88

church-towns, 54, 55, 56
Clement, Percival Wood, 88
Cochichawick, 68, 69
    exploration, 51
comets, as signs, 124
Companies, 34
company (as emic category), 14, 15, 33, 137
company, militia, 36
Concord, Mass., 46
conflict in Andover, 137
Connecticut Colony, 36
constables, in Andover, 134
controversy
    and Chandler's tavern, 142, 144, 145
    and Francis Dane, 139, 141
    and ministers, 139
    over parish boundaries, 157
    over the new meetinghouse, 153, 154
controversy in Andover
    the meeting house, 138
country (as emic category), 18, 24, 26, 28, 29, 30, 31, 137
cousin marriage, 109, 166
    and British regional background, 116, 117, 119, 120, 121
    debate in England, 116, 117
cousin-german (as emic category), 10, 18
cousins-german (also first cousins), 166
covenant
    and women to sign in their own behalf, 171, 172
    of South Parish, 128
Covenant community, 54
covenant dispute, 66
covenant theology, 172
covenanter (as emic category), 18
Covenanters, 142, 163
    house lot inheritance, 92
Cowing, Cedric, 135
Cressy, David, 78, 102
Cromwell, Oliver, 52, 127
Cutshamache, 2, 69
    statue of, in Andover, England, 2

D

Deetz, James, and British regional characteristics at Plymouth Colony, 12
demography, historical
    and E. A. Wrigley, 8
Demos, John, 28, 141

disputes
    among townspeople, 140
    among townspeople over animals, 140
Dorchester Company, 32
Duby, Georges, 45

E

East Anglia, 49
emic categories, 14, 22
Endecott Company, 39
Endecott Fleet, 44
endogamy, 112, 113, 114, 115, 116
English nobility and Puritan sympathies, 42
Essex County, 11, 76
etic and emic categories
    of English colonists, 9
etic and emic concepts, 4, 5
    and Kenneth Pike, 4
exogamy, 112, 113, 114, 115, 116
    and colonial social hierarchy, 119

F

Farber, Bernard, 102
Faulkner List, 19, 20, 21
Field, Edward, 86
firstcomer (as emic category), 18, 22, 82
Firstcomers
    to Andover, 71, 72
first- cousin marriage (also *cousins- german*), 166
Fischer, David Hackett, 13
    Albions Seed, 12
Foster, Stephen, 9
Four Generations, 5
freed holder (as emic category), 18
freemen,
    in New England, 78
French and Indians, 50

G

Geertz, Clifford, 17
generation, as an analytic term, 164
gentry, 43, 70, 79, 109
    in New England, 33
Giddens, Anthony, 15, 34
Gildrie, Richard, 159
    on Salem, 11
Godbeer, Richard, 124, 126, 135

Goodman, Robert L., 10, 31, 55, 133
Green, Joseph
  minister at Salem, 129, 159,170
Greven, Philip, 4, 22, 90, 136, 162
  analysis of marriage, 165
  and concept of kindred, 105
  and demographic analysis, 164
  critique of marriage analysis, 166
  Four Generations, 5
  on Andover marriages, 164
  problems with demographic approach, 165
Guildford, Conn., 133

H

Hall, David D., 83
Hansen, Chadwick, 25, 123, 151
Hansford, Gillian, 22
Harris, Marvin, 17
Harvard College, 9
Haverhill, 87
  as Penticutt, 49
Headland, Thomas N., 17
Heaven's Alarm to the World
  Increase Mather 1680, 124
Hertfordshire, 80
Hertfordshire, England
  Bishops Stortford, 61
Heyrman, Christine, 53
Heyrman, James, 124
Hingham, Mass., 174
Hinman, Barry, 142
History of King Philip's War
  Increase Mather, 131
"Holt's Tree", 154
house holder (as emic category), 18
Hunt, Robert, 9

I

Indians
  and attack on Andover, 127, 130
  and attacks, 149
  and liquor, 69, 143, 146
Indians and Andover, 127
Innes, Stephen, 28, 43
Ipswich, Mass., 10, 12, 49

J

Johnson, Edward, *Wonder-Working Providence*, 24

K

kindred, 105
King Philip's War, 76, 127

L

language
  and social identity, 155
latecomer (as emic category), 18, 22
Latecomers
  to Andover, 71, 72
Lepore, Jill, 76
Lincolnshire, England, 30
Lindholdt, Paul J., 1
liquor
  and Indians, 143
  licenses, 142, 144
  problems with, 143
Lockridge, Kenneth A., 27
Lovejoy, Barrie, 143

M

Madam Knight's diary (1702), 78
Mahoney, Gratia, 9
Maine
  and Indian Wars, 130
Malinowski, Bronislaw, 17
markets
  town and regional, 89
marriage
  after the witchcraft crisis, 167
  alliance as social reconciliation, 175
  and choice of mate, 168
  and emic categories, 101, 104, 107, 108
  and Scots, 144
  and social location, 103, 105, 107, 128, 142, 174
  and social structure, 100
  as alliance, 46, 99, 103, 109
  in Andover's second generation, 112, 113, 115
  with close kin, 109
Massachusetts Bay Colony
  See Bay Colony, 43

Massachusetts Bay Company, 38, 39
Mather, Cotton
    account of Ezekiel Rogers, 148
Mather, Increase, 124, 131
meetinghouse
    and controversy, 138, 153, 154
    and seating arrangements, 138
meetinghouses, colonial, 85
    seating, 85, 181
militia, 36, 37
    and Indian Wars, 130
    rise in importance of, 131
    rise of, 130
Miller, Perry, 11, 54, 159
mills, 83, 84
ministers
    and controversy, 139
    of Andover, 97
"Model of Christian Charity" (Winthrop), 101
Mofford, Juliet H., 19
Molloy, Maureen, 102
Mooar, George, 152, 169, 171
Morgan, Edmund, 65
Moriarty, G. Andrews, 62
murder of Hannah Stone, 145

N

Narragansett, Battle of, 130
Nash, Gary, 8
native categories
    (see also etic and emic categories), 9
New England Tracts, 39
Newbury, Mass., 10, 12, 60, 133
    church conflict, 55
Newtown (Cambridge, Mass.), 50
North and South Ends
    tax lists, 134
North Andover, 3
North End
    tax lists, 136
North Ender (as emic category), 18
Norton, Mary Beth, 172

O

O'Malley, Patricia, on Rowley, 11
oath of allegiance (1678), 133
Old Britons (also Brittains), 13, 25, 64
    and Scots, 135
    and West Boxford, 135

and witchcraft, 151
ordinary (also tavern), 85
    public house, 86
ordination
    Puritan views of, 159
Osgood Hill (North Andover), 22

P

parish division
    controversy over boundary, 157
Parker's Company (Newbury), 59
    settlers at Newbury, 15
partible inheritance, 92
patronage relations, 41
Paynter, Robert, 81
Perkin, Harold, 40
    and vertical social structures in Britain, 14
Perzel, Edward, 10
Phillips Andover Academy, 3
Phillips, Samuel, 168, 169, 171
    and children, 171
    and tavern controversy, 171
    first minister of South Parish, 158–159
    ordination ceremony, 159
    teaching on covenant and women, 171
    view of church, 173
    views on baptism, 170
Pike, Kenneth L., 4, 17, 164
plantation (as emic category), 18, 137
Plymouth Colony, 39
Powell, Sumner, 78
    Puritan Village, 11
primogeniture, 92
Puritan social theology, 55
Puritan Village, Sumner Powell, 11

R

Reversal of Attainder (1709), 170
Rhode Island colony, 130
road maintenance conflict, 88
Rockwell, Forbes, 80, 136
Roger (Indian), 69
Rogers, Ezekiel, 53, 148
Rogers' company (Rowley), 15
Rowley, England, 53
Rowley, Mass., 11, 33, 52
    boundary dispute, 66
    Yorkshire, 33
Roxbury, Mass., 62

Subject Index

S

Salem, Mass., 32, 44
   and witchcraft, 128
Schneider, David, 25
Scots, 26, 43, 80
   and Chandler's tavern, 145
   and Francis Dane, 129
   and South End, 137
   in Bay Colony, 64
   neighborhood in Andover, 144
   in New England, 25, 26, 27, 28
Scots Charitable Association, 27
scottie (as emic category), 10, 18
settlement pattern, 91, 93
   of New England towns, 57
Sewall, Judge Samuel, 22, 129
Shawsheen River, 81
signs and wonders, 124
   and animal behavior, 125
smallpox, 127, 149
Smith, Carol
   Regional Analysis, 87
Smout, T. C., 102
social brokers, concept of, 95
social hierarchy
   and meetinghouse seating, 138
social identity
   and language clues, 155
social location
   and marriage, 142
South End, 136
   and Hertfordshire families, 156
   and Old Britons, 156
   and selectmen, 155
   as voting majority, 154
   tax lists, 136
South Ender (as emic category), 18
South Parish, 136
   and new covenant, 159
   and witchcraft crisis, 170
   calls Samuel Phillips as minister, 158
   covenant, 128
   covenant signers, 170
   incorporation, 156
Southwesterners, 59
Springfield, Massachusetts, 28
Staloff, Dennis, 15
Stearns, Raymond P., 55
Stone, Hugh and Hannah, 145
Sudbury, Mass., 11

T

tax lists, 95, 97 (see also appendix D)
   North and South Ends, 134
Thayer, Christopher, 139
Topsfield, Mass., 135
Turner, Victor, 4, 41
Two Brothers Rock, 100, 175
   (Concord, Mass.), 46
tything-man, 9

V

Vaughan, Alden T., 34

W

Wallace, Anthony, 83
Walsh, J. P., 159
Ward's company, 15
"warning out" of Martha Carrier, 150
Waters, John J., 32, 133, 156, 174
Watertown, Mass., 35
Webb, James, 124
Webb, Stephen, 130
West Boxford, Mass., 134
west-country men, 9
west-country people (as emic category), 32
wills, language of, 132
Winthrop Fleet, 38
   arrival at Salem, 44
Winthrop-Dudley, marriage, 47
Winthrop-Dudley, quarrel, 45
Winthrop-Dudley, reconciliation, 47
witchcraft, 151
   1692 crisis, 123
   and Andover social categories, 151
   and Francis Dane, 126
   and Hampton, N. H., 29
   and Indian fears, 124
   and John Godfrey, 143
   and Old Britons, 137, 151
   and the ship Welcome, 124
   and West Boxford, 137
   and women, 130
   crisis and impact on marriage
      patterns, 167
Wonder-Working Providence, 24
Wrigley, E. A., 8

Y

Yorkshire, England, 53

SIL International and
The International Museum of Cultures
Publications in Ethnography

Other Publications

39. **What place for hunter-gatherers in millenium three?** by Thomas N. Headland and Doris E. Blood, eds. 2002.
38. **A tale of Pudicho's people,** by Richard Montag. 2002.
37. **African friends and money matters,** by David Maranz, 2001.
36. **The value of the person in the Guahibo culture,** by Marcelino Sosa, Walter del Aguila, trans., 2000.
35. **People of the drum of God—Come!,** by Paul Neeley. 1999.
34. **Cashibo folklore and culture: Prose, poetry, and historical background,** by Lila Wistrand-Robinson, 1998.
33. **Symbolism and ritual in Irian Jaya: A glimpse of seven systems,** by Marilyn Gregerson and Joyce Sterner, eds., 1997.
32. **Kinship and social organization in Irian Jaya,** by Marilyn Gregerson and Joyce Sterner, eds., 1997.
31. **Ritual, belief, and kinship,** by Marilyn Gregerson, ed., 1993.
30. **Rituals and relationships in the Valley of the Sun: The Ketengban of Irian Jaya,** by Andrew Sims and Anne Sims, 1992.
29. Not published.
28. **Peace is everything,** by David E. Maranz, 1993.
27. **Mice are men: Language and society among the Murle of Sudan,** by Jonathon E. Arensen, 1992.
26. **Language choice in rural development,** by Clinton D. W. Robinson, 1992.
25. **El arte cofan en tejido de hamacas. The Cofan art of hammock weaving,** by M. B. Borman, 1992.
24. **Development program planning: A process approach,** by David Spaeth, 1991.
23. **Nucleation in Papua New Guinea cultures,** by Marvin K. Mayers and Daniel D. Rath, eds., 1987.
22. **Current concerns of anthropologists and missionaries,** by Karl Franklin, ed., 1987.
21. **Tales from Indochina,** by Marilyn Gregerson, Dorothy Thomas, Doris Blood, and Carol Zylstra, eds., 1987.

For further information or a full listing of SIL publications contact:

International Academic Bookstore
SIL International
7500 W. Camp Wisdom Road
Dallas, TX 75236-5699

Voice: 972-708-7404
Fax: 972-708-7363
Email: academic_books@sil.org
Internet: http://www.ethnologue.com